FOUNDATIONS OF PSYCHOTHERAPY

Foundations of Psychotherapy

An Introduction to Individual Therapy

Roger Horrocks

First published 2005 by
PALGRAVE MACMILLAN
Houndmills, Basingstoke, Hampshire RG21 6XS and
175 Fifth Avenue, New York, N. Y. 10010
Companies and representatives throughout the world

PALGRAVE MACMILLAN is the global academic imprint of the Palgrave
Macmillan division of St. Martin's Press, LLC and of Palgrave Macmillan Ltd.
Macmillan® is a registered trademark in the United States, United Kingdom
and other countries. Palgrave is a registered trademark in the European
Union and other countries.

ISBN-13: 978–1–4039–2189–5
ISBN-10: 1–4039–2189–X

This book is printed on paper suitable for recycling and made from fully
managed and sustained forest sources.

A catalogue record for this book is available from the British Library.

Library of Congress Cataloging-in-Publication Data
Horrocks, Roger
    Foundations of psychotherapy : an introduction to individual therapy / Roger Horrocks.
        p. cm.
    Includes bibliographical references and index.
    ISBN 1–4039–2189–X (paper)
        1. Psychotherapy. I. Title.

RC480.H645 2005
616.89′14–dc22   2005047564

10   9   8   7   6   5   4   3   2   1
14 13 12 11 10 09 08 07 06 05

Printed and bound in China

For my father,
Frank Horrocks,
1920–2003

Contents

Acknowledgements   viii

1   Introduction   1

Part I   Theoretical Foundations

2   Freud and Jung   11

3   Humanistic Psychology   33

4   Cognitive Therapy   50

5   Neuroscience and Psychotherapy   61

6   Psychotherapy as a Profession   71

Part II   Practical Methods

7   The Setting: Time, Space and Money   87

8   Working with Clients   104

9   The Relationship between Therapist and Client   130

10   Thinking, Feeling and the Body   147

11   Negativity   157

12   Symbolism: the Dynamics of the Inner World   172

13   Difficult Clients   182

14   Conclusions   194

Index   199

Acknowledgements

Many thanks go to Jo Campling who helped me throughout the writing of this book; and thanks also to Andrew McAleer at Palgrave Macmillan.

I am very grateful to those colleagues and their clients who gave permission for vignettes from their work to be used; and also to my clients, likewise.

Psychotherapists cannot work in isolation: I am very conscious of many colleagues and friends who have helped me over many years both as a therapist and writer. In particular, I thank Alan Danks, Sybilla Madigan, Simon Jackson, Victoria Zinovieff.

A big thank you to my clients over many years: they have been good teachers.

Roger Horrocks

1 Introduction

Psychotherapy can be seen as a huge continent, with many countries in it, some of which are on speaking terms, and have historical roots in common, and some of which seem almost alien and unintelligible to each other. Another metaphor that comes to mind is one of those massive rivers like the Amazon, which has many tributaries, and which seems to divide at times into many rivers, and at other times, seems to stretch from shore to shore as one huge movement of water. In more prosaic language, I am saying that psychotherapy is not a unified field of knowledge or practice; that it contains many different schools, some of which are inter-related. None the less we are able to recognize that there is such a thing as psychotherapy, which is delimited from other social phenomena such as medicine and psychiatry.

But the vastness of psychotherapy, and the complexity of its history, precludes any one book giving a satisfactorily comprehensive account of it. Rather one must be selective; and the selection is partly subjective and partly objective, by which I mean that this book in part deals with those topics which interest me as a psychotherapist, and also with certain topics which it would be very odd to leave out, for example psychoanalysis and Jungian psychotherapy.

It is worthwhile looking at psychotherapy in an historical context. It strikes me that it has emerged as the Western world became secularized and individualistic. No doubt human beings in all cultures have had their problems in facing the vicissitudes of life, but therapy is a comparatively recent way of dealing with these problems. Previously one can argue that a wide-ranging religious framework, such as existed in medieval Europe, subsumed individual problems, or one might even argue that the notion of the individual having problems would have seemed odd if not alien to the medieval mind.

To put this more metaphysically, if one argues that psychotherapy brings the client into contact with a relatively unknown Other (the therapist), upon whom all manner of fantasies and projections are heaped, and from whom all manner of solutions are sought, then it is surely not an exaggeration to say that a thousand years ago the Other could only have been conceived of as God. It is often said that with the 'death of God' the lot of human beings became intolerably lonely, and again it is possible to argue that psychotherapy, along with all the self-help and self-development movements which exist today, has partly filled that void.[1]

Therapy instead of confession? The comparison may seem trite, but maybe there is something in it. There is an element of confession in the 'talking cure', in the sense that the client often arrives in a pent-up state, desperate to unburden him or herself with their own story; at the same time, is there not an element of absolution also? I don't mean that the therapist forgives the client or offers pardon, but does offer acceptance of all the oddities and the shameful secrets which we all possess and which press upon us, daring to be told to someone. The unbearable becomes bearable in the telling of it.

The psychotherapist is that ideal person to confess to: unknown, professional, rather distant, not normally condemning. In other words, there is no pay-off in one's ordinary life – you don't expect to see your therapist in your local pub or hob-nobbing with your friends. It's not just a question of confidentiality; clients expect more than that – they expect a large degree of separation between the therapist's life and the client's, and of course when this separation is breached in various ways, all kinds of disruption to the therapy can ensue.

I have sometimes also seen psychotherapy as an off-shoot of the Romantic movement, in the sense that the therapy hour places great value on the individual client, not for any great performance that they may enact, not for any great insights or intellectual feats, but simply for being who and what they are. I see this as an inheritance of Romanticism because the individual is valued highly, and surely this is partly a reaction to the alienating and dehumanizing aspects of modern society.

Unity and disunity

The modern psychotherapist has an extraordinary body of knowledge to draw upon in his or her work. For over a hundred years now there have been many theoretical refinements, much working over of strategies and techniques for working with different kinds of clients. Of course, one of the problems that arises here is that psychotherapy is divided into many schools, and the student therapist cannot be expected to study all of them. In any case, we are all drawn to certain ways of thinking about human beings, and these correspond in many ways to the schools of psychotherapy.

Some critics of therapy have seen this disunity as a fatal flaw, and have pointed out a damning comparison with disciplines such as biology or physics, which have a higher degree of intellectual unity. But this criticism strikes me as ill-founded, since psychotherapy is dealing above all with human subjectivity or with subjectivities. Hence it is clear that different people, with different personalities, and with different needs from therapy, are going to require very different approaches from their therapists. I recall many years ago meeting a therapist who struck me as a very cold person, and in my idealistic youth and fervour, I felt that this could not be valuable for clients, but later I came to realize that some clients actually need someone like that, who gives them very secure boundaries and a degree of distance that is quite safe.

One can make a parallel point here with the place where therapy takes place. I have always worked at home, in a room set aside for therapy, but I have come to realize that for some clients, this is far too intimate and 'warm' and unsafe, and they require something more distant, perhaps someone who sits behind a desk, in an institutional setting, and so on.

Psychotherapy therefore is not like biology or physics, since it is dealing with the astonishing variety of human personality and human existence. We need Kleinian and Jungian and Reichian psychotherapists, and many other kinds as well.

But as well as this fissiparous tendency in psychotherapy, there is the opposite – a tendency to draw together, to integrate insights and theories from different backgrounds. One of the best examples of this is the way in which post-war Jungian groups in Britain integrated some of the ideas from psychoanalysis, particularly to do with infantile development. It was felt that this was a theoretical lacuna within 'classical' Jungian theory, and analysts such as Michael Fordham were not afraid to cross the divide which seemed to separate them from the psychoanalytic world.[2]

One can also cite the many humanistic groups and training courses which now as a matter of fact incorporate the study of object relations, transference, psychic conflict, and so on, into their studies. Yet thirty years ago the humanistic movement had partly arisen in revolt against the perceived aridity and intellectualism of psychoanalysis.

It is easy to see the splits in the therapy world, but there are also signs of connection and rejoining, so that the contemporary psychotherapist is able to take ideas and practical techniques from different sources. We see connections being made between psychotherapy and neuroscience, between therapy and spirituality and so on.[3]

Yet this new era of connectedness presents some problems for the trainee, and indeed for all therapists, who are required to keep an ongoing professional development, and one of them concerns selectivity. Psychotherapy is such a vast area that it might seem daunting to pick and choose among the various intellectual movements and technical repertoires which can be found. However, this is in some ways a very mechanical way of looking at it: none of us sits down and intellectually decides which ideas suit us best. We are all emotionally and intellectually drawn to certain areas and not to others. For example, when we select a therapist for ourselves, we may do it in an apparent blind way, but I am sure that normally there is a kind of intuitive sensor at work, which guides us. Some people are drawn to Kleinian analysis; others to Jungian; others to bio-energetics; others to Gestalt. These are deep choices, one might almost say unconscious choices, which connect with quite hidden parts of ourselves.

The same is true once one has begun training; everyone finds that certain areas of the landscape of psychotherapy are attractive, others are not. Gradually one builds up a kind of portfolio of one's own predilections and interests, and later in one's career, these can be synthesized into one's own unique style of therapy.

Old and new

One has to strike a balance in a book like this between the old and the new. On the one hand, trainees and inexperienced therapists and those wanting to find out more about therapy are interested in key ideas, the intellectual landmarks of the psychotherapy paradigm. Of course, one should really say 'paradigms', since we are dealing with a number of interlocking but sometimes opposed views of the psyche and ways in which to work with it.

On the other hand, I believe one should always challenge and provoke students to think for themselves, as they will have to as therapists. One certainly cannot practise psychotherapy by rote, or from memory. It is an improvisational art, not a set of recipes or rules. There are rules, but as in many games, one learns to play creatively within the rules, and at times to bend or break them.

It is also important to think about old concepts in a fresh way, so that we do not fall into the trap of parroting ideas. Take the example of the unconscious – familiar enough outside as well as inside therapy. It is instructive to do a mind experiment where one has to explain it to Martians in everyday English, without recourse to psychological jargon. For example: is the unconscious that which is not known? Clearly that is not true, since there are many things I don't know – for example, my exact weight, or the capital of Peru – which would not be said to be unconscious.

But this is only a beginning. Is the unconscious that which has been repressed or that which has never been known? Could it include both? Is the unconscious an intelligence, with a 'mind of its own'? If so, what does that tell us about the nature of human persons? Are we divided against ourselves? Is the ego partly unconscious?

Of course this discussion could rapidly expand to become a book in itself, but I hope the point is clear – that learning a skill and an art such as psychotherapy is not a matter of rote learning but of thinking things through for oneself. After all, one hopes that one's clients will be able to do that, and will not simply accept one's own words and ideas as papal dicta.

In fact, merely to list the accepted teachings of various schools of therapy would be not only inert and lifeless, but mendacious, as in the living moment of therapy, such formulae will be worse than useless. They must be brought to life, in case studies and vignettes, and in discussion, in argument, in thinking through. One can even say that one must be prepared not to know about them, to feel confused, or in a state of contradiction. That is surely much healthier than some kind of 'examination' correctness. In fact, such a state of mind about the psyche would be very odd, since so often one simply doesn't understand something, or something is mysterious, and one has to wait for clarification.

So I hope this book does not provide pat 'answers' and 'solutions', but rather shows ways in which we can all struggle for insight and understanding, and can see the value in those times when they are elusive. Some mystics have argued that God is present in his absence – similarly I believe that intellectual correctness may miss out on something of great value – the living moment.

The main tool: myself

Psychotherapy is an extraordinary profession. Its aim is self-knowledge, acquired through a variety of exploratory techniques, but in the main mediated through a relationship between two people. This gives it its uniqueness, for it is a subjective exploration, whose goal is one's own subjectivity, and whose medium is also the subjective experience of the two people. Thus there are no objective recipe books for psychotherapy – one cannot simply list a set of problems or psychological conditions and lay down a related group of 'solutions'. This works with machines, but not with human beings. For one thing, we find that what works with one person doesn't work with another, even though their problems may appear to be similar. There is something marvellous about this – that human variety and individuality is reflected directly in psychotherapy, in that every client, every session, has to be approached as if it was the first, as if it was unprecedented. In other words, one cannot become blasé or hackneyed as a therapist; one cannot 'go through the motions', for if one does that, then the relationship between therapist and client suffers, and the aliveness that we are looking for has been subverted.

One might say that the chief tool of the psychotherapist is his or her own person – their personality, their inner resources, their own self-knowledge, their experience of life, as well as their knowledge of human psychology. This is partly because clients come to therapy seeking someone they can trust, someone they can open up to, and one might have a tremendous amount of book knowledge, but lack the authenticity and ability to be present which gives clients that sense of confidence and trust. No doubt clients also look for someone who has also struggled with life, and with their own neurotic tendencies, and therefore understands something of sadness, anger, fear, despair, guilt, and so on.

How unnerving this is! Most beginning therapists feel considerable apprehension at daring to present themselves in this way, and probably most experienced therapists still have times when they wonder at the audacity of this enterprise. How does it work? One might say ultimately that there is a healing power in the human relationship itself, but obviously this is not enough, since one might seek this with friends, lovers, spouses, and so on. The therapeutic relationship is quite different, since the therapist withdraws their own personality to a large extent, thus permitting the client maximum attention. It is a one-sided relationship in many ways – we are not here to attend to the therapist's problems! Or at any rate, this goes on only in the most covert and subtle manner, since one can assume that being a therapist does help the therapist in many ways.

The therapist therefore combines several talents – an expertise in human psychology, or certainly some branch of it, a personal ability to be intimate without being intrusive, an ability to be non-judgmental and allow clients to find their own solutions, and probably an understanding of the human struggle for understanding and meaning. This last quality is the most nebulous, since it refers to a grasp of our perennial attempt to find meaning in life, and many clients come to therapy because they have lost meaning or never had it.

Perhaps the most important quality is humility – a sense that the client is the real expert, that their life is their life, and is not ours to play with or intrude on.

In therapy we range from the sublime to the ridiculous, from the tiniest detail of daily life to the most transcendent issues of our place in the universe; from how to pay the mortgage to the question of the existence of love, or God, or self.

As well as unnerving, it can be seen how attractive a profession this is, since it combines a remarkable intimacy with people with an ongoing quest for life's significance, a quest which obviously allows for an infinite number of answers.

Structure of the book

This book is devoted entirely to one-to-one psychotherapy. It therefore does not consider couples work, family therapy, group therapy, group analysis and so on, and the interested reader can find many books on those subjects. But individual psychotherapy deserves its own treatment, since it is a vast and complex discipline.

The book is divided into two sections. In Part I, I have looked at some of the important schools of psychotherapy, in particular, Freud and Jung, humanistic psychology, cognitive therapy, and neuroscience. Finally in this section, there is a chapter on the nature of psychotherapy as a profession, including issues to do with accreditation, ethics and so on.

In Part II, I have examined more practical issues in therapy. Thus Chapter Seven looks at the basic parameters of time, space and money, which provide a basic structure to therapy. Chapter Eight examines some of the ways in which therapists work with clients; and Chapter Nine looks more closely at the important issue of the relationship between therapist and client.

Chapter Ten looks at the basic elements of thinking, feeling and the body, and how they are dealt with in therapy; Eleven considers the negativity which is found in therapy, in both therapist and client, and how it can be worked with and through. Chapter Twelve takes up the issue of symbolism, including dreams, fantasies and other kinds of symbolic structures, and what role this has in therapy. Finally, Chapter Thirteen looks at some of the particular problems met with in psychotherapy, particularly difficult clients such as borderline clients, narcissistic clients, and those who are very depressed.

Notes

1 See Masud Khan, 'Freud and the Crises of Psychotherapeutic Responsibility', in *Hidden Selves: Between Theory and Practice in Psychoanalysis* (London: Karnac, 1989).
2 See Andrew Samuels, *Jung and the post-Jungians* (London: Routledge, 1985).
3 On neuroscience, see J. Corrigall and H. Wilkinson (eds), *Revolutionary Connections: Psychotherapy and Neuroscience* (London: Karnac, 2003); on spirituality and psychoanalysis, see *British Journal of Psychotherapy* (2002) **18:3**.

Part I

Theoretical Foundations

2 Freud and Jung

The psychotherapies dealt with in this chapter derive from the 'depth' psychologies developed in the first place by Freud and Jung. Although Freud and Jung were to diverge considerably, nonetheless at the beginning of psychotherapy both men developed the notion of the unconscious, which is probably the most important concept in the whole field of psychotherapy.

Thus these therapies posit the fundamental incoherence of the human being, or the divide between the conscious and the unconscious, or the ego and the id in Freudian parlance. This incoherence or contradiction is of such great importance that one might devote the whole of this chapter to it, since it strikes an enormous blow at those rationalist views of human beings which see them as coherent, consistent, following rational goals and so on. In other words, Freud and Jung struck huge blows at the Enlightenment and post-Enlightenment views of human beings.

And the notion of the unconscious still causes shock and revulsion today – the last twenty years have seen many criticisms of Freud, some of which are well argued, but some of which seem to simply express horror that anyone could suggest that we have unconscious motivations, or unconscious wishes, some of which contradict our civilized veneer. No doubt Freud would have laughed at such criticisms, and would have expected them, since he felt that psychoanalysis was a scandalous body of ideas.[1]

What is the scandal? That we all nurture ideas, feelings, wishes, memories, which we have no conscious awareness of, and which go against the grain. One can cite many examples: the man who professes fidelity to his wife, but finds himself full of intense desire for a colleague at work; the person who vilifies pornography, so much so that much time is spent reading and viewing it; the peace-loving Christian who unexpectedly is in favour of aggressive military action by his country; the doting mother who suddenly smothers her child. Examples of comparable internal psychic conflicts are legion, and fill the consulting rooms of therapists, and the more lurid of them the columns of the tabloid press.

Freud and psychoanalysis

Without doubt, psychoanalysis is the most important school of psychotherapy. It has the richest theoretical system, and a very complex and sophisticated set of clinical tools. It is difficult to see how anyone today can practise psychotherapy without some acquaintance with the notions of the unconscious and the ego, object relations, the psychological defences, therapeutic containment and management, envy, transference and counter-transference, resistance, and so on.

Freud articulated a causative and developmental psychological scheme. That is, he argued that the adult neurosis has infantile roots. In fact, Freud argued that the whole of our psychic life has a causative hinterland – thus, dreams, slips of the tongue, many 'accidents', jokes – could be analyzed by Freud in the same way, as betraying unconscious motivations.[2]

In his development of psychoanalysis as a therapeutic discipline Freud laid great emphasis on the association of ideas – that the patient would unwittingly lead to the core of the neurosis by the chain of associations which would be produced, so long as the patient said what came into his head. Of course, everyone breaks that commandment, and then the analyst is able to examine the resistances which go on in the patient.

One of the brilliant discoveries of psychoanalysis has been that every apparent stumbling block to the progress of the analysis in fact proved to be a further rich source of information. Thus resistance itself, which does clearly block progress, in fact gives us a great insight into the patient's issues and problems. In what areas do we find the resistance? What form does the resistance take? The principle of the therapeutic microcosm is at work here – we can assume that the same resistances go on in the patient's life in general as go on in the consulting room. Thus, if a patient is particularly shy of any sexual references, it is likely that there are sexual problems. If another patient is resentful of the time schedule which therapy keeps to, we would expect the same issue to crop up in life. Most tellingly, if the patient is unwilling to have much contact with the analyst, that is, avoids intimacy, this normally indicates that intimacy is a serious problem.

Similarly transference and counter-transference, which originally were seen as obstacles to the smooth running of analysis, were eventually seen as further rich sources of information. One might say that key unconscious material is revealed in the resistance, the transference and the counter-transference.

Freud posited a sexual aetiology to adult neurosis – that it had its origin in a disturbance to the sexual development of the infant. Freud based this theory on the notion of drives – instinctive forces originating in the body which impact on the mind – and the disruption which occurs when those drives are blocked. Freud concluded, in one of his famous pessimistic lines of thought, that civilization was compelled to repress the sexual and the aggressive drives, and so we are all compelled to be neurotic.[3]

However, this sexual aetiology has been marginalized in many versions of psychoanalysis, although it can be still be found (in a considerably altered form) in the psychology of Melanie Klein. Instead, object relations became the dominant school of thought, arguing that abnormal infantile development (leading to adult neurosis or psychosis) occurs as a result of faulty relationships with others, particularly in the original family. The 'object' referred to in object relations is the other – in the case of early life, the mother or father, who form the basis for the first relationships.[4]

But object relations becomes much more complex with the postulate of the inner world, or 'inner objects', that is, bits of the psyche which relate to each other. Thus, one can conjecture that many people have an 'inner critic' which persecutes the ego; there may be an 'inner child' who probably retains much of the distress and pain of early childhood; there may be 'internal parents' who have complex relationships to the inner child.

The development of object relations has been a key gear-shift in psycho-analysis and psychotherapy as a whole, since it represents the socialization of psychological theory. Where Freud's drive theory was to an extent atomistic, and saw the individual as isolated, dealing as best they can with their own inner drives, object relations sees the individual as indivisibly connected with others. One might even say that individual identity actually emerges from early relationships – one's sense of self, for good or ill, is founded in childhood care, or the lack of it. Thus those patients whose sense of self is fractured or self-destructive are invariably found to have had early relationships which were disturbed in some way. Sexuality is part of this, but no longer has the key role given to it by Freud.

Transference and counter-transference dovetail into object relations, since both concern a kind of misrecognition of the present, or a fantasy relationship that is not appropriate. Transference involves the patient seeing the analyst as someone or something else; counter-transference involves the analyst receiving feelings and thought belonging to the patient. Of course, it is likely that all human beings do this to an extent – here Freud's repetition compulsion is important, arguing that we repeat the past, especially those aspects of it that are undigested or deeply repressed. If you like, we repeat in order to understand, and we keep on repeating when understanding is not happening. Thus we find those distressing scenarios where an individual keeps getting into situations that are very harmful – for example, the woman who meets men who beat her up.

But Freud also argued that this repetition can be broken. Analysis can investigate the covert feelings which are forcing the person to repeat the malign situation, and the early experiences which are at the root of it. The remembering of what has been forgotten can break the neurotic compulsion; the understanding of the hitherto repressed experiences can permit one to choose another way of life.

Of course, there is no guarantee that this will happen. Those critics who argue that therapy often doesn't work, or doesn't work with everyone, have failed to see that it is not a panacea and it is not a medical or surgical procedure. In other words, the patient/client is not a passive recipient. Analysis and therapy work when the patient is determined that it will work, but we are all able to prevent this happening. Therapy is a tool which one can put to one's advantage – or not. And without doubt there are those who step back, prefer to retreat into their own depression or neurosis; if you like, prefer death to life.

The unconscious

The unconscious is not simply that which is unknown; both Freud and Jung, in different ways argued that the unconscious is of a different order from the rest of the psyche. For Freud, it is disorganized, chaotic, full of infantile wishes, which may directly contradict each other, and certainly contradict our adult façade. For Jung, it is full of archetypal forces, innate, universal structures which are in fact unknowable, yet which give our experience structure and order.

In therapy, we appreciate the importance of the unconscious when we see people who are in a crisis because some unknown part of their personality is beginning to emerge, or is perhaps causing trouble. The repressed returns, Freud said, and its return is often marked by intense emotional upset and distress, since I find that I am not the person I thought I was, or that I am going through a change which I have neither planned nor wished for.

In one of his case studies Freud uses the phrase 'a mutilated telegraph message', to describe a communication from the unconscious.[5] The phrase summarizes Freud's attitudes to psychological work – that the task of the analyst and patient is to restore the mutilated text to its full sense.

The mutilation occurs because of repression, or the censorship which is forced upon the unconscious by the ego, and it can take different forms. It can involve gaps – or missing parts of the text; or metaphoric substitutions, but the key issue here is that the communication of the unconscious is impaired and has to be repaired, so that the patient can come to terms with the full contents of their own repressed psyche.

The relationship with the analyst is one of the key areas where this restitution can go on, since in the transference the patient produces many mutilated texts from the unconscious, in the form of dreams, slips of the tongue, associations, and simply what is being talked about.

> Jim bursts into the consulting room and lets go of a vehement series of complaints about the railways, the nature of public service, telephone manners, and so on. The therapist begins to suspect that Jim is partly complaining about him, and ventures this interpretation. Jim is at first reluctant to see the parallels, but eventually concedes that he is angry with the therapist.

Here the 'mutilation' occurs by displacement. That is, instead of venting his anger directly about the therapist, Jim displaces it onto other areas of his life.

The key philosophical idea in psychoanalysis is the dichotomy between the covert and the overt, and the ways in which the former can be inferred from the latter. That is, the unconscious is repressed, but leaks, and the therapist is able to detect the leakage, and the client eventually can do the same. We might say that therapy aims towards a greater intimacy with our own unconscious, thereby helping us not to act it out. By 'acting out' is meant the blind dramatization of unconscious contents, so that in fact they remain unconscious, or one remains cut off from them.

This is one of the key insights of Freud, and one which still drives much of contemporary psychotherapy – that I am concealed, not only from others, but from myself. In fact, being hidden from myself is a kind of alienation which produces feelings of loneliness, meaninglessness, and so on. In more modern idiom, we talk about being 'out of touch with myself', being cut off, and so on, but the fundamental idea is not knowing and not accepting myself, and therefore experiencing the pain and dislocation that this causes. It also leads to poor relationships, since if I am out of touch with myself, it is unclear to me what effect I have on others, and how others affect me.

But matters are much more complex than this in therapy. It's not as if the therapist studies from some Olympian detachment the client's unconscious and delivers penetrating observations on it which the client gratefully receives. In the beginning, the unknown pervades everything and everyone. Of course the client is unaware of himself – that is partly why he has come to therapy; but the therapist is also unaware of the client. In addition, the therapist is also unaware of herself in the relationship with the client – unconsciousness reigns supreme! Of course, the therapist has worked to gain some self-knowledge, so that she is able to use her own psyche as a kind of radar or sounding board.

What I mean is that both therapist and client begin in a state of not knowing. The client does not know himself, to a greater or lesser extent; the therapist does not know the client; but the therapist does not know herself in that relationship with the client. She is full of unconscious information about the client from the first meeting or the first phone call, but it is unconscious! The therapist is not Superman, able at a moment's notice to consult her own psyche and read off it as if from a radar screen. The screen is partially obscured, and much time and effort must be spent before more clarity is achieved.

Of course the therapist is using her own unconscious as a key tool in the therapy, but has to struggle with it just as we all have to struggle with the unconscious. It takes time and effort and mistakes and false moves and retreats to achieve any kind of insight into one's unconscious, and even more so someone else's.

The therapist is there to help the client to deal better with his own unconscious, and one way this is achieved is that the therapist shows in practical ways how she deals with her own unconscious. This does not happen in an explicit way usually – I mean that the therapist does not tend to say 'I am getting a kind of semi-conscious feeling here that I want to punish you out of rivalry' or some such interpretation. Such interpretations are very powerful, and can be used at the right time to great effect, but early on in therapy they are usually too powerful.

But the therapist contains her unconscious, reads off it, uses the information from it, is not freaked out by it, has a relationship with it, instead of being overwhelmed by it, or forced to crush it. That is the way in which the therapist demonstrates concretely how one can relate to the unconscious without being consumed. Furthermore, the therapist uses her unconscious particularly as it relates to the relationship with the client. If you like, two unconsciouses meet, interact, collide, interpenetrate, and so on, and the therapist hopefully is in a position to use the information that is coming her way both from her own unconscious and also from the client's.

The therapist therefore has made a profession out of studying her own psyche, being able to contain it and withstand it without having to act out.

When she is in a professional relationship with someone, she is able to use her own psyche as a forensic tool.

> After several years therapy with James, his therapist began to experience feelings of sadness and rejection. His first thought was this must be how James felt, and there was much exploration of this to good effect. But still the feelings persisted, and the therapist began to think that this was the effect James has on people, since he was quite detached and cool, and did not acknowledge the importance of the therapist to him. The therapist felt guilty about wanting to be recognized by James, but was able to deal with this guilt internally, and then was able to broach with James that coolness which people found off-putting.

Note that in this case the therapist did not say something like 'I feel upset because you reject me', which is not to say that such an interpretation is always ruled out. But he felt that this was a bit too strong for James at present, who could not really bear anyone directly relating to him. Other therapists might go for a more confrontational approach. One can also notice in this example the complexity of the feelings aroused in the therapist – sadness, guilt, and probably some anger at being disturbed in this way. Clearly, the therapist has to have acquired the ability to process their own internal state, without blurting it out or acting it out.

One can have very strange experiences as a therapist in relation to unconscious feelings. I recall sitting with a client for months in the grip of an eerie feeling, without being able to put a name to it, until eventually something changed, and I was able to identify it, and could then relate it to our relationship. But not being able to name a feeling was of great importance to this client, who often was in the grip of things he did not recognize. Here the importance of not knowing is underlined – one should not rush to judgement, for then something important is being jumped over – that the client is often in such a state.

Repression and repetition

It is repression which creates the unconscious in Freudian psychology; those infantile desires which are forbidden are repressed and go into the unconscious. If that was the end of the story, there would be no problem with the unconscious, but in fact these covert wishes create trouble in adult life – they press on the conscious mind, wishing for fulfilment, they haunt our dreams; as we get older they can become very troublesome and demand attention.

But in addition, the atmosphere and feelings of our childhood are often repressed if they are too painful, and then can survive as a barely felt depression or low-level anxiety, or indeed as a high-level anxiety. Again, many people get through their early life without paying attention to such feelings, but middle age often forces us to begin to look at them.

> Elizabeth describes her life as having been a question of survival, but she says she has never felt desperate. However, after she got divorced, she began to experience a new kind of emotional intensity – a sense of loneliness and futility which were quite debilitating. She says these feelings forced her to seek help in therapy.

This example also demonstrates the issue of repetition – that the repressed feelings or circumstances begin to emerge again. Indeed, one finds that repetition can go on not just emotionally, but in relationships, in work, in fact in any area of life. It is as if an unresolved issue or a dark corner of the psyche forces itself into our awareness by compelling us to go through it again in life. It is common to find that difficulties in relationships are a rerun of some childhood problem – for example, emotional distance, guilt, fear, and so on. But the 'rerun' is usually quite unconscious, and it is only when we have hit the buffers that we are compelled to begin to give it attention.

Thus repression seems to be a temporary solution in some cases, although it is very likely that all of us have successfully repressed certain things and will never deal with them. But the troublesome material demands to be raised to consciousness, one might say.

But what is repression? It is not simply 'forgetting', for forgetting is often reversible, but repression acquires a semi-permanent nature. A more modern version of it would refer to 'cutting off', 'splitting off', 'disassociation', and such terms. In other words, the repressed material may be actually compartmentalized, and placed in a different area of the psyche from the normal conscious mind and the normal forgotten stuff. I may well forget the names of my primary school teachers, but that is different from repressing them.

Thus the combination of repression and repetition means that eventually some of the repressed returns to us, and then we are compelled to deal with it. It can return in many forms – such as depression, illness, accidents, bizarre events in life, impulsive behaviour – it is often said that 'acting out' is taking place, when the repressed is ejected through action rather than being contemplated upon.

One might say that parts of the unconscious actually drive towards consciousness – this is presumably the force of a dream – and then psychotherapy is in an enviable position, since the therapist is actually helping a process that is already underway. At the same time, this drive upwards is usually met with an opposite force downwards, which wants to perpetuate the repression.

In other words, most clients in therapy have a contradictory view of their own unconscious, both wanting and not wanting to come to terms with it. The conservative side of them is used to not dealing with it, but then again, that has probably become unbearable or unworkable. Quite simply, for many people their life has become unsatisfactory and demands some kind of resolution. One may be unhappy for the first part of life, and be able to endure it stoically, but then sometimes a kind of rebellion sets in, since the individual knows at some level that happiness is not too much to ask for, or becomes fed up with being denied it.

However, it is quite likely that many people do not experience such a conflict, and seem to settle for a vaguely unhappy life, or an intensely unhappy life even. In other words, one cannot predict who will turn to therapy and who will not – it does not correlate with degree of unhappiness. In fact, I have noticed a curious phenomenon in large families, that often the most unhappy members do not do therapy, but somebody else does, almost as if on their behalf.

Often this is the most sensitive child of the family, for it is they who have been half-aware of the unconscious feelings and issues in the family, and therefore have a head start, so to speak. Certainly, sensitivity to the unconscious varies enormously. Some people seem to have a very acute radar – they speak of knowing what their parents were going through for most their childhood, whereas others were in the dark, and were perhaps kept in the dark. But some children seem to have a very acute awareness of unspoken issues in the family, and again these may have to be dealt with at a much later stage in life. The unconsciousness of the parents is visited upon the children!

The issue of repetition becomes of direct importance in therapy, since one finds that the therapy itself has become the arena where the unconscious material is projected. Thus all of the covert feelings and structures of the early family can be recapitulated – aggression, guilt, fear, seductiveness, hate, distance, and so on. One might even say, within the psychoanalytic paradigm, that it is impossible not to recapitulate one's early life.

That of course is a very bold claim, but it goes to the core of Freud, and provides the therapist with an invaluable tool or set of tools – the principle of microcosm. It is very difficult to keep one's troubles out of the therapy sessions, even if one is not aware of them and one is not referring to them directly. In fact, one might argue that psychotherapy begins with the troubles which the client is aware of, and then proceeds to the troubles which they are not aware of, against which there is often much resistance by the client, who in part does not want their early life (or their unconscious) exhumed.

It is interesting and indeed important to question the principle of repetition or recapitulation. Why should this go on? Why should repression not be totally successful?

I have already mentioned the astonishing idea that the unconscious presses towards consciousness; one can argue that human beings have an innate need to process psychic material, and the unprocessed causes great discomfort and demands attention in the end. If it does not get this, then it turns into symptoms, both psychological and physical. It is probably not too strong to say that an unattended neurosis can in the end make you ill. One can indeed make a parallel with physical digestion, in that just as we continually take food and liquids in, we also need to evacuate waste material, and if we do not, we become very ill. Both the body and the psyche can be seen as organisms which take in material, process it, and then let it go, but human beings have acquired the ability to interrupt this process in the psychological realm, so that they become considerably 'constipated'.

The defences

Repression is one of the key defences found within the psyche, but post-Freudian work has considerably amplified the notion of defensive mechanisms, and analysts such as Klein and Anna Freud were able to show that while repression is probably the central means of defence, there are many others which operate both within the psyche, and as a defence against the outside world.

This distinction is interesting, since while I may need to defend vulnerable areas of my personality from others, so that for example, I may become rather intellectual or sarcastic when someone gets too close to me, different areas of the psyche also have to be protected against other areas, often to prevent intense anxiety. For example, a number of analysts have pointed to the mechanism of 'splitting', whereby a child may split its mother into 'good' and 'bad' versions, since it seems intolerable that the same person may be a mixture of the two. Such mechanisms often carry over into adult life – so that we find men who divide women into idealized saints and whores. Of course, such a split also represents a split in oneself – in this example, the 'whore' can be lusted after, while the 'saint' cannot, showing that the man concerned finds his own sexual desire distasteful.[6]

It should be pointed out of course that defence mechanisms are not in themselves pathological; in fact, all human beings need various kinds of psychological defences, just as they need protection from inclement weather, wild animals, and so on in the external world. For example, it is interesting to consider Jung's notion of the persona – that mask which people put on when they wish to hide, particularly in a public setting.[7] One can say that there are two extremes in the use of the persona – there are those people who are dominated by it, so that they have no choice over it. An example of this is the buffoon, who is the life and soul of the party, but who in fact cannot not be the buffoon. But there are also people who lack a reasonable use of persona, or who find it difficult to put one on in a public setting. For example, I have had clients who felt so vulnerable that they found going round the supermarket an excruciating experience, as they felt exposed to the world. We all need to be able to use a persona (or a number of them), but not to be dominated by it.

This shows that some kind of defence is essential to psychic health, but we can also see that it is a matter of discrimination – there are situations where I need to be defensive, but also situations where I can take my defences down, for example if I am being intimate with someone. And of course it is the issue of intimacy which connects so deeply with the psychic defences, since so many people in Western culture find intimacy very frightening, and therefore employ a variety of defences.

We might say that defences become pathological when they are rigid, automatic, when we have no control over them, and when they prevent us from any intimate meeting with another. In other words, they are maladaptive.

One can speak therefore of 'mature' defences, which are needed in all human beings, and more primitive mechanisms such as splitting and projective identification, which aim to get rid of certain aspects of the self, either by walling them off, or by placing them in someone else. For example, paranoia clearly takes aspects of one's own psyche, such as criticalness or anger, and places it out there, usually in a hostile world. This obviously turns into an endless cycle, since when one treats other people suspiciously and with hostility oneself, they often react badly, thus confirming one's prejudices.

The issue of how one deals with such defences in clients is a very complex and controversial one, since one cannot simply tear them down or even refer to them in the early period of therapy. This is too forceful and too direct, and for many clients represents a frightening assault on the integrity of the self. Even neurotic or quasi-psychotic defences exist for a good reason, in the sense they have helped the individual survive hostile circumstances, particularly in childhood, and no-one who has had to get through life like this will thank a psychotherapist who sets out to demolish them. In fact, this can be quite dangerous, since behind the defences may lurk all manner of primitive or even quasi-psychotic feelings, impulses and fantasies, and one cannot simply open these up willy-nilly.

One way of looking at our psychological defences is that they represent in part a kind of self-cure which we have constructed to deal with the deficits which we experienced in early life. In other words, they are both maladaptive and adaptive. They are adaptive since they help me to avoid those intense feelings of anxiety, vulnerability, shame, need, rage, and so on, which may have occurred to me as a child. Yet this survival mechanism, which can be seen as self-protective, is also self-damaging, since it stops me being open to others or to life, experiencing vitality and excitement, being able to love and be loved, and so on. The psychoanalyst Masud Khan made the brilliant comment that curing people's illness wasn't so difficult, but what was very difficult was curing their own self-cure.[8]

Another interesting aspect of psychological defences is that the therapist also needs to be aware of how much their own defences are being elicited with a particular client, and what implications this has for the client's own psychological state. The therapist also needs to have a good grasp of their own defensive repertoire, since with some clients they will need it! I mean that some clients attack their therapist forcibly, and it is not the therapist's job simply to accept this attack in a martyred way.

But every therapist will be aware of the changing nature of their own defensive system with particular clients – with some it is on high alert; with others, it comes right down, and there can be an atmosphere of intimacy and trust.

Object relations

The theory of object relations is one of the most important post-Freudian developments in psychoanalysis. The turn from the drive theory of Freud to a theory of the object – that is, something to which the human infant wishes to relate, or has an innate need to relate to – changes psychoanalysis into an interpersonal psychology. Object relations therefore has considerable explanatory power both in relation to childhood – where we can argue that human beings begin to emerge as selves out of early relationships – and in relation to psychotherapy, where it can be argued that these early object relations are inevitably brought back to life, so that they can be examined and made more conscious, and to some degree rectified.

But in addition, a number of analysts such as Klein, Fairbairn, Winnicott, and others, formulated the view that there is an inner world, which contains objects, which have various relations to each other, and to which the ego also relates (in fact the ego is one such object). This theory has very dynamic consequences. For example, the theory of projection assumes great significance and power, since we can argue that the objects of the inner world are projected onto the external world. If my inner world contains a very fierce inner critic, then I will tend to see such figures in the outer world – I may in fact be drawn to them, or I may see some people as such, who in fact are not. Many psychoanalytic concepts can be reconceptualized in terms of internal object theory – for example, one can argue that transference fantasies – whereby the client treats the therapist in an inappropriate way – do not simply represent a repetition from the past, but also a projection of relations between objects in the inner world. This marks a shift that is liberatory in some senses, since one does not have to delve into the past in order to make connections between the client's external life and their psychic life. The past may be a very shadowy realm, but the inner world, while elusive, presses upon all of us with its imagery, its interrelations and its emotional qualities.

Thus it can be argued that for many people, their neurotic or psychotic disturbance represents not simply a hangover from a difficult childhood, but also a contemporary event in the inner world, whereby they attack themselves, or more precisely, one component in the psyche attacks another. One often comes across a diabolical figure in the inner world, who hates the individual, resents anything positive they experience, and sets out to sabotage it. This kind of psychological disturbance is therefore something going on now within the client, and must be explored and dealt with through a sense of the client's own agency – in other words, that we are called upon to take part in our own civil war and attempt to neutralize these negative figures.[9]

The development of object relations marks not just a kind of technical shift, but a philosophical one, in the sense that Freud's quasi-biological concept of 'drives' was replaced by a more interpersonal theory that posited relating at the heart of psychic life. In other words, for many object relations theorists the human infant has an innate need to relate to an object, and the quality of its early object relations will in part determine its psychic health. It is interesting therefore that object relations has been appropriated by other schools of therapy, for example humanistic psychology, who were repelled by the notion of the Freudian drive.

Different schools of psychoanalysis

Psychoanalysis has become a very rich and complex body of ideas, and post-Freudian analysts have developed many new concepts and working methods, so much so that one can speak of 'schools' of psychoanalysis. For example, Melanie Klein focused on the very early psychological development of the child, and inferred that powerful forces such as guilt and envy were at work from a very early age. In this sense, Klein considerably enriched our understanding of the unconscious and its contents. On the other hand, ego psychology, particularly as developed in the United States, focused more on the development of the adult ego, and the ways in which psychoanalysis could abet this.

One can also mention the interpersonal school (Karen Horney, Fromm, Sullivan), which plays down the influence of the internal world, and emphasizes the importance of early relations for the child's development. In particular, the child is seen as attempting to negotiate between feelings of anxiety and security, which arise as a result of its environment, rather than as a result of internal drives.

Kohut's self-psychology has been influential in Britain outside psychoanalysis, no doubt in part because Kohut's concept of the self offered non-analysts a more approachable way into psychoanalytic ideas. One of the key ideas in self-psychology is the self-object, that is, a relationship with another which sustains and nourishes the self. Originally this analysis was applied to narcissistic patients, but has been expanded beyond that to cover the normal development of self-worth and security, which are seen to arise from one's dependency on others.

Relational psychoanalysis has begun to debate many of the issues which were raised in humanistic psychology, in particular, empathy, self-disclosure by the therapist, and the role of touch. This school is also much less restricted in membership than orthodox psychoanalysis – one finds in its ranks Jungians, psychologists, and others, so that it represents a kind of 'integrative' strand within psychoanalysis.[10]

A paradox

There is a paradox at the heart of Freud. On the one hand, he formulated and developed the theory of drives, which are quasi-biological forces impinging on the mind; he also attempted to marry psychology and neurology. We can call this the hard-edged scientific side of Freud. But in his invention of the psychoanalytic space, he developed a forum which encouraged intimacy between the two participants, and at the same time exposed the resistances to intimacy in both people. That is, the psychoanalytic session is a brilliant and profound exploration of our being with each other, and also our not being with each other.

This contribution has been passed on to psychotherapy as a whole, which whether it has agreed with Freud on many issues or not, has generally retained the sanctity of the hour long session, within which two people connect, and do not connect with each other, and are able to explore in a self-reflexive manner, those connections and disconnections.

This strikes me as an amazing invention. There are many disagreements about the technical means with which we analyze that space which two people inhabit together, and many disagreements about the attitudes of the psychotherapist, their aims, and so on, but most psychotherapies retain the intensity and the focus of the session, which is both like an X-ray machine and yet also a means of promoting intimacy, and ultimately human love. Of course, our route to love takes in many negative resistances to love, but then that is being human also!

Criticisms

One major criticism of the psychoanalytic mode is that it is reductive, that is, it traces many aspects of the client's personality to infantile origins, or to psychoanalytic principles. But in fact, one might argue that all psychological models are reductive, in that they seek to explain phenomena by means of their model, but certainly it is true that the Freudian model can be applied sometimes with a certain crudeness. This is so with symbolic expressions such as art and literature, where Freud himself often offers explanations which today seem rather simplistic. To say, for example, that the play *Hamlet* is concerned with Oedipal relationships – Hamlet is unable to form a relationship with Ophelia because of his incestuous relations with his mother – strikes me as both bizarre and naive. *Hamlet* is about much more than that – for example, it is very much concerned with Hamlet's self-consciousness, elaborated in a series of brilliant soliloquies, almost as if we are watching the dawning of modernity itself in Hamlet's self-questioning and anguish.

However, contemporary psychoanalysis and psychoanalytic criticism have become in general less crude, and offer many penetrating insights into contemporary culture, for example in film criticism, literary criticism and so on.[11]

The many rebels against psychoanalysis have often argued that the analyst is too detached and arid a figure. Analysts such as Ferenczi wanted to introduce a warmer, more intimate atmosphere, and also wanted to bring the analyst's own personality into the room. But Ferenczi anticipated later rebellions, such as in humanistic psychology, which also argued against the over-intellectuality of psychoanalysis, its sidelining of the body, the unequal relations between analyst and patient, the actual coldness of some analysts, and so on.[12]

It strikes me that a lot of these criticisms are concerned with fantasies which people have about Freud and psychoanalysis. No doubt there are cold psychoanalysts, but whether this tells us anything interesting about psychoanalysis itself is debatable. Without doubt, there are strange, bizarre, over-detached or over-involved, therapists in all of the main schools – I am not sure we can actually draw any general inferences from this about one school over another.

One might also say that the rebellions against psychoanalysis have been inevitable and necessary, since all movements such as psychoanalysis tend to become conservative. Without doubt, in some parts of the world, psychoanalysis became a very Establishment force, for example in America, and would probably have horrified Freud himself, who no doubt had a secret pride in being the head of a scandalous body of ideas and a scandalous profession.

Jung and analytical psychology

Jung seems to inhabit a different universe from Freud, so much so that it is surprising, not that these two giants became estranged from each other, but that they were able to co-exist for a number of years. Whereas Freud looks back to the history of a neurosis, Jung looks forward to its possible meaning in the future; where Freud takes a quite materialistic view of the psyche, seen as containing various quasi-biological drives, Jung's psychology is much more concerned with images and symbols as things in themselves. I mean that Jung sees the psyche inherently as a symbol-producing organ, and these symbols determine in large part the course of our life. Thus for Jung the myths and legends of a culture tell us much about human motivation, and are not seen a la Freud as derived from infantile experience, but in fact as determining it.

The Jungian concept of the archetype is critical here, since for Jung this is a given, an innate universal principle of the psyche, which again is reflected in various images and symbols. But the archetype is not derived from experience, but rather gives our experience its structure and its value.

One might say rather simplistically that for Jung our experience of fathers is mediated by a father archetype which is simply inborn in us, and is not derived from our own father. In some ways, this is the exact converse of Freud, who would argue that the ways in which I think about fathers is largely determined by my experience of my own father.

Jung's psychology also shows its anti-materialistic quality in its notion of the Self. This is conceived as the organizing principle of the psyche, the superordinate force which overlooks it. In fact, the ways in which Jung talks about the Self reminds us of our images of God, and Jung argued that human ideas about God are reflections of the Self. But crucially here Jung has brought into human psychology the idea of transcendence, something which to Freud is anathema, or which can explained by infantile experiences.

One might almost say that for Freud a transcendent experience is an avoidance of something else; for Jung it is the summation of human life. Thus Jung was profoundly interested in mythology, mysticism, alchemy, and other collective expressions of inner truths, or in Jung's terms, expressions of the collective archetypes.

So there is a kind of inversion of Freud in Jung. Where Freud saw infantile sexuality as highly determining of later mental structures, Jung saw it as the outcrop of deep symbolic pre-existing structures.

The Self

Jung's notion of the Self is one of the most extraordinary ideas developed in human psychology, not least since it connects with many religious and spiritual ideas. The way in which Jung describes it – as the centre of the psyche, and also the totality, as the ultimate source of knowledge and symbolism – reminds us of nothing so much as traditional descriptions of God, and Jung freely admitted that the Self had a God-like existence. In fact, normally the individual cannot directly perceive the Self, but can perceive images of it, which often give that sense of the 'numinous' which Jung speaks of. Thus I recall clients who had 'big dreams', which filled them with awe and wonder and fear, and which seemed without doubt to presage some important shifts in their life, and which seemed to act as transcendent guiding forces. This kind of dream reminds us of the ancient belief in oracles and divination and other means of understanding one's destiny.[13]

If we compare the Jungian notion of the Self with Freud's division into ego, id and superego, we can see that the Jungian view offers something more sweeping, even transcendent. The ego has a relationship with the Self, and this relationship, in the Jungian view, is of great importance, and fractures in it cause great unhappiness and lack of fulfilment in the individual.[14]

We might say that whereas Freud's unconscious is chaotic and primitive, Jung's unconscious is mediated and governed by the Self. Thus we are led to Jung's ideas about the purposive or teleological nature of psychological disturbance, including neuroses, in human beings, since the Self, as it were, strives to bring about a balance in a psyche which is imbalanced. Neurosis therefore can point the way towards the resolution of inner conflicts.

The Self is one of those ideas which attract some and repel others. It certainly attracts those who have spiritual leanings, and probably repels many who do not, but then this is true of Jungian psychology generally, which is much less factual and empirical than psychoanalysis, and more concerned with the symbolic life of the individual.[15]

The collective unconscious

Another of Jung's original and provocative contributions to human psychology is the idea of the collective unconscious, the notion that some psychological forces are not simply produced in the individual, but exist in a mass
of people.[16] A good example of this in relation to Western culture is the tide of
Puritan thinking which swept across Europe three centuries ago, and then was
exported to the United States. One can adduce all manner of explanations for
the rise of Puritanism – economic, political, sociological – but its psychological
impact has been immense and affects everyone who lives in the West. One
might say that it has inculcated strong feelings of guilt about pleasure, particularly sexual pleasure; it has instilled a strong sense of duty in people, so that life
is seen very much to do with work and routine and obligation; it has also produced a heightened sense of individualism. The Puritan rejected the collective
womb of mother Church, and replaced it with the individual's private relationship to God. Indeed, it is not fanciful to look forward from the early Puritans
to the individualism of liberal capitalism, and its 'privatization' of many
cultural and social areas.

Whatever the origins of Puritanism, it is undeniable that it has been of
great importance psychologically, and one could argue that every individual
in psychotherapy in Western culture has to grapple to an extent with its
tenets and stipulations, particularly to do with guilt and duty. Can we say
that Puritanism represents an aspect of the collective unconscious? To my
mind, it is exactly that, since its dynamics are profoundly unconscious, so
that we have to painfully and gradually uncover them in therapy, and it is
clearly a movement that has taken over whole nations, indeed continents.

But is it useful to point out in psychotherapy that one is grappling with
something that is a collective phenomenon? I think it is, since then one no
longer feels bizarre and freakish, say for example, if one is grappling with ferocious guilt. People may ask why they are being subjected to such attacks of
guilt, but one answer to that is that the culture has demanded it. Jung used
similar reasoning to explain the rise of Nazism and Communism, and it is clear
that the human propensity to war and the barbarism that is found in war
cannot simply be explained in terms of individual psychology. There are mass
psychological movements and forces, which in fact are difficult to deal with for
individuals, precisely because they are collective phenomenon, so that some
people feel swept away by them. Indeed the Jungian idea of individuation, the
process whereby the individual realizes their full self, in part consists precisely
in resisting some aspects of the collective. Thus people often find that they
need to move away from their family, or they become reclusive as they get
older, or no longer want to work in a large organization. The shift from youth

to maturity is often accompanied by a move away from a collective way of life to a more individual and indeed solitary one. Thus students tend to hang around in bars and clubs en masse; but the middle-aged person often shuns such gatherings, and prefers the company of one other person, or prefers their own company.

These developments are of great importance in therapy, since many clients are beginning to experience the first steps in this process, and find it very painful and bewildering, since the edicts of the collective no longer carry the weight they formerly did. It is as if one is being born anew.

Individuation

Jung's psychology projects forward, and is concerned with the destiny of each individual. This destiny is something like a calling, that is, something born inside us which gives meaning and purpose to our life. Jung conceived of the idea of individuation to mean the self-realization of each person, and I have found it one of the most useful of Jung's ideas, since one meets in therapy so many people who are struggling with their own destiny, or are trying to find out what it is.[17] By 'destiny' in this context, I do not mean any kind of external destiny, but an internal one, a sense of one's innermost strivings and talents.

I mean that quite a number of people realize, often in mid-life, that they are not following their own inner calling, and then they enter into a crisis, in which they are forced to re-evaluate many things – their relationships, their work, their creative output, the actual fabric of their life. One might say that early in life we tend to do what others say, or we tend to have identities derived from parental or other social influences, but then in mid-life we can begin to find ourselves as we really are. In Jungian terms, the individual begins to separate from the collective, and begins to find their own true identity, which may be quite different from that defined by others. This also means that the Jungian unconscious does not simply contain repressed material, but also forces that have never been conscious, and which begin to struggle towards consciousness at a certain point in our development.

Clearly Jung's psychology is much less deterministic or causative than Freud's. It is more concerned with the inner life of the individual, and the inner core which desires expression and realization. This is given, not learned. So my destiny is in fact to become fully the person that I am and to express that. This obviously produces conflict, either because society at large is not very interested in that development, or is hostile to it, or because my own family and friends are hostile to it. In fact, I myself may be hostile to my own individuation, because it is frightening and runs counter to what I have been told about life.

Therapy according to these ideas is very much concerned with the symbolic life of the individual, since it is through symbols that these deep inner meanings are revealed. Thus the study of dreams, fantasies, and other symbolic structures in our lives is of great value.

Having said that, it is remarkable that some kind of rapprochement has occurred between Freudian and Jungian ideas, in that many Jungian training courses today have a considerable amount of developmental ideas in them. Many Jungians felt that 'classical' or symbolic Jungian analysis neglected the individual's development, particularly in infancy, and that psychoanalysis had produced a very important collection of theories and research methods which were essential in the understanding of a person's present problems.[18]

This rapprochement has been largely one-sided – although many Jungian schools have absorbed large amounts of psychoanalysis, the return process has not occurred, and many psychoanalysts traditionally have been deeply suspicious of Jung. However, the contemporary school of relational psychoanalysis shows signs of relaxing this barrier, as it begins to open up to ideas outside the analytic canon.

The shadow

An important part of individuation is the confrontation with one's own shadow, that is the aspects of one's personality which have been hidden away, which are shameful, which one does not like to think of as oneself. This includes all the negative feelings such as envy, hatred, and so on, but some people have a positive shadow, that is they feel very embarrassed about feelings of love and affection, and have therefore shunned such feelings. But the human need for such emotional connections is very powerful, and tends to push up against the repression.

We might say also that the human need for negative connections is very powerful! I mean that the denial of envy, hatred, dislike, and so on, can lead to a knotting up of the personality, since the effort of denying the negative side of one's character can turn one into a caricature of good behaviour, which is inauthentic. Without the shadow, human beings are insipid and featureless. It reminds me of food without salt – it lacks flavour, yet we do not want to pour tons of salt on food – that is inedible. Similarly, we hope that the negative aspects of the personality can be assimilated so that they form a part but not a domineering part.

Freud/Jung

Freud and Jung form an amazing polarity in psychotherapy. Freud tends to look back, Jung forwards; Freud looks for the concrete roots of a neurosis, Jung looks for its symbolic meaning; Freud looks at relationships with others, Jung at the inner relations in the psyche; Freud is tied to the earth, Jung looks more to heaven; Freud is an empirical researcher, Jung is a visionary.

One can in fact produce a whole series of oppositions of this kind, but while it is often true that therapists and clients tend to be attracted to one pole or the other, I have always thought that Freud and Jung are two halves of a whole – that clearly we need both poles if we are to be authentic witnesses to the whole human being. One must look at early development and also at the innate abilities in the client which are struggling to flower; one must look at the transference and counter-transference processes going on, and also at the symbolic life of the client; one must look at the relationship between ego and unconscious, but also at signs of the Self.

FURTHER READING

- A. Bateman and J. Holmes, *Introduction to Psychoanalysis* (London: Routledge, 1995).
- S. Freud, *Introductory Lectures on Psychoanalysis* (Penguin Freud Library Vol. 1) (Harmondsworth: Penguin, 1991).
- S. Freud, *An Outline of Psychoanalysis* in *Historical and Expository Works on Psychoanalysis* (PFL Vol. 15) (Harmondsworth: Penguin, 1993).
- C. G. Jung, *Two Essays on Analytical Psychology* in *Collected Works* Vol. 7.
- Andrew Samuels, *Jung and the post-Jungians* (London: Routledge, 1985).

Notes

1 See for example R. Webster, *Why Freud was Wrong: Sin, Science and Psychoanalysis* (London: Fontana, 1996); J. Masson, *The Assault on Truth: Freud and Child Sexual Abuse* (London: Fontana, 1992); F. Crews, *The Memory Wars: Freudian Science in Dispute* (New York: New York Review, 1995).

2 S. Freud, 'The Unconscious' in *On Psychopathology* (Penguin Freud Library Vol. 10) (Harmondsworth: Penguin, 1993).

3 S. Freud, *Civilization and its Discontents*, in *Civilization, Society and Religion* (PFL Vol. 12) (Harmondsworth: Penguin, 1991).

4 See J. R. Greenberg and S. A. Mitchell, *Object Relations in Psychoanalytic Theory* (Cambridge, Mass.: Harvard University Press, 1983).

5   S. Freud, 'Notes upon a Case of Obsessional Neurosis', in *Case Histories II* (PFL Vol. 9) (Harmondsworth: Penguin, 1991).
6   See H. Segal, *Introduction to the Work of Melanie Klein* (London: Hogarth, 1973).
7   C. J. Jung, *The Archetypes and the Collective Unconscious* in *The Collected Works of C. G. Jung*, Vol. 9 (London: Routledge and Kegan Paul, 1953–79).
8   Masud Khan, 'Towards an epistemology of cure', in M. Khan, *The Privacy of the Self*, (London, Hogarth: 1986).
9   Donald Kalsched, *The Inner World of Trauma* (London, Routledge: 1986).
10 A fuller account of psychoanalytic theories can be found in A. Bateman and J. Holmes, *Introduction to Psychoanalysis* (London: Routledge, 1995). On relational psychoanalysis see Patricia DeYoung, *Relational Psychotherapy: A Primer* (Hove: Brunner-Routledge, 2003).
11 See for example E. A. Kaplan (ed.) *Psychoanalysis and Cinema* (New York: Routledge, 1990); B. Creed, *The Monstrous-Feminine: Film, Feminism and Psychoanalysis* (London: Routledge, 1993).
12 S. Ferenczi, *Further Contributions to the Theory and Technique of Psychoanalysis* (London: Karnac, 1994).
13 For an example see Marika Henriques, '"The lions are coming"– the healing image in Jungian dreamwork', in *British Journal of Psychotherapy*, (2004) **20:4**.
14 See E. F. Edinger, *Ego and Archetype* (Boston: Shambala, 1992).
15 C. G. Jung, *Two Essays on Analytical Psychology* in *Collected Works* Vol. 7.
16 C. G. Jung, *The Archetypes and the Collective Unconscious* in *Collected Works* Vol. 9 Part One.
17 C. G. Jung, *Two Essays on Analytical Psychology* in *Collected Works* Vol. 7.
18 See K. Lambert, *Analysis, Repair and Individuation* (London: Karnac, 1994).

3
Humanistic Psychology

Humanistic practitioners have not necessarily rejected the idea of the unconscious, but they have tended to see the psychoanalytic means of uncovering it as too cerebral and detached. Humanistic psychology was originally a rebellion against the perceived aridity and intellectualism of psychoanalysis, and against the mechanical nature of behaviourist psychology, and advocated direct emotional expression, a greater use made of the body, and in some ways a more dramatic approach to the human personality. For example, in encounter groups, which were important in the late 60s and early 70s, the group itself became a kind of theatre, where one's emotional conflicts and disturbances could be played out.

But humanistic psychology has many influences behind it, including existentialism, Zen, Jung, and American management techniques. For a period it led to a heady explosion of therapeutic techniques and a determination to overthrow the psychoanalytic establishment, seen as elitist and word-bound. But one of the great ironies in the contemporary developments of psychotherapy has been the turn back to psychoanalysis by most of the humanistic training courses, and in particular the incorporation of object relations which has become de rigueur on most courses.

One might argue in fact that such rebellions are healthy and necessary, and that humanistic psychology was part of the post-war movements against the conservative status quo which occurred in many areas of culture. There is also ironically an intergenerational or Oedipal dimension to this – the young Turks overcome their elders and proclaim a new liberation and a new revolution. The fact that eventually humanistic psychology turns back to psychoanalysis is also part of this dynamic, since many rebellions eventually turn back to the source, since ultimately they owe their existence to it.

Authenticity, autonomy, empathy

These have been some of the battle cries of the humanistic movement – that its way of doing therapy offers the client a greater degree of choice and involvement, and less of a sense of being the passive recipient of expertise from a disengaged interpreter. It is unclear to me how much of this is correct, in the sense that cold neutral therapists – the fantasy figures who were to be over-thrown in the humanistic revolution – probably exist in all schools, and no doubt psychoanalysis contains many warm engaged analysts.

Nonetheless, fantasy or not, the humanistic movement has been very impor-tant in bringing forward such issues, and has probably forced psychoanalysis to consider its own values more closely. It is also interesting that similar criticisms had been made many years ago by analysts such as Ferenczi, who had also advocated a greater involvement by the analyst, and even a kind of mutual analysis by analyst and patient.[1]

Certainly humanistic psychology, with its emphasis on empathy, the im-pact of the person of the therapist, which includes a limited amount of self-disclosure, and the use of touch, has articulated a very different set of values from psychoanalysis, although interestingly relational psychoanalysis has begun to explore such issues.[2]

Humanistic psychology also moved away from the use of interpretations, and certainly in its early days did not analyze transference and counter-trans-ference phenomena. Humanistic therapy has emphasized the notion of the 'real self' in the client, which emerges as defences come down. Here the very positive nature of humanistic psychology is shown – as John Rowan says in his book *The Reality Game*, 'what is true in the person is always OK'.[3] In his book *The Mind Gymnasium*, Denis Postle says something similar: 'humanistic psy-chology takes a more optimistic view, regarding human beings as fundamen-tally good and as having been born with a huge potential'.[4]

From the psychoanalytic point of view, one could argue that this ignores the existence of very negative feelings and wishes in many people, including quite destructive and self-destructive feelings. Of course, from the humanistic point of view, we can say that such feelings are not 'what is true in the person', but form part of their defensive armouring. However, we are now thrust into a very difficult debate about what truth is and is not, in relation to the human person-ality, since it is arguable that my defences are as much part of my truth as my loving core, if such there be. Or indeed, that aggression and destructiveness are as intrinsic to human beings as love and kindness.

Humanistic psychology has also criticized psychoanalysis as having adapted to a conservative bourgeois set of values, so that people are encour-aged to 'fit in', rather than encouraged to find their own way through life, even if this means bucking the norms. This certainly seems to have some truth, when we consider the homophobic nature of psychoanalysis, since gays and lesbians have often been condemned by analysts for not conforming to the heterosexual norms.

It has also been argued that psychoanalysis itself was hierarchical, elitist, and imbued with bourgeois values, and the humanistic movement therefore appealed to a certain anarchistic current which existed from the 60s onwards. But again, this seems to have changed considerably in the last twenty years, since humanistic therapists in the UK have found themselves, rather uneasily maybe, joining in the attempt to construct a profession of psychotherapy, to be certified by government. There is a certain irony in this, just as the political rebels of the 1960s often became bankers and accountants.

However, it is obviously true that one cannot be in a permanent state of rebellion, or if one is, it becomes a kind of protracted adolescence. Humanistic psychology has had to grow up therefore, and has largely shed its former associations of hippy values, libertarian aims and utter eclecticism of technique.

The present moment

The notion of the 'here and now' achieved iconic status within humanistic psychology, perceived as an antidote to the cerebral explanations of psychoanalysis. Schools of therapy such as Gestalt encourage clients to focus on the present, on the body, on feelings going on now, rather than speculating about the past or worrying about the future.

It is likely in fact that most therapists see the present moment as a vital part of the therapeutic endeavour, since it gets people out of their head and rescues them from over-intellectuality. Hence it is of great value with those clients who approach life in a very cognitive way, and therefore tend to see therapy as a problem-solving practice. Such people tend to get disappointed and fed up when problems are not being solved, and when obvious cognitive working out is not taking place. It is worth asking them whether the present moment has any value for them, for one will often find that it has little, since their mind is already focused on the next goal or the next problem to be solved. This is particularly true of men who spend their working lives engaged in this kind of mental activity, and are often very good at it.

For such people, the present moment may seem of little or no value, or may seem quite empty, unless it is filled with mental work. If one asks them if they ever do nothing, they often say that sometimes they read a book or watch TV – in other words, they never do nothing, and therefore the present moment is usually lost behind a haze of mental activity.

One might call this the Western disease, since we are all prone to overvalue the mind and its workings, and feel proud when it solves problems or proposes elegant theories. Compared with this, the present moment may seem mundane and disappointing, in fact something to be avoided.

This seems to be a vital point – that many people in our culture fill their lives with distractions, so as not to feel empty or isolated or 'bored'. Thus in therapy, silence fills them with dread or impatience, for something should be happening. Of course, there is a partial legitimacy to these demands. People come to therapy to achieve certain things, and that is part of the contract between therapist and client. But if the therapist detects an avoidance of the present, a tendency to drift off into clouds of speculation, or an over-active use of the intellect, thereby avoiding this moment, then we can infer that this is affecting the client's life adversely.

Of course, part of the present moment is that two people are sitting in a room, and this in itself fills some clients with dread, for it may seem too intimate. They may say that it is too uneventful, or mundane, or 'nothing is happening', but I tend to think that these are roundabout ways of complaining about and defending against intimacy.

The other major reason for avoiding the present, is that we find ourselves having feelings, since they tend to rise up spontaneously, if we allow them to, so that we find all kinds of methods used to stop this happening. Quite often, this involves never being alone, and such a phobia indicates a dread of repressed feelings beginning to emerge.

Direct intervention

In its early years, humanistic therapists often advocated more direct interventions than a psychoanalytic therapist would. For example, one might use role-play, or suggest that the client say certain things, or shout them aloud, or one might suggest that certain body postures and movements be tried. These techniques are particularly suitable for groups, since the more theatrical atmosphere of the group lends itself to a kind of dramatic performance. In fact, one of the humanistic streams is psychodrama which has at its core the dramatization of the client's problems with others, or with parts of their own psyche.

But do these techniques work in one-to-one therapy? Many psychotherapists I have asked have told me that they abandoned them, since they make clients embarrassed, very self-conscious, and also tend to break up the focus of the sessions. In a sense, the dramatic technique militates against the intimacy between therapist and client. Nonetheless the tradition of direct techniques still survives in humanistic therapy, and of course in certain branches of it, such as bodywork, is very important.

> Elizabeth kept complaining about her sister, who criticized her all the time. In an attempt to make the scenario more explicit, the therapist asked her to play her sister, while the therapist played Elizabeth, and then they switched roles. In fact, what emerged was Elizabeth's scorn and vindictiveness towards her sister.

One might object that such techniques change the therapist's role considerably, so that some clients might feel dismayed or frightened by the sight of the therapist playing herself or another person. Even the fact that the two participants are busy changing chairs and roles could be disturbing for some clients, but clearly the sensitive therapist would not suggest such techniques for such clients.

In fact, such direct techniques are precluded for many clients, it strikes me, who find it too embarrassing, or who simply cannot change their own identity with the required fluidity. None the less, they are a useful part of therapeutic armoury, which can be held in reserve.

Experience

If one is asked to point to the most important theme that separates humanistic psychology from psychoanalysis, I would say it is the emphasis on experience rather than explanation. Thus key questions for humanistic psychology, certainly in the early days, were: 'How are you feeling now?', 'How do you feel in your body?', 'What is it like being with me now?'

The focus here is on the client's experience, and humanistic psychotherapy seeks to promote emotional awareness rather than cognitive understanding and explanation. One can see of course that this can also become a cul de sac, since one has not said anything about the context of the feelings going on, their history, their causes, the relationships which give rise to them. Thus I recall encounter groups in the 70s which were emotionally dynamic, even theatrical, but lacked any sense of intimacy or reflectiveness. There was a lot of pressure to have feelings, and to express them, but in fact this could become another kind of defence against contact with others and with oneself.

There was also the danger of seeing emotions as ipso facto good, and rationality as bad; but this meant that the expression of feelings, particularly hostile ones, could easily become destructive. In fact, the destructive power of negative feelings was poorly dealt with in such therapy groups, which often tended to suggest that expressing a feeling was somehow self-fulfilling or self-justifying, whatever the effect on others.

In other words, the inner world was often projected onto the outer world in a quite theatrical manner, without the space in which one might reflect on one's own feelings, before expressing them. Of course, the feeling of emotional liberation was understandable, since humanistic psychology felt it had to throw off the shackles of rationality and inhibition, which it believed psychoanalysis fostered.

But for some humanistic practitioners, thought itself was suspect, since it interrupted the dynamic flow of feelings. However, looking back, which is of course a great luxury, it can be seen that humanistic psychology in its early years threw out the baby with the bathwater. I mean that it encouraged impulsiveness, which can easily become destructive.

Sometimes I work with couples who function in this way – they hurl abuse at each other; they release their negativity willy nilly. In therapy, one tries to help them to deal separately with their own feelings, before they are discharged to the other. Couples like this are playing a very dangerous kind of emotional tennis, and in fact have not learned to contain their separate psyches. This produces a sense of boundaryless confusion or fusion, which then tends to impel people to get away from this mess.

But I am speaking about an early and primitive form of humanistic practice; and certainly the last twenty years have seen an increasing sophistication in humanistic training and theorization, and in particular a return to psychoanalytic ideas in some areas. The anti-intellectualism once so prevalent in the humanistic movement has abated, while its emphasis on emotional authenticity has been preserved.

The emphasis on experience also connects humanistic therapy with spirituality, since the experience of the present moment can be seen as a transcendent experience. I mean that one can let go of one's cognitive turmoil, and one can surrender to life itself now. No doubt this kind of experience is found in all kinds of psychotherapy, but the humanistic movement has prized it, and in some ways has counterposed it to conventional notions of life as goal-driven. Furthermore, in the surrender to now, one's conception of oneself as a tightly delimited ego, separate from everything else, begins to dissolve, and a larger or more profound sense of self may emerge. Writers such as Ken Wilbur have articulated this transcendent development, and have been influential on humanistic psychology.[5] Hence transpersonal psychology can be seen as a part of the humanistic movement, and underlines its ideological dislike of 'business values' and the general ethos of late capitalism, which is less concerned with personal development than with mercantile development.

But one also has to issue a word of warning about transpersonal psychology – that it is dangerous for disturbed, unstable or chaotic clients. In order to transcend the ego, one must have developed a stable and strong ego! I have come across people who seemed quite fragile to me, who were exploring various kinds of spiritual practices, meditation systems, and so on, and while one can argue that belonging to a spiritual group or having a regular spiritual practice is a grounding and stabilizing factor in one's life, for fragile people it can bring up very uncomfortable and upsetting experiences about the nature of the self. It is fine for Buddha to exclaim that there is no separate self, but not for someone who has barely managed to acquire a sense of self at all. I have to admit that with such clients I usually avoid discussion of spirituality like the plague – far better for them to find a grounding in the ordinary world, so that they can take care of themselves physically, financially and emotionally. In fact, Zen practice recognizes this fact, and is very insistent that students have regular jobs, carry out their work conscientiously, pay their bills, and in general are well grounded.

Catharsis

The notion of emotional catharsis or release formerly held great sway in humanistic psychology, particularly in the more body oriented disciplines, where it seemed to offer tangible, even dramatic, results, in that the client, formerly emotionally blocked and inhibited, was encouraged to get in touch with feelings and express them energetically. This was also the basis for much group work, where again an underlying philosophy seemed to be that the clients were there to express feelings which had been repressed.

However, historically the humanistic movement has had to acknowledge that catharsis cannot be the basis for an in-depth psychotherapy, since the assumption that neurosis is simply about blocked feelings is palpably untrue. One might instead define neurosis as a set of self-limiting or self-damaging systems in the person's mind or inner world. This self-limitation might well include emotional inhibition, but one cannot change that simply by encouraging emotional release, since one has not investigated the mental systems which perpetuate the inhibition.

There is a further drawback to catharsis – it can become abusive of other people. I have already referred to those couples who certainly are able to hurl emotional invective at each other, but whose relationship is in fact in a terrible mess, because they are using catharsis as a weapon. One therefore has to find out why such weapons are being used towards each other, why there is so much anger, and so on. In fact, therapy with such people might well encourage the curtailment of emotional catharsis, since it has become a kind of mutual punishment.

I recall also groups of friends, who spurred on by the discovery of emotional catharsis in therapy groups, would regularly vent anger towards each other, in the belief that this 'cleared the air', got rid of one's emotional blockages, and so on. In fact, it often led to feelings of hurt and betrayal, and even the ending of friendships.

Catharsis is therefore something to be handled very carefully. Without doubt, some clients are emotionally pent up, and their feelings begin to spill out in therapy, and this process is entirely healthy. However, for the therapist to make catharsis a central plank of therapeutic technique strikes me as dangerous, since it tends to leave out so much else, such as the client's capacity for intimacy, their ability to be in their own company, and in fact their ability to contain feelings. Containment does not mean repression, for it denotes being in touch with feelings, without venting them on others necessarily.

The notion of catharsis can also go along with a rather crude view of psychological neurosis – that people have suffered trauma as children, and now need to remember this, and express the feelings surrounding the trauma – 'healing the pain of childhood'. This is a kind of 'naïve realism', and is often found in the writings of 'Freud-bashers' such as Jeffrey Masson, who are infuriated that Freud rejected such a theory of neurosis in favour of something more complex and more internal. Freud rejected his early theory of child seduction or abuse as he realized that many patients had not been sexually abused, but suffered from self-damaging internal processes. Without doubt, many people who come to therapy have suffered some kind of neglect or worse in childhood, but it is not sufficient to investigate that, for we are still left with the ways in the which the person abuses or restricts their own person and their own life.

Going back to the pains of childhood, exploring them, working through them and healing them is undoubtedly part of psychotherapy, but it is not something that can be done quickly or easily. Some 'regression' therapies seem to suggest that it can, and furthermore, that this healing is the core of psychotherapy. It may be for some clients, but I think for many clients there are other things which need to be looked at and explored.

Schools of humanistic therapy

Humanistic Psychology has become a very complex collection of different disciplines. Sometimes it is difficult to see what they all have in common, but probably there is a shared concern with authenticity, the autonomy of the client, and perhaps still a suspicion of overly analytic approaches.

Probably the most important are Gestalt therapy and bodywork. Gestalt began as another breakaway from psychoanalysis by Fritz Perls, who advocated a greater emphasis on the here and now, and also began to employ much more directive techniques in therapy, such as role-play, to articulate the different parts of the client's experience. Thus Gestalt has a connection with the philosophical current of phenomenology, which focuses on personal experience, rather than the interpretation of experience.[6]

In addition, Gestalt is centred on the 'dialogic relationship' between therapist and client, that is, a relationship where the therapist is present and focused on the client's experience, rather than distancing him or herself from it by means of interpretation. In particular, the therapist will pay attention to the rhythms of contact and withdrawal made by the client, since these give us vital information about the client's contact or non-contact with life.

Bio-energetics

Bodywork was in part developed by Wilhelm Reich, who also initially received a psychoanalytic training, and again developed techniques which were much more directive, and led the therapist to work with the client's body directly, something which is pretty much inconceivable in psychoanalysis, where the 'don't touch' rule has tended to dominate until recently.

Of course, one can see why therapists tend to stay away from clients' bodies, because of the dangers of seduction and sexual exploitation, but at the same time it would seem very odd if clients could not find a therapy which dealt with their own bio-energy and its expression (and repression).

Bodywork or bio-energetics is in some ways the quintessential humanistic discipline – it is concerned with the release of feelings in the body, as against their neurotic blockage; it is concerned with energy in the body, its pulsations and its repressions; it sees the organism very much as a physical one. Ironically, one might even argue that in some ways bodywork goes back to Freud's formulation of the human being as a biological entity, subject to certain drives.

Bio-energetic therapy in part stems from the perception that in the West, human beings have become deeply alienated from the body, and have therefore incurred many psychological and physical ailments. Its founder, Wilhelm Reich, continued Freud's emphasis on sexuality, but located sexual dis-ease in the body itself, or rather in the turning away from the body which our cerebral culture has inculcated.

Reich therefore advocated the healing power of the sexual orgasm, and saw sexual dysfunction very much as a physical, or energetic, problem. One obvious problem with this is that the issue of relationship, and its dysfunctionality, seems to be avoided, and one of the problems with bodywork therapy, or bio-energetic therapy, is how the relationship with the therapist is dealt with.

Most humanistic therapists do not practise bio-energetics in their therapy sessions, but an awareness of the body, and of the potential of bodywork therapy, could be said to infuse much humanistic work. For example, one's emotional state is always a physical state, as well as a mental one, and most humanistic practitioners would pay some attention to this. I quite often ask clients who are describing a feeling, what it feels like in their body, since this often gives some grounding to otherwise rather nebulous emotional experiences.

But to practise bodywork techniques in therapy marks a dividing line between bodywork and non-bodywork therapists, and there seems little doubt that the past 15 years or so have seen many humanistic therapists turn more to a psychodynamic mode of working. Thus there is a tendency for the various streams in humanistic psychology, such as bodywork and Gestalt, to become specialized disciplines in their own right, and the trainee tends to undergo trainings in them directly. The eclecticism of humanistic psychology in the 70s has probably been reduced, partly from professional exigency – I mean that it is difficult to practise a pick and mix psychotherapy, since potential clients are not sure what this is.[7]

The wild fringe

The psychotherapy world has always had a wild fringe – one could even argue that in nineteenth century Vienna Freud was considered wild. Today it is made up of a very mixed bag of shamans, psychics, astrologers, healers, and so on. Many psychotherapists view them with alarm and scorn as charlatans, but I am convinced that therapy always needs such a movement on the fringes, as it were to explore the less respectable branches of human psychology. It's interesting that Jung took an interest in such areas as flying saucers and Marian visions, not particularly because he believed in them, but because he was fascinated by the psychological disturbances in the collective unconscious which he believed they corresponded to. One might say that people obviously have a need to believe in flying saucers, alien abduction and so on, and it is likely that these are attempts to get in touch with the unconscious in an indirect way.

One obvious example of such parapsychological tendencies today is the crop circle movement. It combines a 'green' tendency with a mystical belief in aliens, outer space communication, and above all a sense that there are many things in reality we cannot comprehend. Thus it appeals to people who are repelled by the more rational areas of psychology, and this is why Jung kept an eye on such movements, in the belief that the unconscious expresses itself in them. One might say that crop circles have absolutely nothing to do with therapy, but there are people such as shamans and healers who, as it were, straddle the worlds of more orthodox therapy and less orthodox New Age thought. The fact that orthodox psychotherapists tend to shun such movements may show in fact that they are articulating important areas of non-rational experience which are difficult for psychotherapy to deal with.

A parody

One can make up an interesting parody about the ways in which the humanistic movement has regarded psychoanalysis. One must imagine a patient, lying on a couch, with the analyst sitting behind. The analyst is rather bored, disengaged, but occasionally makes a comment about the patient's lack of engagement. Both parties are completely in their heads, disembodied. In fact, their bodies are disregarded completely. The patient is unaware of sensations in the body, and of how feelings are rooted in the body, but then so is the analyst. The patient feels increasingly lost, bored, frustrated, at the lack of contact with the analyst; but the analyst feels likewise. At the end of the session, the analyst makes a brilliant interpretation that the patient has been cutting off in order to drive him (the analyst) mad. The patient leaves the room feeling enraged by this last interpretation.

Is this a parody? Yes, it is, but something like it has been a very powerful force in the humanistic world, and one wonders where it comes from. No doubt there is a grain of truth in it, in that there are disengaged and rather cold analysts; but one has to reply to that by saying that there are flaky, chaotic and uncontained humanistic therapists – I have met a number of them! What I am really saying is that the mutual suspicion and hostility felt by different schools of psychotherapy towards each other often consist of fantasies and projections, since this seems to be a universal human method of demonizing others. It is often overcome by actually going into the enemy camp and experiencing for oneself the nature of the beast – thus I began in the humanistic world, but eventually did a long psychoanalytic therapy, and found it to be as warm and engaged as a humanistic one.

Another way of looking at these divisions and conflicts in the psychotherapy movement is as a class system. The psychoanalysts are like a ruling class, dominating everyone else with fear and elitism. The psychoanalytic therapists are the middle class, aspiring to join the upper class, but obtaining plenty of comfort just by being near them, being trained by them, doing supervision with them, and so on. The humanistic therapists are the proletariat, apparently full of rage and rebelliousness, yet secretly also yearning to join the Establishment, be respectable, wear suits, and earn a decent salary.

This is another parody, yet there is probably a grain of truth in it, in the sense that psychotherapy is a highly stratified profession, with a strong hierarchical structure. One can get a sense of this by going to seminars and other events run by different groups – at some, one finds middle-aged affluent ladies wearing strings of pearls; at others, one finds those in jeans and sweaters; and there is a middle group who try to steer between the other two.

Existential therapy

Humanistic psychology has been heavily influenced by existential therapy, and ideas such as authenticity and choice can be traced back to the existential 'project' of human freedom. The number of existential therapists is small in most countries, but the influence of existentialism has been disproportionately large, in part because of the philosophical background. Philosophers such as Kierkegaard and Nietzsche had attacked the moralistic stance of Christianity, and had propounded instead a radical emphasis on human existence itself, and the freedom which human beings have to change their existence, and such ideas have proved attractive to many looking for alternatives to Freud.

More influential on psychotherapy have been a later generation of existential philosophers, such as Heidegger and Husserl, who also introduced the current of phenomenology, which argued that the split between subject and object, which had obviously nurtured the development of scientific thinking, had had a disastrous effect on human beings in other ways. This is because the actual experience of people tends to be ignored in rational or scientific discourse, and abilities such as intuition are undervalued. Phenomenology is therefore a valuable philosophical underpinning to those psychotherapies which stress the value of actual experience, and which nurture a poetic rather than a scientific sensibility. In part, one can see the split between Freud and Jung as a split between the hard-line scientific approach of Freud's, as against the more mythical and poetic approach of Jung's.[8]

Existential therapy has tended to reject the idea of the Freudian unconscious as rendering human beings too puppet like, and as a denial of our ability to choose a way of life, a freedom which causes much anxiety. Existential anxiety is therefore seen as inevitable in modern post-Christian society, and the existential therapist would not attempt to dispel such anxiety, but would seek to put it into its historical context.[9]

The issue of self-disclosure was brought into focus by existential therapy, since the quest for authenticity has been seen as paramount, and therefore the therapist cannot hide behind the traditional veiled anonymity. However, the issue of self-disclosure is highly controversial, and in humanistic psychology it has probably been curtailed in the last twenty years, under the influence of analytic thinking. I mean that with certain clients, self-disclosure by the therapist is quite ruinous, and in fact my experience is that the majority of clients are not that interested in the therapist, certainly to begin with, and any attempt at therapist self-disclosure can be jarring. At the same time, self-disclosure can be a very potent therapeutic tool, particularly with very disturbed clients, some of whom seem to be seeking such authenticity (see Chapter Thirteen).

Another reason in Britain for the importance of existentialism has been the influence of the charismatic and intellectually brilliant figure of R. D. Laing. Laing was highly unusual in a British context in that he incorporated quite difficult and complex ideas from philosophy (often derived from Sartre) into his psychological approach. In addition he published a series of books, such as *The Divided Self* and *The Politics of Experience* which caught the imagination of a wider public in the 60s and 70s, and seemed to suggest that a new radical psychology might be born out of this heady mix of philosophy, psychoanalysis, and Laing's own flamboyant and iconoclastic thinking. However, although Laing's influence still continues in the humanistic movement, his own particular therapeutic approach has rather fizzled out. This is partly because Laing was imbued with romantic ideas about madness and the repressive nature of society, and therapists have in practice found them to be unworkable or unpalatable.

Shortcomings

One of the shortcomings of humanistic therapy historically has been that it was often contact-driven, and hence did not leave much room for reverie and silence. It was very attuned to the contact between therapist and client, and was therefore a rather extravert kind of therapy, and dealt badly with introverts and creative people. Historically, there has also been a kind of triteness sometimes in the injunctions to 'be good to yourself', and so on, which have been purveyed in the humanistic world, somewhat akin to the advice found in self-help books. Positive thinking is all very well, but many people find in practice that it is continually sabotaged by internal negative forces, which seem ungovernable. Humanistic psychology has often spoken of love and intimacy, but it has until recently been theoretically and technically rather impoverished in dealing with hatred and destructiveness.

One can therefore suggest that one reason for the partial turn back to psy-choanalysis has been that mutuality and empathy work fine with clients who are themselves well-intentioned, but become much more problematic with clients who show hostility to the therapist. What does the well-intentioned humanistic therapist do then? One cannot simply appeal to the 'better nature' of the client – that may well excite more scorn. The clearest way ahead is to interpret the hostility, and attempt to find out what it is that excites it in the client – but here we have walked across into psychoanalytic territory. In other words, humanistic therapy found itself lacking in certain tools when dealing with difficult clients, and in fact, when dealing with transference in general – since it is negative transference that can be described as the source of such difficulties. But if we admit the notion of transference into our theoretical and practical armoury, then it seems odd not to admit more of the psychoanalytic body of theory. In fact, one might argue that the positive transference is just as difficult to handle, since one cannot simply rely on the two participants' good will to each other, since some clients in fact find positive feelings more difficult to deal with than negative ones. And of course the well-intentioned client may well change in the course of therapy, and may need to show hostility to the therapist.

What we are saying is that the therapist cannot simply be the client's ally. One cannot build one's therapeutic approach solely on empathy and congru-ence. The therapeutic alliance is obviously important, since it helps cement a kind of contract that we will work together, through foul weather as well as fair, so that a good foundation early on will help us get through more stormy waters later on. But one cannot rely entirely on this alliance, since that curtails the client enormously. He has to feel free to feel hostile to the therapist, or to want to become more separate, or to feel alone while with the therapist, and so on. In other words, there is a danger that relying on trust, caring, love, warmth, and so on, can become cloying and actually restrictive. In fact, the therapist also has to feel free to hate the client, or in fact to have any kind of negative feeling – otherwise, therapy becomes a kind of 'tea and comfort' kind of counselling, which for many people is actually quite disastrous. I say disas-trous because so many clients have to be allowed to vent their negativity onto their therapist in some way in order to find out what it consists of. Someone who offers smiles and sympathy is quite out of tune with this.

Perhaps also one can say that the humanistic movement had been orig-inally anti-intellectual, and had therefore rejected much of the drive for understanding which is found in the analytic movement, but humanistic therapists have had to come back to this, since authentic feelings are not enough for personal growth. I can learn to get in touch with my feelings, but I also need to know where they come from, what place they have in my internal geography, how I am to deal with them, express them, and so on. This is a complete package, which involves a considerable amount of thinking and understanding. One might say that understanding provides an essential container for feelings, which otherwise might become too raw and primitive and tend to be acted out, or vomited onto others, as the following example demonstrates.

> Every time his wife goes back to work after the holidays, Sam goes through powerful feelings of abandonment and grief and anger. This used to cause considerable disturbance in their relationship since Sam used to vent his anger on his wife, who felt confused and guilty about this. But in therapy Sam connected these feelings with his childhood feelings about his mother's many absences, and had therefore considerably reduced his attacks on his wife. He became able to tolerate the feelings without having to give vent to them.

This example is interesting since the client does not in fact get rid of those infantile feelings, although they may reduce in intensity, but becomes able to contain them. If you like, as an adult he is able to look after his infantile side. This is an invaluable part of our healing, as otherwise we are all tempted to launch our childlike protests at others, often with unfortunate results. I am not saying that we are never allowed to express such feelings, but that they also need some containment. Sam's wife may sometimes have a maternal role towards Sam, and she may be sympathetic to his feelings of abandonment, but she is not his mother, and that distinction is probably crucial to the well-being of their marriage. Sam must look to his internal 'mother' and 'father' to take care of his inner child, and then he can meet his wife adult-to-adult, as well as child-to-adult, and adult-to-child. But here again, in our turn to the inner world and inner objects, we have entered a definitely psychoanalytic domain; however, not to enter it condemns us to a psychology that is ultimately too superficial to get to the roots of people's problems.

Humanistic psychology is like the rebellious child who runs away from home, spends years scorning parents and home, and yet in the end has to make some accommodation with this ancestry. It is necessary to rebel at times, but also it is necessary to make use of the great gains made in human psychology in the last century. However, one can also speak of the amazing ability of the humanistic movement to absorb influences from other sources. In that sense it has been something of an eclectic school, taking its ideas from a wide range of philosophical and psychological disciplines, and from other areas such as management training, work with addicts, meditation, Buddhism, and so on.

This is therefore a great virtue and strength of humanistic psychology, and the fact that it has latterly incorporated a considerable amount of psychoanalytic thinking into its training programmes and its intellectual remit, should be a cause for congratulating it rather than belittling it. The humanistic movement has been extremely porous to ideas and influences from elsewhere, and whilst at times this makes it seem rather pick and mix, it also gives it a richness and elasticity which is very productive in the working milieu. Thus, speaking for myself, although I have absorbed many ideas from Jungian and Freudian psychology, I still consider myself to be a humanistic psychotherapist, and the fact that one sets out to analyze the transference, (or counter-transference), or that with some clients one uses concepts such as individuation and introversion, and with others one might be involved in a very intense and authentic encounter, is neither contradictory nor confusing.

But such a coming together of ideas and methods and techniques is very much an individual issue. I mean that the individual therapist follows a path which is unique, and is able to blend together different influences so as to produce eventually a personal style. In fact, the boundaries between schools of therapy seem less clear cut today, as ideas and clinical methods have interpenetrated.

Humanistic psychology has become something very different from its incarnation in the 60s and 70s, partly under the pressure of 'professionalization' and the stricter control over accreditation. Maybe something has been lost – a freewheeling spirit, a kind of libertarian ethos that anything goes – but in terms of individual (one-to-one) psychotherapy, one can see that the need for firm safe boundaries has demanded this. The vast majority of people who come to therapy certainly do not want a libertarian atmosphere, since that is frightening and chaotic.

FURTHER READING

A. H. Maslow, *Motivation and Personality* (New York: Harper and Row, 1987).

J. Rowan, *The Reality Game* (London: Routledge, 1998).

Denis Postle, *Letting the Heart Sing: The Mind Gymnasium* (WLR: 2003) (CD-ROM).

Carl Rogers, *On Becoming a Person* (Constable: 1961).

Notes

1 S. Ferenczi, *Further Contributions to the Theory and Technique of Psychoanalysis.*
2 See Patricia DeYoung, *Relational Psychotherapy* (Hove: Brunner-Routledge: 2003).
3 John Rowan, *The Reality Game* (London: Routledge, 1983) p. 61.
4 Denis Postle, *The Mind Gymnasium* (London: Macmillan, 1989) p. 165.
5 Ken Wilbur, *No Boundary: Eastern and Western approaches to personal growth* (Boulder: Shambhala, 1979).
6 See P. Joyce and C. Sills, *Skills in Gestalt Counselling and Psychotherapy* (London: Sage, 2001), pp. 16–26.
7 On bio-energetics see J. Rowan and W. Dryden (eds), *Innovative Therapy in Britain* (Milton Keynes: OUP, 1988); A. Lowen, *The Betrayal of the Body* (London: Macmillan, 1969); A. Lowen, *Bioenergetics* (Harmondsworth: Penguin, 1975).
8 See R. Brooke, *Jung and Phenomenology* (London: Routledge, 1991).
9 E. Van Deurzen-Smith, 'Existential Therapy' in W. Dryden (ed.) *Individual Therapy: A Handbook* (Milton Keynes: OUP, 1990) pp. 149–74.

4 Cognitive Therapy

It is likely that most therapists work with cognitive problems for some of the time, for many clients show a degree of faulty thinking or faulty logic. But cognitive therapy makes the rectification of such fault lines the core of its work, and it has proved extremely powerful in dealing with certain problems.

Examples of faulty thinking are very common.

> Jim always imagined that if something good was coming up in his life, somebody else – who was unspecified usually – would envy him, and would therefore attempt to spoil it for him. Jim therefore decided to spoil it first, thereby pre-empting the other person. The result was that Jim continually sabotaged himself.

In fact, such a train of thought and action can be found in many self-destructive people. The fear of envy leading to the pre-emptive strike produces a kind of ersatz safety, since I have caused my own destruction, which is preferable to it being caused by others, which is much more frightening. If you like, the saboteur has taken control of destruction, has wrested it out of the hands of others, of course at a huge price, since one's life is subject to much damage.

Of course, one can immediately see a psychoanalytic approach to such a problem – that one would attempt to trace back the origins of this behaviour. Who was it who envied Jim to begin with? When did Jim make the fateful decision to take the task of destruction into his own hands? Or in terms of inner world analysis, one can attempt to deal with the fierce critic which exists in Jim's psyche.

But one can also work with the material in the present, by tackling the issue of 'faulty thinking'. One can see the flaws in Jim's logic – there are quite a few!

First, he has generalized the issue of envy and destruction, so that from one person doing that to him, he has inferred that everyone is going to, or that it will invariably happen. Second, he has assumed that envy leads to destruction, when this may not be true. Many people are able to have feelings of envy without necessarily needing to make destructive attacks. Third, Jim has decided that it is better to do the destruction himself.

In short, Jim deprives himself of good things, so that no-one else can take them away from him. Of course, this sounds absurd, but it is not absurd in Jim's world; in fact, it provides a kind of comfort and safety.

Jim can look at this faulty logic and attempt to correct it, if he has reached a point in his life where it has caused him much harm, and he has become weary of the self-destructiveness. In fact, we can say that this is crucial – if there is still life in it for Jim, then any therapy will make little headway. It's rather like the alcoholic – who has got to have reached rock-bottom and is prepared to admit defeat, and that alcohol has power over him. As long as the alcoholic denies he/she is an alcoholic, as long as they are still making those familiar excuses – I can stop any time I want; I'm not really an alcoholic, I just drink a lot – then it is impossible to help them.

The neurotic person is in the same boat. They can look at their faulty thinking, and take steps to correct it, when they have exhausted it, and themselves.

Differences from other therapies

Certain key differences stand out in relation to cognitive therapy. First, it is usually time limited, and the number of sessions is often around twelve, but certainly much less than the traditional psychoanalytic period, which often amounts to several years or more. Cognitive therapy sets itself the task of identifying and changing the client's maladaptive thoughts and beliefs, and there is no need for lengthy periods spent in allowing the relationship to build up, allowing the client to do nothing, and so on, which may go on in other therapies. Cognitive therapy is brisk and business-like.

This connects with the much more active nature of cognitive therapy. It is much less contemplative than analytic therapy; it gives the client homework to do, of a written or practical nature; it suggests that changes are made by the client to their current neurotic thinking and behaviour, and that these changes can be made immediately; the therapist is much more interventionist than the analytic therapist. For example, one can begin in the first session to reflect back to the client those cognitive flaws and traps which the client is manifesting.

It is much less concerned with the past, and sees itself as intervening directly in the present life of the client, particularly in those areas which are self-damaging, and particularly those areas of repetitive harmful procedures.[1] The historical antecedents for such self-harm can often be sidestepped, as one can penetrate directly to the core of beliefs, thoughts and actions which are damaging the client.

One of the key principles of psychoanalytic thought is the distinction between the covert and the overt, but this distinction is absent from much cognitive therapy. The cognitive therapist is more prepared to accept at face value what the client presents, and much less concerned with investigating hidden motives, thoughts and feelings.

The cognitive therapist is more practical, concerned with problems which the client brings, and finding solutions to them. This means that much less attention need be given to the client's childhood, parental influences, their dream life, and so on, since one is concerned with the client's life now and ways in which it can be improved. In addition, much less attention needs to be paid to the transference relationship, although cognitive analytic therapy, which has incorporated many psychoanalytic ideas, does attend to this.

Is cognitive therapy only suitable for the less disturbed client? In fact, short term work in the cognitive mode may be found more acceptable by some severely disturbed clients, since it provides a safe container, it does not stir up excessive needs and dependency, and it tends not to excite very negative transference.

Cognitive faults

Every therapist of every persuasion will be familiar with the fault-lines in thinking and belief which afflict certain clients, particularly those who are severely depressed. They can be outlined as follows.

Automatic thoughts comprise those subliminal thoughts which go on much of the time in depressed people, telling them that things are pointless, that nothing will work, that they are a failure, and so on. The word 'automatic' is quite accurate here, since most of the time we are not aware of them, even though they seem to govern much of our behaviour. Of course, there are positive automatic thoughts, which tell us that we are valuable, lovable, that we are productive and creative, and so on, but of course such thoughts tend to bolster up our self-esteem, and in the face of life's disappointments, they help us to get back on track.

But the negative automatic thoughts have the reverse effect – they are basically sabotaging, and even when good things are accomplished, and some happiness is found, such attacking thoughts can quickly spoil things.[2]

A terrible cycle can ensue, for the negative thoughts make us depressed, and then we are less motivated to try new things, go out and meet people, be creative, and so on, so then we feel dissatisfied and unfulfilled, but of course the sabotaging thoughts come in and tell us that this is all our fault.

There is a twin task in therapy: first, to identify such thoughts, and second, to counter them in some way, change them, defeat them, neutralize them. The first task is no easy matter, as 'automatic' can be interpreted in analytic language as 'unconscious'. In other words, they are automatic since they go on below the surface of our conscious awareness. In fact, many people have a vague sense of them, so that they could be described as 'semi-conscious'. And the fact that one is doing therapy tends to focus people's minds, so that they quickly become more able to identify such thought patterns. The cognitive therapist helps considerably here, since the evidence for such thoughts going on is often apparent in the demeanour and the speech of the client, so that the therapist can intervene directly, by asking the client what he or she has just been thinking, by pointing out the indications of negative thinking which are apparent to the therapist, in fact by challenging the client's habitual mind set.

> Joan presented herself in a doleful weary manner from the first session. Her therapist immediately confronted her with this, and asked her what thoughts she linked with this state. Joan said she had thoughts such as 'what's the point', 'nobody cares about me', 'I never get anywhere', but in fact she was shocked to be confronted so quickly. But it had an invigorating effect, and Joan began to enjoy the task of identifying her 'bad thoughts', as she called them, and her weary manner began to improve.

One might say about this example, that whereas Joan has become an habitual victim of her own negative thinking, her therapist refuses to collude with this, and immediately provides an opposition to it, which provides Joan with much needed ego-strength, and the basis to confront her own 'bad thoughts'.

In a cognitive framework, the client can also be set homework tasks, such as identifying automatic thought sequences, writing them down in a diary, constructing dialogues, in which they are challenged, and so on. The point here is that the client becomes habituated to the task of identification of automatic thoughts.

The second part of the therapeutic task is to combat such harmful thoughts. This can be done in various ways, but one is mainly concerned with two tasks, one, to take to pieces the faulty logic and examine all its stages, its faulty assumptions, its faulty syllogisms, and so on; and second, to provide in its place a more positive kind of thinking.

> Helen was convinced that when she went out, everyone was looking at her, and everyone thought she was ugly. Her therapist suggested that they adopt

a two-pronged approach – first, to look at how Helen's thinking was distorted; and second, that Helen could do a series of experiments, by going out, noticing how people reacted, writing down her own thoughts and feelings, and even asking people what they were thinking. As the experiments continued, it began to emerge that what upset Helen most was when people didn't even notice her! Her therapist suggested that being ugly was a way of being special for Helen, and she wanted everyone to look at her.

This example shows how cognitive work can be combined with more analytic work, since the therapist's interpretations are a way of dealing with Helen's unconscious thought processes, whereby a fear is shown to be in part a wish. That is, Helen is partly afraid of everyone looking at her, because that is what she wants.

Can we then go on and suggest something more positive? Why not? I don't mean that the therapist tells Helen she is pretty – that would be too interventionist, and would probably provoke a huge backlash, and certainly is far too seductive, but it is possible to suggest that Helen entertain such a thought – that she is attractive. Again, analytically speaking, this is the 'shadow' thought to the overt thought that I am ugly. Secretly, perhaps I think that I am attractive, but I have never dared to articulate that idea, so I have covered it up with its opposite.

Vignettes such as this demonstrate that cognitive therapy can be subtle, can explore unconscious thoughts and feelings, and is much more sophisticated than the crude distortions of it that one sometimes sees. It is not a question of sitting a client down and telling them that they are really OK, and their negative thoughts are rubbish. That is a sure way of provoking the client's own backlash.

Irrational beliefs

All human beings possess irrational beliefs, but again we are concerned here with those which are debilitating. Examples are not hard to find:

> If I achieve something good, it will be taken from me.
> Achieving something isn't worth it, because I don't enjoy it.
> My neighbours are suspicious of me.
> The whole world is against me.
> Women are predatory.

Such beliefs form underlying assumptions which govern our lives. We also have many positive beliefs, but these tend to make our life positive and productive, since we are obtaining a kind of positive feedback internally. One must however distinguish here those over-optimistic beliefs which some people possess, which actually prevent them engaging in the world in a real way – beliefs such as 'if I keep gambling, eventually I will become a millionaire', 'I don't need to get a job, since my real ability is being psychic about other people's thoughts', 'it's alright to steal from shops, because I'll never be caught'.

But negative beliefs can be remarkably resistant, and one can suspect with some clients that they provide a kind of bulwark which the client can cling to. But in such a case, we can expose a further belief: 'if I give up believing that the world is against me, I'll be hoodwinked'.

Clearly it is not a question of the therapist counterposing their own positive beliefs as an antidote to the client's negative ones, since that can easily excite the client's suspicions ('I am being indoctrinated'). But it is a question of finding out if the client has the resources to marshal their own resistance to such belief. Thus some clients will be found to possess alternative beliefs which are more positive, but which they keep hidden away, for fear of being scorned or attacked. Many clients are in fact eager to entertain alternative beliefs, and are willing to carry out 'thought experiments', involving positive assumptions about the world. We can go on and suggest that the client carries out experiments in the real world, based on the positive beliefs.

Fred was convinced that no girl would go on a date with him. Some time was spent in therapy going through the cluster of beliefs which Fred possessed here – that he was unattractive, that he was clumsy, that he didn't understand women. But Fred was not entirely hopeless, since he had female friends, and he had had sexual relations with women. After exploring his beliefs, and trying out alternative ideas – that he liked women, and some women like him, Fred set himself the task of asking a girl at work out for a drink, and she accepted.

But of course the girl might say no, and then Fred may be thrown back into his pessimistic beliefs, which seem confirmed. However, here we come up against other cognitive distortions, particularly the power of generalization.

Over-generalization

Over-generalization forms the basis for many neurotic beliefs and ways of living. For after all, all of us have probably generalized from our childhoods as to the nature of the universe. If someone's parents were critical and depressed, one tends to expect everyone to be like that, or indeed one might go out actively seeking such people.

Karen had had a number of boyfriends who she described as cold and distant. She had become very depressed as a result of this, and felt it was pointless to look for another boyfriend. However, in therapy she was able to exhume some of her core beliefs – that all men were like her father; that she somehow owed her father something; that she didn't deserve anything better; that she could thaw out these cold men. She also had the hope that there were men who were not like this, and that perhaps she deserved something better.

This example shows the value of painful experience. In a sense, life is the foremost therapy, since it is here that we test out our beliefs, and in fact often keep retesting them.

This means in fact that if we take someone like Karen at a young age, and give her therapy, that it will not be successful, since Karen has not yet done that testing out in life that is required. In fact, Karen probably would not go to therapy, since at a young age most people possess that sense of immortality and divine destiny which is so intoxicating, but which eventually life erodes, until perhaps we are ready and able to look into ourselves more realistically. Karen had inferred that all men are cold and distant like her father, but she had also developed a kind of grandiose belief that she could change them, and this is what she has been acting out for a number of years. But now the grandiosity has begun to shrink, and she is ready to be more realistic.

Human beings are shown to be philosophers, in that they base their lives on inferences made from experience. However, many of these inferences are faulty and lead to much painful repetition of early experience. At a certain point in life (particularly when one has suffered enough), cognitive therapy can strike at the heart of this inferential logic, and can demonstrate that it is bad logic.

Pessimism

Pessimistic thinking forms one kind of automatic thinking, but it is so important that it often forms the core target of therapy. It is of course very common in depressed people, who often possess clusters of pessimistic beliefs and ideas.

Today went alright, but that means the rest of the week will be bad.
There's no point in asking that girl out, since even if we get on, things will go wrong in the end.
We all die in the end, so what's the point?

One of the interesting things about pessimism is how it is used to under-mine positive achievements. There is a kind of 'backlash' phenomenon, whereby something good is immediately negated by a pessimistic thought, and in analytic therapy, one would want to investigate the presence of envy in the client, and in the client's family, since the backlash as it were wards off envy, or pre-empts it.

We are aiming to help the client deal with their own pessimistic beliefs and thoughts. It may be unrealistic to set the goal of getting rid of them completely, but if one can find ways of neutralizing them, then that is a battle half-won.

The first step is to become aware of them, and then to accept that they are part of one's own attitude to life. This is quite a difficult step, since our uncon-sciousness makes us see it as simply the way life is. 'It's not that I'm pes-simistic, it's that life is awful' is a good paraphrase of this. Hence it is quite a step forward to accept that 'I am the pessimistic one', or indeed 'I am the author of my pessimism', and then we are quite close to suggesting that there are alternatives to pessimism.

Here one encounters other negative beliefs, particularly that 'nothing can be changed'. This affects many people in therapy, who may secretly believe that all this psychological work is pointless, since everything is set in stone, and cannot be changed. But again to bring that belief from out of the darkness into daylight is a partial victory in itself, for then one can begin to challenge it.

In fact, pessimism often has at its core this resistance to change. The belief that I cannot change myself conceals the wish not to. Here one can see again the close proximity between cognitive therapy and psychoanalytic therapy, and it is not surprising that cognitive analytic therapy has been able to integrate the two successfully. Pessimism has a kind of shadow wish inside it – I don't believe that things will ever get better, because I actually don't want them to.

If one can extract such beliefs and thought processes from a client, the result can be astonishing, and there is often a sense of surprise and relief. How amazing it is that we live our lives according to such outlandish beliefs – that being happy is too dangerous, and I am better off miserable. But the awareness of these beliefs is already a partial neutralization of them, and the therapist provides a powerful reinforcement of this neutralization, and then the client is able to take that away so that the neutralization becomes second nature. 'Here is that pessimistic thought again, well I'm going to ignore that, as it's just stupid and self-destructive'. Instead of being a victim of one's own negative thoughts, one takes up arms against them – one learns to fight them, resist them, get angry at them, and so on.

Other methods

Cognitive therapy is quite elastic in its techniques, as it has been able to borrow methods of working from other therapies. For example, it is possible to use role play, as used in Gestalt therapy, in order to go further into a particular situation which causes anxiety. A common scenario where this can be used is bullying.

> Jane often feels inhibited when she is with her friend Gale, as Gale tends to undermine her, drops rather insulting remarks, and is quite sarcastic. The therapist sets up a role play and plays the role of Gale, and proceeds to browbeat Jane, who at first appears humble and beaten. But it becomes clear that Jane is quite irritated, and the therapist comes out of role and asks Jane what she is feeling. Jane is feeling angry and annoyed at Gale, and so the two go back into role, and Jane is able to voice her annoyance.

It is also possible to reverse such role play, so that the therapist plays Jane, and Jane plays Gale, and then the therapist can show a different possible way of replying to the bullying friend. But such work is quite subtle, and clearly requires the therapist to have some proficiency and experience in role play.

Another technique which can be used is visualization. In the above scene, one could get Jane to imagine being with Gale and being more assertive, or she could imagine being browbeaten, and then trying to change things. Visualization is particularly powerful since it involves visual images rather than words and thoughts, and for some people this is a more approachable way of tackling their most anxious scenarios.

Cognitive therapy does not shrink from actual exposure to anxious situations. For example, if a client is anxious about being outdoors, some cognitive therapists might ask the client if they would like to go outside, accompanied by the therapist, and then the client can continue to talk about how they feel, the level of anxiety, and so on. Obviously this doesn't work with some situations – one cannot accompany the client who wants to have a row with the boss. But the client can be given the assignment of doing this, and can be prepared for it by discussing possible strategies, things that need saying, how to respond if the boss becomes angry, and so on. This approach is quite refreshing, for a link is made with the real world of the client.

Cognitive therapy often uses homework of different kinds to keep the client involved in the tasks which have been agreed on. The homework can take different forms – keeping a diary of one's thoughts and feelings; carrying out a difficult task, and recording one's reactions; in the case of depressed clients who are rather passive, carrying out various activities in order not to become paralyzed; carrying out experiments, to test out one's fears and expectations. Thus a common experiment involves telling a friend something which one fears will drive them away, as the fear is often unfounded.

Meanings not events

One of the most succinct descriptions of cognitive therapy is provided by Neenan and Dryden in their book *Cognitive Therapy*, when they say that it is not events that determine our feelings, but the meanings we attach to those events.[3] This strikes me as a very useful summation of psychotherapy as a whole – it is really saying that we make our own universe. This can be seen very clearly if one compares different people who have had difficult or traumatic childhoods, and one finds in fact that while some react negatively, become very depressed or angry, and, as it were, refuse to engage with life, others do not do this, but are able to make something of their life, despite its unfortunate beginning. The second group have refused to over-generalize, and have not inferred that a bad childhood implies a bad universe.

The problem here however is that one cannot simply evangelize about this to clients. One cannot simply hector them, and tell them the fault lies within themselves and within their faulty thinking. Clients will interpret this quite rightly as a kind of blame, and many clients are fed up with being blamed as it is. But what we can do is to penetrate to those hidden beliefs and thoughts which help to sabotage the client's life. In a sense, the client with many negative beliefs and thoughts constructs a universe which is hostile to him or her, but then argues that this universe is an objective one, out there, and has not been constructed at all. One may disagree, but in the first place, one cannot criticize the client for having constructed such a universe. But one can begin the process of taking that universe to pieces and examining its component parts.

In fact, by doing this, we are implicitly subjecting the client's universe to a critique. We are suggesting that it is not an objective world, but a world of meaning. In fact, we can say that we all inhabit a world of meaning, and the meanings are given by the beliefs and thought processes which are adhered to. Often such beliefs and thoughts seem like concrete – they seem permanent, never changing, objective, and therefore simply by subjecting them to examination, by suggesting they can be altered, or that one can take up other beliefs about reality – one has already implicitly cast doubt on their permanence. At times, the therapist may become quite confrontational in this respect, in the urge to cast doubt on the absoluteness of the client's beliefs.

In this sense cognitive therapy is a post-modern discipline, in that it forensically examines our beliefs and ideas, and suggests that they are not fixed for all time, indeed that they have been chosen by us. Therapy in this manner deconstructs our meanings, and leaves it open to us to find or construct other meanings.

Of course, many clients exhibit resistance to this idea, for it strikes at the foundation of their own beliefs, particularly if those beliefs are partly paranoid. For paranoia always insists that the fault is out there, and I am the hapless victim. 'It's not my fault, I just keep meeting these unsuitable women, or finding unsuitable jobs'. Thus cognitive therapy confronts this kind of objectivism by its own brand of subjectivism – arguing that reality is not determined or laid down or fixed, but is affected by our own beliefs and thoughts and feelings.

Whether or not an individual is able to make the shift from victim to energetic instigator of their own life seems to be a mysterious choice in the end. I think that many clients are able to make a partial shift of this kind, and can accept that they have lived by a set of beliefs which are partly false. It is possible then to overturn one's pessimism and self-sabotage. Others cannot make this shift, for without doubt it is a frightening one, and involves a partial change of identity. As one client said to me, 'don't take away my depression, it's who I am'.

FURTHER READING

- A. T. Beck, *Cognitive Therapy and the Emotional Disorders* (New York: New American Library, 1976).
- K. Davidson, *Cognitive Therapy for Personality Disorders* (Oxford: Butterworth-Heinemann, 2000).
- M. Neenan and W. Dryden, *Cognitive Therapy: 100 key points and techniques* (Hove: Brunner-Routledge, 2004).
- A. Ryle, *Cognitive-Analytic Therapy: Active Participation in Change* (Chichester: John Wiley, 1991).

Notes

1 A. Ryle, *Cognitive-Analytic Therapy: Active Participation in Change* (Chichester: John Wiley, 1991), p. 2.
2 M. Neenan and W. Dryden, *Cognitive Therapy: 100 key points and techniques* (Hove: Brunner-Routledge, 2004), pp. 75–142.
3 M. Neenan and W. Dryden, *Cognitive Therapy*, p. 3.

5 Neuroscience and Psychotherapy

Neuroscience has had a long interaction with psychotherapy, since Freud himself had originally been a neurologist, and had been deeply interested in the relationship between brain and mind. Freud's notion of the drive attempted to bridge the gap between them, since the drive was conceived as a physical impulse which impacted on mental phenomena. And Freud attempted, in his *Project for a Scientific Psychology*, to construct a neurological theory which would account for mental processing, but it remained unpublished in his lifetime, although subsequent researchers have argued that it was an original and fruitful contribution to the area.

Subsequently, psychotherapy and neurology parted company, partly because neurology was insufficiently developed to be able to provide models of the brain which could be used in psychological research. However, this impediment was lifted, as neurologists became able to use scanning technology, which could reveal changes in the brain in living subjects. Now it became possible to match mental and neurological processes.

In addition, once the worst excesses of behaviourist psychology – which had professed a lack of interest in such unobservable entities as thoughts, assumptions, intuitions, minds and so on – had given way to a new cognitive psychology, it became possible to examine areas such as children's development of concepts (already pioneered by Piaget), the relation between language and thought, and so on. In addition, new disciplines such as psycholinguistics reawakened interest in 'mentalist' theories of language, that is, the view that the human brain is specially designed to process language.

Psychotherapists for their part have become interested in two main areas of brain/mind interaction. First, do childhood trauma and deprivations cause changes in brain structure and organization, so that there is actual neurological impairment, or impairment to the operation of certain brain functions? This would give empirical backing to the developmental basis for much therapy – in particular, the idea that a bad childhood gives us a handicap in life in our relationships to others, our work, our creativity, sexuality, and so on.

The second area of interest concerns psychotherapy itself – is it able to improve those damaged brain functions, either by reawakening areas which have been damaged, by using other areas to carry out functions which have been impaired, or by facilitating a reorganization within the brain?

But neuroscience might not simply offer empirical backing to psychotherapy – it may also in the long run actually change some of the focal points or targets of therapy, if it is found that therapy is able to stimulate certain neural areas more than others. In other words, it is possible that therapy works for some things and not for others, and neurological evidence may help us to make that distinction.

Out of all the very rich and complex research in neuroscience certain issues stand out as relevant to psychotherapy theory and practice, in particular, the child's early development of relationships and its own sense of self; the influence on the child of deficits in early caretaking; the relation between thought and emotion; the notion of the unconscious; the effects of brain damage on personality; and the role of enriched environments in repairing neurological malfunctioning.

Plasticity

By plasticity is meant a particularly receptive period in which the brain is able to receive and organize information. One can make the analogy with language learning, for it is clear that young children can acquire foreign languages with no effort, given enough exposure. Thus if young children go to live in a foreign country, they will pick up the language without instruction, just by being with their peers. However, at the age of puberty this plasticity towards language disappears, and then begins the very laborious struggle to learn a language – in other words, foreign accents begin at about this age. We can say that the young child does not need to 'learn' a language, since it can acquire one, for its brain has a 'wired in' capacity to do so.[1]

Something similar seems to happen with personal intimate interaction, except that the zone of plasticity is very early and doesn't last so long. It begins at birth and lasts several years. This means that if a child of eight years has not been in an intimate relationship, it is very difficult to introduce it to one. Similarly the adult client who shuns intimacy, is cut off from their own feelings, and is generally schizoid, proves usually to be a very difficult subject for psychotherapy.

Much research has gone on into parent/child interaction at a very early age, particularly mother/child interaction, showing the remarkably delicate and detailed mutual 'fine tuning' which goes on between the two. That is, the mother tunes into the infant's emotional and physical needs, mirrors them back to the infant, who also tunes into the mother's communications and responds to them. It has been compared to a musical performance, in that voice and body are used in an alternating manner by mother and child, each eliciting responses from the other in a sort of duet.[2]

In addition, there is a rhythm of engagement and disengagement. That is, the infant needs periods when it is left alone just as much as it needs periods of intimate contact. The mother who attempts a continual kind of relating to her child is in fact overloading it, and not allowing it its own space. This can have very negative consequences, as the child either has to construct formidable defences in order to keep people out, or may in fact split itself into different parts, in order to keep something private and hidden from the intrusive parent. One can have too much contact just as much as too little.

The argument about plasticity proposes that the infant's brain has a special facility which deals with interaction, communication with another person by means of voice and body, and very intimate fine tuning, so that two individuals get to recognize each other's signals in great detail. It is not an accident that the brain has this facility, for the human infant uses it to construct its own sense of self, its sense of others, and its knowledge about the world. Its curiosity about reality is stimulated by such a relationship, as is its ability to love and be loved. It is possible therefore to speak of the 'social brain', meaning the way in which the brain organizes itself in response to social interaction at an early age, and with the corollary that if this interaction is lacking or of a negative quality, brain organization is impaired.

Generally most parents have a 'good enough' ability to meet their child in this way, but of course there are those who do not, because of their own psychological damage, and then their own child stands a good chance of being damaged.

At this point, one can make an interesting point about psychotherapy, which is also an engaged relationship, in which a lot of learning or relearning can take place, but again not in a neutral or cold manner, but in a human and empathic manner. In other words, it's no good having a therapist who gives you the correct information, but is cold and detached, for you will be repelled. What people want is someone who is there, present, involved, full of feelings themselves. We need a therapist who is alive, not shut off from life.

The parallel between early intimacy and the nature of psychotherapy seems unlikely to be a coincidence. Rather, the establishment of the psychoanalytic space, and the use by the early analysts of the couch, so that the patient could regress, unconsciously reproduced the early period of intimate communication with a parent. One might argue that this infantilizes clients/patients, so that the therapist becomes an august figure of parental wisdom, but this is only one possible transference fantasy by the client. It certainly permits the client to become vulnerable, to explore issues about early childhood, and so on, but the key word here is 'permit', since it by no means compels the client to do so.

But certainly it looks as if psychotherapy has found ways and means of going back to the early period of interaction and identifying faults therein and to some extent repairing them. Thus although brain plasticity for relationship tapers off in childhood, it does not absolutely end, and adults are able to an extent to 'relearn' how to relate and can partly overcome old deficits.

Deficits

We can therefore make a contrast between those psychological disturbances involving early problems with intimacy (that is in the first two years of life), and those involving later ones. Generally the former, termed 'pre-oedipal' in psychoanalytic language, are much more severe, whereas the latter can often be termed neurotic and are amenable to treatment. Early deficits in intimacy, communication, and love can lead to very severe damage to the actual sense of self, and one's awareness of others, so that for example one might not have much of a sense that others have feelings too. One might come to live in a very narcissistic world, cut off from others. In other words, the neurotic client generally has a stable sense of self, can relate to others adequately, can work reasonably well, and so on, whereas the more disturbed client may have problems in one or more (or all) of these areas.

This means that psychotherapy with the more disturbed client is more difficult, is much slower, and has less obvious results. It doesn't mean that it doesn't work, but it is gradual, laborious and frustrating. However, here we come up against the exigencies of time and money. For example, the American analyst H. F. Searles spent many years with his very damaged schizophrenics, and obtained good results, but which health organization or insurance company is going to pay for such long therapy? We find instead of course that such organizations, as with employer funded counselling, think in terms of giving clients twelve sessions!

But going back to the arguments about plasticity, we can see a plausible hypothesis here: that if the early receptivity of the brain to intimate relations is not made full use of, because the parents are not able to relate to their child with warmth and sensitivity, that child suffers a kind of brain damage, since the period of plasticity comes to an end. Information about relation-ships, one's sense of self, emotions, curiosity towards the world, and so on, is not incorporated into brain structure and organization.

Thus the close observation of mother/infant interaction has apparently confirmed some of the key hypotheses of psychoanalysis, concerning the influence of early deficits in child-rearing, the fracturing of the self which can ensue, and the long term nature of such damage. It may not simply be a ques-tion of 'bad habits' or 'faulty learning', but something to do with impaired brain development.

Thought and emotion

One of the most interesting aspects of research into mother/infant relations is that cognition and emotion are seen to be closely related. That is, the mother who instructs her child in a neutral or cold manner will cause considerable damage to it, even if her instructions are nominally correct. The infant does not simply require knowledge about the world – it needs this to be given in a loving manner, which respects the infant as a separate person. This is why some of the Victorian child rearing methods, which treated the infant as a rational adult, and subjected it to a rather didactic and formalized series of inputs, left something crucial out – which we might loosely call warmth and sensitivity. Feeding babies every four hours actually leaves out of the equation the baby itself! Or the instruction to leave crying babies to 'cry it out' now strikes us as cold and heartless to both mother and child, since the mother's instinct is usually to go to her child.

We also obtain a striking perspective on the Western splitting of thought and emotion – I mean that intellectuality which characterizes our culture, particularly in its education system, in many of the great professions, and even in private life. One of my clients was told by her father not to cry at her mother's funeral, as it was letting down the family. Thus emotion came to be seen not simply as private, but as shameful, whereas thought and under-standing and intellectuality became respectable and dignified. What a curse the Cartesian dictum – 'I think, therefore I am' – has been for us!

Anyone who has had children will recognize that they need warmth and contact continually. I don't mean that sometimes we don't get mad with our children or shout at them, and so on, but that coldness and withdrawal are like poison to them, particularly if this is sustained. One meets many clients in therapy who have had depressed mothers – I am not saying that that is the only cause of the client's problems, but undoubtedly the depressed mother is usually a withdrawn mother, and then the child is lost, afraid, and often withdraws in turn, and then its ability to form good relationships is impaired.

The conjunction of thought and emotion can be seen in children's play, which is both a very rich learning environment, and also great fun. The two things are not separable, for if it's not fun, one doesn't learn. The same is true of personal relationships – one learns to treat others considerately and so on if one has been treated oneself as a child with dignity and with love, not because one has been instructed to do so. Knowledge cannot therefore be divorced from one's ability to respond to life and to others, or if it is divorced, one finds oneself to be only half-human, in the sense that one is cut off from oneself and others.

Again, this argument gives us a considerable insight into psychotherapy and how it works – that it combines a kind of relearning experience, in which one is able to look closely at one's attitude to life and to others, and one attempts to rectify some of the deficits which can be seen therein, with a relationship which is intimate. In fact, the two are not separable – the relearning occurs *because of the intimacy and through it.* This explains why different schools of psychotherapy seem to be equally effective, since all of them, whatever their theoretical and technical apparatus, operate through the one-to-one intimate setting. This also suggests that it is very difficult to go through a healing process or growth process by reading books, since one is lacking that meaningful other, with whom one can interact.

One might object here that some people go through a growth process or healing process (for example in bereavement), without doing psychotherapy. Of course this is true, but it is probably true that such people have had the experience of intimacy in their life, and have been able to incorporate it into their psyche and make use of it. If you like, their brain has been attuned to intimacy, empathy, emotional vitality, and well-being. It is very likely that the schizoid person or the sociopath does not get through bereavement successfully at all, since they are cut off from the feelings which they need to go through in order to grieve.

And in fact one meets in therapy people who have never grieved the loss of a parent or a partner or a child, because they had not been educated emotionally to have feelings and go through them.

The unconscious

One of the most intriguing aspects of neurological research is the evidence for the existence of the unconscious systems in the mind. Allan Schore, one of the foremost neuroscientists of our age, has argued that the well-known specialization between the left and right hemispheres of the brain – the right hemisphere organizing emotional representations, and the left, linguistic and logical systems – also means that in young children (up to three years of age) the right hemisphere is dominant. But he also argues that 'neurobiological studies are revealing greater right than left hemispheric involvement in the unconscious processing of affect-provoking stimuli'.[3]

Startling evidence concerning the neurological basis for unconscious processes is found in certain kinds of brain damage, which seem to lay bare those characteristics which Freud described as inherent in the unconscious, that is, contradiction, timelessness, and replacement of external by psychic reality. Certain brain-damaged patients show such features in their feelings and their speech, and seem to exist primarily in a state of fantasy, as if the normal ego control over such processes has been removed.[4] Such research seems to confirm Freud's idea that the unconscious and conscious systems of mental representation have neurological substrata which are quite distinct. The authors of the book *Clinical Studies in Neuro-Psychoanalysis* conclude that 'the ventromesial frontal cortex performs the fundamental economic transformation that inhibits the primary process of the mind'.[5] The term 'primary process' here is a reference to Freud's description of the unconscious, which is conceived of as a primitive mental aggregate, which has to be organized by the ego in order to become coherent. But the above authors argue that with certain kinds of brain damage, 'the very fabric of the ego and superego unravelled'.[6]

Clearly research of this kind provides an interesting not to say surprising back-up to Freud's ideas, and even suggests that there are anatomical correlations to some of his key concepts, such as the ego and the unconscious. This not only seems to contradict those 'Freud-bashers' who have argued that the notion of the unconscious is a quasi-mystical and unverifiable nonsense, but also seems to point the way forward to further research concerning the development of mental systems and various kinds of disruption to this, which may occur. It also points forward to an overall 'grand theory' of mental development in children, involving the elaboration of both unconscious and conscious systems, and specifically a sense of self, which includes the ability to think about oneself and one's feelings and thoughts, the ability to express these internal events, and the ability to act appropriately.

Brain damage

It has long been known that brain damage affects speech and language. In particular, stroke victims show recognizable symptoms in speech, which has allowed neurologists and linguists to correlate certain cortical areas with particular linguistic functions. Thus Broca's and Wernicke's aphasia came to be distinguished as separate conditions, depending on the area of brain damage. It is also clear that language is organized mainly in the left hemisphere, since this is where those strokes occur which cause aphasia.[7]

Contemporary neurology has also shown that patients with certain lesions, often acquired in car accidents, develop so-called 'acquired sociopathy', in other words, they lose empathy with others, their relationships are poor, and their career loses meaning for them.[8] In addition, interestingly, such patients often lose the ability to dream. This provides compelling evidence that such emotional/cognitive functions are organized in certain areas of the brain.

There is also a kind of reverse argument from the use of recreational drugs such as cocaine and ecstasy – that such drugs heighten interest in the world, empathy for others, and so on, showing that one can chemically affect one's emotive stance to reality. The same argument can be made about the range of drugs now used to control depression, schizophrenia and so on.

The arguments about 'acquired sociopathy' are particularly interesting, since one can draw a parallel with those people who become sociopathic, not from lesions to the brain, but from developmental failure. It is tempting to argue that the same brain functions have been affected in the two cases, thus returning us to the conclusion that childhood neglect or abuse causes brain damage.

Enriched environments

The notion of the 'enriched environment' has been used in psychology for a long time to describe those experiments on animals, which show that a stimulating environment 'enables the animal to build and shape a more enriched, complex and potentially more resilient brain'.[9] In humans, it has been shown that a stimulating environment, such as higher education, improves brain functioning and can reduce the risk of dementia later in life. Those who have suffered strokes can be helped to partially recover by going to stroke clinics, which help with speech and language practice and other skills.

Again, we can view psychotherapy as an environment which is enriched in many ways, but especially in terms of emotional expression, intimacy with another, self-awareness and cognitive understanding. That is, it is part of the aim of psychotherapy to facilitate those abilities, especially in those people who have suffered deficits and damage in their early life.

The new discipline of neuro-psychoanalysis seems to be suggesting that psychotherapy not only provides support and helps the client to reorganize their mental world to a degree, so that they are not inflicted by the same negative thoughts and feelings, but that it can actually modify brain functioning. Undoubtedly the weakest area of research in this new field concerns the neurological impact of psychotherapy, but perhaps in the not too distant future it will be possible to obtain neurological confirmation that a particular type of treatment is or is not beneficial for certain clients.

One should probably issue a word of caution here about the potential 'imperialism' of neuroscience. We certainly do not want to return to the outmoded arguments of behaviourism – that everything mental is in fact only a neural event. To be told that love or pain or fear are 'really' going on in the brain, and that subjective experience is a chimera, would take us back to an unwelcome extreme reductionism. The cogent reply of psychotherapy to such arguments has always been that mental events have mental causes.[10]

Fortunately the new generation of neuroscientists show few signs of such an attempted intellectual coup d'etat, and in fact show great sensitivity to the discipline of psychotherapy.

Certainly the new neuroscience provides exciting and tantalizing evidence concerning the interaction of thought and emotion, the effect of relationships on early development, the organization of personality in the brain, and so on. Psychotherapists have understandably seized on some of this research, since it seems to give empirical information about ideas which have been previously theorized upon in psychotherapy. It is too soon to herald a new age in which neurology and psychotherapy work together for the benefit of clients, but certainly the ancient split between brain and mind seems to be being partially healed.

FURTHER READING

J. Corrigall and H. Wilkinson (eds), *Revolutionary Connections: Psychotherapy and Neuroscience* (London: Karnac, 2003).

A. Damasio, *Descartes' Error: Emotion, Reason and the Human Brain* (New York: Avon Press, 1994).

K. Kaplan-Solms and M. Solms, *Clinical Studies in Neuro-Psychoanalysis* (New York: Karnac, 2000).

A. Schore, *Affect Regulation and the Origin of the Self* (Hove: Lawrence Erlbaum, 1994).

Notes

1   See C. J. Doughty and M. H. Long (eds), *The Handbook of Second Language Learning* (Oxford: Blackwell, 2002).

2   C. Trevarthen, 'Neuroscience and intrinsic psychodynamics: current knowledge and potential for therapy', in J. Corrigall and H. Wilkinson (eds) *Revolutionary Connections: Psychotherapy and Neuroscience* (London: Karnac, 2003).

3   Allan Schore, 'The seventh annual John Bowlby memorial lecture' in J. Corrigall and H. Wilkinson (eds) *Revolutionary Connections*, p. 10.

4   K. Kaplan-Solms and M. Solms, *Clinical Studies in Neuro-Psychoanalysis* (New York: Karnac, 2000) pp. 200–39.

5   Ibid., p. 230.

6   Ibid., p. 238.

7   Ibid., pp. 73–115.

8   O. Turnbull, 'Emotion, false beliefs and the neurobiology of intuition' in J. Corrigall and H. Wilkinson (eds) *Revolutionary Connections*.

9   L. Cozolino, *The Neuroscience of Psychotherapy* (New York: W. W. Norton, 2002), p. 298.

10 See Warren Colman, 'Consciousness, the Self and the Isness Business' in *British Journal of Psychotherapy*, (2004) **21:1**, pp. 83–102.

6

Psychotherapy as a Profession

The professionalization of psychotherapy has gathered pace in the last twenty years – many more training courses exist; whereas most therapists used to get into the profession through doing their own therapy initially, it is now considered as a profession along with others; organizations of therapists have mushroomed, and have drawn up descriptions of their own professional conduct, including codes of ethics, complaints procedures and so on.

One might describe this process as two-sided. On the one hand, it is clearly a step forward for the profession to be recognized as such, and not simply as a disparate collection of different schools; it means that trainings are now regulated, codes of ethics harmonized, and both therapists and clients have a clearer idea about what is being offered.

However, one might also point to a certain disillusionment among some psychotherapists, that bureaucratization and politicization have become an inevitable part of the process. Thus in the UK the original forum for all psychotherapists (UKCP) split into two, as the more psychoanalytic therapists decided that they should be organized separately. Other therapists have complained about such organizations as a form of elitism; in any case, if splits go on happening, the same picture of apparent chaos and disunity presents itself.

But some therapists have also complained that the actual process of professionalization, involving consultations with government, working parties, formalization of accreditation, and so on, involves something anti-therapeutic.[1]

Certainly when I look back on my thirty years involvement in this movement, there is a sense in which that heady sense of adventure and exploration has been replaced by caution and conservatism. This is probably inevitable – pioneers cannot remain such forever. One hopes that the inevitable steps towards a professional body of psychotherapists, with all its concomitant regulations, does not crush the enquiring spirit which has characterized psychotherapy for most of its history. Then again, there can be little doubt that pioneers and mavericks, who have always existed within psychotherapy, will continue to rise up to castigate the prevailing paradigm, in order to create a new one – the best example of this in recent years has been Jacques Lacan in France, who eventually founded his own psychoanalytic organization.

Centrifugal and centripetal

From one point of view, psychotherapy appears chaotic and disorganized, split as it is into hundreds of different factions. Furthermore, the main schools of psychotherapy, such as psychoanalysis and Jungian psychology, have themselves undergone various splits, some of them painful and traumatic. One can cite the battle royal waged between the respective followers of Melanie Klein and Anna Freud in the 1940s, which led to a split within psychoanalysis which still exists today. Jungian therapy now exists in a number of different organizations which have split from each other.

However, simply to see this history of splits in a negative light would be quite a shallow judgement. Psychotherapy is not a monolithic profession, and there are very good reasons for this, principally that it is catering for a very wide and diverse range of human personalities and problems. In other words, human beings are not a monolithic group of individuals, but show remarkable diversity.

One can argue that the human psyche is so vast and complex that it would be impossible to have a 'unified theory' of it, or that if there were such a thing, it would be trivial, because it would be highly abstract. For example, I might make as a basis for such a theory that 'childhood relationships affect adult relationships'. However, I have not really said anything very profound, and until I start to put detail on this claim, my theory is not very helpful in a practical way. But it's in the detail that divergences begin to emerge.

In fact, one can say that there are two powerful forces at work in psychotherapy, the centripetal and the centrifugal. I mean that there is both a tendency to draw together, and a tendency to pull apart. This paradox can be seen at work in most organizations, for the existence of the organization itself is testimony to the first principle, but often after it has existed for a period of time, it begins to fragment.

But one can argue that splits are often a sign of health not decrepitude. I mean that splits occur because of important theoretical disagreements and also because of power politics, the need for one's own development, and the struggle to control organizations. A prime example is Freud's attempt to control psychoanalysis, which involved many splits from erstwhile colleagues, such as Jung, Rank, Adler and so on.

In Jungian terms, one might relate the centrifugal force to the notion of individuation – that need in human beings to leave the collective and find one's own identity. Thus Freud and Jung had to split from each other in order to pursue their separate development. The monolithic all-embracing organization often becomes a suffocating influence on talented individuals, who are compelled to dissent, and in the end to break away.

Of course, these two forces – of unification and splitting – are without doubt found in all social organizations, such as political parties, commercial organizations, nation states, and so on.

Mavericks

The centrifugal forces in organizations are often conducted, as through a lightning rod, through those unusual individuals who are seen as mavericks, or more politely, as exceptionally talented people who do not fit easily into conventional organizations, and are compelled often to found their own group. In fact, one might argue that most of the great figures in the last one hundred years of psychotherapy have been of this kind – Freud, Jung, Klein, and so on. However, such figures attract many others to their cause, and they often become the standard-bearers of a new paradigm in psychology. There are of course other figures such as D. W. Winnicott, who while exhibiting a considerable originality in ideas, are able to remain within the main organization, and who in fact probably need such a containing group.

One might say that important new developments are usually pioneered by maverick figures such as Lacan. Thus it is correct to say that in their day both Freud and Jung were such iconoclastic figures, who revolutionized human psychology, and there are a host of more minor leaders who turn against the status quo, and establish a new paradigm. The history of humanistic psychology contains a litany of such figures – Fritz Perls, Wilhelm Reich, Alexander Lowen, Roberto Assagioli – but in fact psychoanalysis, that apparently most conservative of disciplines, is full of pioneering spirits who changed ideas radically.

The centripetal

The reasons why professional organizations exist in so many areas such as the law, medicine, education, and so on are very complex, and no doubt have benefits and drawbacks both for the practitioners and the clients. Thus it has often been said that professionalization protects the clients of psychotherapy, since rigorous training and accreditation tends to filter out charlatans, quacks and crooks. It is unclear to what degree this is true, since one can also cite the evidence of crooks in all professions, and certainly the existence of manipulative people who are perfectly able to pass through training procedures. Nonetheless, it is true that in a professional organization, the injured client has redress to a body which is able to investigate complaints, and can carry out sanctions. This is clear enough in the medical profession, where patients are able to take action against unethical behaviour. Whether or not medical training filters out criminals such as the serial killer Harold Shipman, and sexual exploiters, is more doubtful.

But the organization also of course benefits its members. It is a kind of closed shop, meaning that fees can be raised, committees formed, professional literature produced, and so on. This tends to be emphasized less, since it paints a less flattering picture of the profession – not so much concerned for its clients and patients, but for its own members. One might call this the shadow side of all organizations, that self-protective and self-regulating aspect which at its worst, can become incestuous and actually collusive with malpractice. This is of course when the state tends to step in and takes upon itself the task of regulating certain key professions such as the law and medicine. The relations between the state and psychotherapy vary widely, but it can be seen in Europe that some attempt at harmonization is now being made.

Psychotherapy and the state

On 11 February 2004 the European Commission added psychotherapy to those professions for which it issues directives – 'this means that European training standards and ethical guidelines will be decided in Brussels, and will be applied in all member states.'[2] It appears that directives will be based on a wider interpretation of psychotherapy than is applied in many European states, for example Germany and Italy, which restrict it to psychiatrists and some psychologists. It remains to be seen how long it takes for such directives to be issued and to really take effect, since there have been many indications previously that the European Commission would take an interest in psychotherapy, but it has been and remains a very complex area, since qualifications and accreditations vary so much from state to state. One of the most contentious areas is whether psychotherapy is defined as a 'medical treatment', to be practised largely by psychiatrists, since if that is the case, many psychotherapists in Britain will have to close their doors.

This echoes an earlier debate within psychoanalysis, when some analysts argued that psychoanalysis should only be practised by qualified doctors, but Freud, interestingly, argued against this, and for 'lay analysts'. It is hard to believe that Europe would be able to restrict psychotherapy across the whole continent, since the tradition of non-medical psychotherapists is a long one in some countries, for example Britain and Austria.

In France the situation has become very confused, since a law had been introduced to define psychotherapy as a medical procedure, but after much protest, this was changed so that non-medical therapists would be permitted to practise. However, many European countries do have very tight restrictions, so that the British situation – where in fact anyone can set up as a psychotherapist, whether qualified or not – is quite anomalous.

One can see a spectrum here ranging from tight regulation at one extreme, and a kind of free market at the other (Britain). The arguments for the former set up are clear-cut – that it protects clients from charlatans, and provides for an ethical framework for therapeutic practice – but again one can make an argument for the British situation, in that its apparent laissez faire and anarchic attitude to psychotherapy is part of a libertarian stance which traditionally protects individuals against the state. Continental Europe, of course, tends to take the Napoleonic attitude that the state organizes life for individuals in many ways.

It can be seen how complex the relationship between psychotherapy and the state has been and has varied from country to country. In Britain, although medicine itself has been largely state controlled since the war, psychotherapy has been largely carried out in the private domain. But this is changing, and there has been a considerable impetus for the state registration of psychotherapists, so that the clients are given safeguards about the training of therapists and so that ethical considerations are looked after.

There has been some opposition to this drive towards state registration, since there is a long tradition in Britain of private practice and private organizations of psychotherapists who have regulated themselves. Hence a number of therapists have questioned the need for state registration.[3]

Work contexts

The work contexts in which psychotherapists work have broadened considerably in some countries, so that one can work in private practice at home, or privately in a rented room, possibly in a therapy centre; one can work in a hospital or attached to a doctor's surgery; in the UK working in the National Health Service is an increasing possibility; there are also private clinics; social work settings, such as probation and prisons; work for private companies, and so on.

These different work contexts have very different implications for many aspects of therapy, for example, the relationship between therapist and client, relations with other professionals; the way in which mental illness is viewed; differing political and legal implications about very disturbed people and how they are dealt with. If say one is working in a hospital which is dealing with disturbed patients, who are sectioned, that is, compulsorily detained, one has to be conversant with all the ramifications which apply to such patients, including the patient's rights not to be treated, the pharmacological treatments which may be given, and the importance actually given to psychotherapy in that institution. This is obviously very different work from the psychotherapist who works at home, does not generally work with very disturbed people, and does not have to deal with social workers, police or medical staff.

In general, it is clear that institutions such as hospitals offer much greater containment than private practice, and are therefore more suitable for very disturbed clients. In fact, there is no doubt that some clients like this find therapy in someone's home too overwhelming in its offering of apparent intimacy, homeliness, and so on. The 'colder' atmosphere of the institution feels much safer in such cases.

Of course in institutions, one has to also work alongside colleagues, who may or may not share one's own ideas about psychotherapy, and this can be both frustrating and stimulating. In addition, one's actual therapeutic work can be affected by the presence of other staff, since one's clients are also aware of them, and are not averse to making unfavourable comparisons about oneself, or feeling jealous of other clients and staff, having rich fantasies about others, and so on.

Confidentiality

Confidentiality is the most important ethical issue in psychotherapy, for it provides for both therapist and client that sense of a safe container without which therapy cannot be sustained. But confidentiality is subject to many riders and qualifications which set the therapist many ethical problems, since there is rarely an absolute bar on disclosure. For example, those therapists doing supervision are making a palpable opening in the container, in that their clients are discussed regularly with their supervisor. Of course, there is no objection to this, but perhaps we need to consider at times what effect this has on the work. And at times clients become aware of supervision and may become curious or alarmed by the fact that their innermost secrets may be being discussed with an absolute stranger.

Then there is the issue of gossip, to which psychotherapists seem to be as prone as any other profession. How many therapists mention a particularly annoying or upsetting client to their partner? Or how often when therapists get together professionally or socially does the conversation turn to those clients who are troublesome or bizarre or amusing?

The issue of publication has become a difficult one, and it seems that there are fewer and fewer articles published in journals which cite clinical material, since it involves asking clients for permission to publish, and possibly having to disguise their identity anyway.

Thirty years ago I recall that the bar on 'incestuous' work, that is taking on clients who had some kind of relationship with existing or former clients, was poorly maintained in humanistic psychology. It was not uncommon for therapists to see a number of individuals who were mutual friends, with all the attendant feelings of rivalry which that engenders, and it was not unknown for a therapist to see both members of a couple separately, again setting up unhealthy triangular forces and feelings.

This was the downside of the 'anything goes' atmosphere in the 70s in humanistic psychology, but thankfully such ethical issues have been tightened up, as professional organizations have drawn up codes of ethical conduct, including the important statement that clients should not be exploited, financially, sexually or emotionally. Without doubt, seeing the friend of an existing client is a form of emotional exploitation, since the therapist is given privileged access to two differing accounts, and can easily fall into a kind of grandiose position.

But confidentiality can be subverted in many other ways. For example, information can be requested by other professionals.

> Helen's psychiatrist wrote to Helen's former therapist requesting a brief account of how things had gone in therapy, and how the therapist now viewed Helen. Since Helen was no longer a client, the therapist replied that he could not comply with this, since he could not ask Helen's permission.

However, this example presents other complexities, since even if Helen was an existing client, the therapist might not want to ask her permission to divulge information to the psychiatrist, and even if Helen gave permission, might still not want to. If for example, Helen was a particularly vulnerable and paranoid person, hearing that professionals were writing to each other behind her back would not be helpful to her.

> Joe's solicitor wrote to Joe's therapist asking for a copy of his notes, as Joe had been in an accident, and was claiming compensation, and the solicitors were trying

to use every available weapon at their disposal. The therapist discussed this with Joe, who was amenable to it being done, but the therapist felt uncomfortable with such disclosure, and refused to give a copy of his notes.

One of the problems with cases like this is that the other professional is non-medical and non-therapeutic, so that one would wonder about the degree of confidentiality which the notes would have in a solicitor's office.

No doubt there are innumerable examples like this, and there are individual judgements to be made about each case, but in general I take a conservative line on confidentiality – in other words, I would maintain it as a firm barrier, except in exceptional circumstances. Such circumstances are usually stated to be that the client is in danger of harming someone else or themselves, that is, committing suicide. But even here there can be difficulties.

> Mary often had fantasies about harming her children, but she seemed able to distinguish between fantasy and acting them out. Nonetheless, her therapist felt alarmed at times at the intensity of the fantasies, and was unsure at what point he would feel compelled to inform someone about the dangers.

This is a terrible judgement to have to make, since while in general people who are able to talk about their fantasies are less likely to carry them out, this is not an invariable rule. On the other hand, one cannot take emergency action every time someone has such a fantasy, since in a sense one encourages them to come out in therapy. But I think there is an emotional quality to the dangerous fantasies – a quality of fear and danger and anger – which should alert the therapist. Clients who are liable to commit violent acts are usually either in a disturbed state, or may be icily calm – in any case, the therapist's own reactions and feelings are critical here, since incipient violence is nearly always preceded by disturbed feelings which should be picked up in counter-transference.[4]

Exploitation

The exploitation of clients by therapists falls into several categories, of which the most important are financial, sexual and emotional. Financial exploitation does not refer to charging high fees, but to accepting financial gifts, being included in someone's will, receiving gifts towards the establishment of therapy centres and so on. Such financial transactions undoubtedly pollute the therapeutic relationship, even if they occur after therapy has ended. The therapist is always indebted to the client, consciously or not, and this will affect any therapy that is ongoing. If therapy has finished, it may affect the possible return of the client to therapy.

Sexual exploitation is a big issue, since it seems to go on with a relatively high frequency, and is also found in the medical profession, and no doubt in other professions. We can define sexual exploitation as any form of seductive attitude towards clients by therapists, whether or not any physical contact takes place. But it does not refer to sexual feelings, which are inevitable in some therapeutic relationships. But such feelings are quite different from seductive behaviour by a therapist, and any therapist who cannot tell the difference needs not only to deal with this in supervision, but needs to go back into therapy, since this is a personal as well as a professional problem, since it involves the difference between having a feeling and acting it out.

One can see why sexual exploitation arises in professions such as psychotherapy and medicine, since the relationship between practitioner and client is intimate, may be intense, and in the case of psychotherapy, often uncovers many ancient sexual problems, trauma, and so on. There is also the issue of seductive clients, or clients who idealize their therapists, which can affect some therapists adversely, in the sense that the idealization or the seductiveness is interpreted by them as a licence to be seductive themselves.

One interesting area of confusion is that of sexual fantasies, since again many therapists will experience these with some clients, and they can form an important part of the therapeutic process. Again, one can say that there is a cardinal distinction between fantasy and action, or there is a firm boundary between them, and those therapists who cannot deal with this boundary securely need to do more work on themselves.

Emotional exploitation is difficult to define, since it may refer not only to sexual seductiveness, but can also refer to power domination, the mishandling of fragile clients, aggressive abuse of clients, deliberate frightening of clients, and so on. These issues are very hazy and often difficult to separate from legitimate emotional reactions – it doesn't mean for example that one is not allowed to have a blazing row with a client, but this would be exploitative if the client cannot fight back and is crushed. In other words, bullying by a therapist is out of court.

Complaints procedures

The issue of exploitation naturally brings up that of complaints procedures, since the aggrieved client must have recourse to a method of making complaints against a therapist which is fair to both parties, explicit as to its procedures and its possible sanctions, which must include in the last resort the expulsion of a therapist, in the case of severe abuse.

At the same time, it is advisable to have some kind of reconciliation procedure as part of the whole system of complaints, since some very angry clients who make complaints are in effect continuing an argument with their therapist, and there should be some means whereby in such a case the two parties can find some peace with each other. In the end, however, clients must be permitted to make complaints, whether or not this is part of a transference gone wrong.

Diversity

The clientele for psychotherapy used to be predominantly white, affluent and middle class, and their therapists were similar. But in the last twenty years, this has changed considerably, as therapy has widened its social catchment, and as counselling has become available for many groups, such as alcoholics, drug addicts, disaster victims, and so on. Thus whereas the therapist might formerly have expected to see sitting opposite a mirror-image of their own identity, this is definitely not the case today, and therapists have to deal therefore with many issues to do with prejudice. Issues of racism, homophobia, and sexism are dealt with in many training courses, since it can be assumed that most, if not all, people have some unconscious prejudice.

If for example a therapist has a strong antipathy towards a certain group of people, it would be as well not to work with them. One might argue that psychoanalysts formerly had such an attitude towards gay men and lesbians, but this example shows some of the difficulties in this area, since many analysts would have argued – and would still argue today – that this is not prejudice, but an honest analysis of the roots of homosexuality.

Perhaps the real issue here is dislike. If one dislikes a certain group, then one's therapeutic efforts will be blunted or worse. At the same time, one might have to question the suitability of a candidate in training who manifested gross prejudice of a racial, religious or sexual nature. The homophobic person could be said to have many unresolved conflicts within them which might prevent them being good therapists, not just for gay people, but for heterosexual people as well.

At the same time, psychotherapists are aware that the shadow exists in all of us, and we can assume therefore that we all possess some prejudices, and again these should be worked over in one's own personal therapy, and should not disbar someone from working as a therapist.

Personal qualities

Are there any particular personal qualities which a psychotherapist might be expected to have? Certainly, we should not expect an unmitigated saint, since that would be disastrous for clients, just as a saintly mother would be a disaster for her children. I mean that someone with infinite patience, attentiveness, understanding and empathy would be scarcely human, and would therefore present the client with an idealized picture, rather than a real person. Furthermore, there would be little resistance from the therapist in this idealized state – no irritation, no boredom, no anger, and so on – so that the client would in fact exist in a boundaryless or limitless state.

But one does hear strange stories about empathy from therapists in supervision. For example, I recall one saying to me that a client kept getting angry with him, and he found it hard to maintain his empathy at such times! I was flabbergasted by this, partly by the emotional unreality of the therapist's own responses. Of course, the simple question to put here is 'what did you feel, when the client berated you?' And most therapists will reply that they don't like it, or they feel angry in turn, or frightened, and so on.

In other words, therapists have to be authentic, and cannot shelter behind their vaunted 'empathy'. The client is often after something real and concrete, not some abstract kind of response which has been learned on a training course. Of course, young and inexperienced therapists are understandably afraid of their own authentic feelings, especially when these are negative and decidedly not empathic. It is important therefore that training courses should contain instruction about responses to clients which are not positive and loving. One certainly has to learn to deal with hostile clients, for whom one's empathy has run out.

The issue of authenticity brings up many issues. For example, the fact that I am able to have my authentic feelings with clients does not automatically mean that I share them. That is another issue altogether. In fact, with certain clients I may have to mull over my own negative feelings for a long period before I communicate them, partly so that I can struggle to understand where they come from, if they are simply my own feelings or perhaps are projected from the client. Then I may have to deliberate on the fragility of the client – are they in a state that can take my own feelings?

Therapist authenticity also brings up the question of the therapist's own therapy. One can expect every therapist to have dealt with their own big emotional issues in therapy, to have dealt with blind spots, with areas of experience which they feel uncomfortable with. For example, we do not expect a therapist to feel uneasy with someone's tears, because their own tears have not been experienced. One can say the same of all major feelings and areas of human life, including sexuality, hatred, love, intimacy, fear, and so on. One can guarantee in fact that if there are unexplored areas in one's own psyche, that a client will come along who presses those buttons, and then one might have to take emergency action over this, which might include going back into therapy.

Conventional wisdom states that one should have done as much therapy as one will dispense. Thus if you are going to do short-term therapy, you need to have done it; if you are interested in long-term therapy, then clearly you must have done it yourself. However, this is not enough – one might argue that one should have done more than one's clients, so that one knows the way ahead with some confidence. These are obviously personal matters, but they are also professional ones, and many training courses have requirements about personal therapy.

Therapists go through life crises like anyone else – divorce, bereavement, professional successes and disappointments, marriage, and so on. The question here is whether such crises impinge on one's work as a therapist, and what can be done about this. For example, some therapists who begin to sexually exploit a client are found to be going through a very rocky time in their own personal life, for example a messy divorce. In other words, when a therapist is going through a time of great personal need and loneliness, they are particularly vulnerable to some professional aberration such as sexual exploitation. What is the solution to this? The obvious point is that if a therapist is really having a rocky time, they should go back into therapy, and they should make sure that the therapy is dealing with their own crisis, so that it doesn't impinge on their work more than necessary.

There are also times when therapists feel the need to suspend their work for a period, if a personal crisis gets too much. This often happens because of a major illness, but it can also happen because of bereavement or other personal tragedy.

Sometimes people ask: 'how can I be authentic and professional at the same time?' At first glance, these appear to be contradictory requirements, but that is only because we have a fantasy that 'professional' denotes a grim mask of neutrality, when in fact this is not so. Being professional means first getting all the parameters and boundaries of psychotherapy right, and keeping them intact, so that neither party feels afraid or engulfed. Second, it means keeping my own personality out of the therapy sessions, to ensure that the client is given their own time and space, which is after all what they are paying for. Thirdly, it means helping the client with their psychological problems in ways which are not intrusive, but which are not collusive. In other words, I am not here to smash down a client's defences, but neither am I here to placate them.

These requirements in fact do not contradict being honest. One might even say that they provide a buttress to one's personal honesty, in that the root of psychotherapy is about treating the client with emotional and cognitive truth. But there is also a need for flexibility in being a therapist – there are times, for example, when not very much needs to be said at all, since the client is doing all the running, and doing it very well. But there are other times when one might be very interventionist and forceful, if that seems to be required. Similarly, at the emotional level, one might vary in one day between being rather passive and gentle with one client, and having a row with another. One has to have a considerable emotional and intellectual repertoire to be a thera- pist, so that one can deal with different situations. Thus in fact I may find that with a certain client, my own personality comes into the session in an unusual way, since that seems to be what the client requires. For example, I have had clients with a passionate interest in football, and I have been quite happy at times to talk about football with them. Of course, one then has to deal with all the attendant guilt – in both of us – that we are being so apparently non- therapeutic! In fact, in the end we can also find out why this is very therapeutic for a certain client, as clearly it represents a kind of play, which he has been starved of.

FURTHER READING

H. M. Solomon and M. Twyman, *The Ethical Attitude in Analytic Practice* (London: Free Association, 2003).

Notes

1   See R. Mowbray, *The Case against Psychotherapy Registration* (London: Trans Marginal Press, 1995).
2   H. Oakley, 'Worrying developments in Europe' (letter), *British Journal of Psychotherapy* (2004) **20:4**.
3   See R. Mowbray, *The Case against Psychotherapy Registration*.
4   See C. Bollas, 'Confidentiality and professionalism in psychoanalysis', in *British Journal of Psychotherapy* (2004) **20:2**.

Part II

Practical Methods

7

The Setting: Time, Space and Money

I have known therapists who were rather casual about the physical parameters of psychotherapy, particularly time, space and money, and I think they are making a mistake. This is because many clients need a place and time of safety and reliability if they are to release painful material, and one way in which safety is established is through the physical arrangement of the sessions. If things are a bit slapdash or even anarchic, clients will definitely not feel safe, and they are likely to tighten up psychologically.

> An analyst found it difficult to keep track of the money she was owed by her patients, and sometimes made mistakes, and occasionally found that she had to be helped by some patients to work out their bill for the month. Some of them simply went along with this, feeling flattered no doubt; but others began to feel enraged, feeling that they were being manipulated or even seduced, but perhaps more pertinently, that they had to carry out some of the adult functions which they wished the analyst to carry. To make matters worse, the analyst didn't raise the issue, and was surprised when a couple of patients became distressed and angry over it.

This example shows a deeper psychological aspect of the management of the setting – that it is part of the management of the whole therapy by the therapist. If the client in some way has to take on board some of this responsibility, one of the messages being transmitted unconsciously by the therapist is: don't regress, because I am not completely sure that I can contain you.

We are obviously speaking here about a 'holding environment', or a containing environment, which will enable clients to let go more easily, in the trust that there is a firm support available. The client is being held safely.

One might also refer to the issue of being grounded – the analyst above seemed to give the impression of not being very conversant with the normal world of money and business. While some of her patients were not alarmed by this, some definitely were. There is a sort of 'head in the clouds' atmosphere about it, which gives a rather flaky impression.

Thus while time, space and money and other aspects of the physical and business arrangement of psychotherapy may seem 'non-psychological', this is not true at all. One might say that they form the foundation of the whole therapy. If there is a solid foundation, then something can be built; if the foundation is shaky, then the therapy is under threat.

Of course, some clients object to this 'management' of therapy on the grounds that it is dictatorial on the part of the therapist, and some critics of psychotherapy make the same objection – that there is a subtle and perhaps not so subtle power trip going on in therapy, whereby the therapist indoctrinates the client. This is a powerful critique, and I am sure that sometimes it is merited, but this means that all therapists have to be alive to these issues, and have to be very sensitive to issues to do with intrusiveness, bossiness, and so on. After all, there is always the danger of repeating something from the client's childhood, in particular that sense of being overpowered by someone more powerful.

Nonetheless, we have to state that psychotherapy in the sense in which it is understood in this book, will not work if it is carried out in some anarchic way, where all parameters are continually subject to change on the part of both therapist and client. For example, it is well known that if the times of sessions are being changed all the time, the psychotherapy suffers considerably, since neither party can settle down to the work. In fact, one becomes familiar with clients who do try to change times all the time, and it is usually a sign of some deep-seated reluctance to be committed to the process.

Let me take the dimensions or parameters of time, space and money in turn.

Time

Therapy works best when it occurs at a regular time; when the sessions are the same length; and when the therapist keeps good time. Of course, within that and around that many clients disrupt the timing of therapy – they arrive late, sometimes they don't turn up at all without any warning, they get restless before the end of sessions, they want to keep changing the time of the sessions, often with irreproachable reasons ('I have to work late that night'), and so on. There are many ways in which acting out occurs in relation to time, and in a sense every client has the right to do this. One might even say that every client has the right not to turn up, although the therapist also has the right to attempt to find out what the meaning of this is.

A lot of time disruption by clients is do with commitment. Some clients feel claustrophobic at the regularity of the sessions, and unconsciously or consciously want to keep changing things around.

> Every few months Alan would simply not turn up, with no warning. The next session would find him rather sheepishly admit he just 'didn't feel like it'. His therapist was tolerant of this behaviour, because he felt that Alan was trying to express something with his behaviour that was completely unconscious, and if the therapist became overly censorious, the meaning of it might be buried again.

This example illustrates the dangers of being too critical of 'acting out' – that it simply makes the client feel guilty and disapproved of. At the same time, the therapist cannot simply passively endure such types of behaviour – after all, we are here together to find out the meaning of the client's actions, especially those meanings which have lain undiscovered and have probably caused the client problems in life.

One of the extraordinary things about our relationship to time and money and space is how quite small aspects of our behaviour may in fact reveal very significant attitudes to life, to other people, and to ourselves. We probably all know friends who are consistently late, and some who are usually early, and some who are rigorously punctual. If we follow such behaviours back to their origins in the psyche, we often find complex and rich significance to them.

As well as relating to commitment, the disruption of the time arrangements can also refer to control issues – some clients feel resentful that the therapist appears to wield so much power in relation to the time and space. There may be also a rebellion against feelings of dependency – if you turn up regularly every week, there is a sense in which you are accepting some kind of dependence on the therapy and the therapist, and some clients find that disturbing.

There is also the interesting phenomenon of people who are in fact puzzled by time and space, who find it mysterious or incomprehensible. We are talking here about people who are not 'logged on' to the physical world, who may be floating above it in airy speculation, who have never become grounded. To them, these issues of being late or early, meeting at a regular time, may seem odd or irksome or too much of a trap.

Let me not forget those who are rigorously punctual, and never late. This is in itself strikes me as a little inhuman, and merits some enquiry as to how this pertains to the rest of the client's life. There is obviously something rather obsessional about it which without doubt will be found in other areas, and probably in the thinking process itself, leading to endless ruminations.

Obviously one cannot produce a comprehensive list of meanings of time disruption – as in so many areas, there is no recipe book which can be consulted. One has to take each client individually, and attempt to find out what lies behind and beneath such attitudes to time.

But it is interesting to pause here and question why regularity of time seems to matter so much to therapy. Imagine that therapist and client met on a different day of the week every week, and at a different time. One thing that happens is that everyone gets confused – this tends to happen even in the simple case of a rearranged session. But there is more to it than that – it seems that the psyche needs a kind of constancy and regularity, if it is to begin to submit to the discipline of therapy, and if it is to 'pour forth a horn of plenty'. In other words, in psychoanalytic language, the unconscious begins to release its contents when there is a containment, and a firm set of boundaries. If conditions seem less contained, less safe, somewhat boundaryless, then the repression continues.

Many clients comment that they get into a rhythm, particularly when we begin again after a break, such as Christmas and Easter, and we can relax, as it were, into the three months of regular sessions. It is noticeable that if this period is broken up, by illness or holidays, the sense of rhythm is disrupted to an extent.

Breaks

This brings me naturally onto the subject of breaks. Clients differ widely in their reaction to the breaks at Christmas, Easter and summer. Some profess indifference to them; some are apparently relieved; some are distressed or angry. It is a rather delicate issue here as to how much the therapist comments on the client's reactions, and again, this depends on how much psychoanalytic influence the therapist has received. The more analytic therapists will look quite closely at reactions before and after breaks, in the belief that they stir up ancient and primitive feelings about separation and attachment. If one believes that most clients have a regressive relationship to the therapist, whether it is apparent or not, then one is inclined to make some inferences about the effects of breaks.

However, let it also be said that one should not be too heavy-handed about the breaks. If a client doesn't seem interested in the topic, or shrugs it off, then quite often it is best not to pursue the subject, unless the therapist has strong feelings that the client is going through something quite powerful in relation to the break.

> Barry was bad-tempered after the summer break. He produced a list of reasons for this, which were convincing enough, to do with his marriage, work situation, and so on. However, the therapist thought there was a kind of extra residue of anger, which might be connected to the preceding break. He made an interpretation along these lines, and Barry denied it vehemently, at which point the therapist felt confident enough to say that he thought Barry was angry about the break. But when Barry continued to deny it, the therapist left it alone.

This example shows the balance that one must find between interpreting a certain situation, whilst not being too heavy-handed about it.

Beginning therapists tend to take short breaks, out of fear that clients might leave, and possibly some guilt that they are looking after themselves by having a holiday, but generally as one becomes more experienced, breaks lengthen. In fact, therapists need to take decent breaks, to recharge their batteries and get away from the work situation.

Length of therapy

Most therapists will have a subjective attraction to certain lengths of therapy, although this can change. I have known both therapists who shifted from doing long-term work to short-term, and vice versa. Of course it is also possible to do both, although usually one will have a temperamental leaning to one or another.

In general, those who are more psychoanalytic in their approach will do more long-term work, although one does find today short-term work that is cognitive and analytic. The non-analytic therapies traditionally worked in more short-term therapy, but this is changing considerably, as more and more non-analytic therapists are influenced by the analytic paradigm.

There are of course practical considerations as well here – short-term therapy is cheaper. This appeals not only to private individuals, but naturally to companies and institutions which finance therapy and counselling. Thus in the UK, the NHS tends to allow psychotherapy of a fairly short duration, and those private companies which pay for their employees to receive counselling also tend to want short-term work.

In fact, there is something of a bias against long-term work today. These terms are variable, but by 'long-term' I mean therapy over four years. One hears some therapists argue that therapy that lasts six or seven years or over, is collusive, that is, it is somehow pandering to the client's wish to be dependent, not to become independent, to remain regressed, and so on. I find these arguments unconvincing. I am convinced that there are always a number of clients who eventually want to do long-term work for the purposes of exploring issues of intimacy, trust and love, or who want to explore issues to do with the meaning of their life, and the nature of their identity. One might argue that one should not be using psychotherapy for such exploration, but why not?

Another important area where long-term work occurs is in relation to creativity. Certain creative artists come up against recurring problems in their work – such as guilt, creative blocks, post-creation depression – and may choose to stay in long-term therapy so that they can come back to these issues again and again.

Many clients begin therapy with a considerable amount of anxiety about the length of therapy. They are afraid of staying for over six months or over a year, or whatever. Quite often there are anxieties about dependency, commitment, trust, and these can be explored in relation to the vexed question of 'how long will it take?' One cannot of course give a direct answer to that, and any notion of the 'average length of time' is actually meaningless. One answer that I have found useful is that it depends on how far you want to go – if you want to deal with a particular problem and find a solution to it, then we are in for quite short-term therapy; if you realize that you undergoing a marked personality change or change in lifestyle, then this can take years to go through. So it is not so much that therapy is short or long term, but that the developments we all go through in life differ in the amount of time they take up.

Frequency

Many of the same issues arise in relation to frequency of therapy as to length. The more psychoanalytic therapists tend to favour twice or three times a week therapy; traditionally, humanistic therapists worked once a week, but this has changed considerably, as so many have been influenced by analytic work.

Again, one finds therapists who change their stance on this. I used to work a lot with twice a week or three times a week clients, but now I find a lot of once a week clients come to me, which I assume must reflect a change in me.

The traditional analytic view of once a week therapy is that it keeps the client in a defended state – they may open up in the session, but then they have a whole week in which to close up again, forget what happened in the session, and as it were start all over again next week. There is also what I call a 'News at Ten' flavour sometimes with once a week therapy – whereby the client goes through a description of the week's events – the quarrel with the boss, the disagreement with the wife, the kids playing up again – and then it is the end of the session. Certainly, with two sessions, the second session permits the client to get away from pure event description, and allow some deeper stuff to come up. One might say that it gives the unconscious a bit more room to spread itself or find its voice.

As against that, some clients are frightened and disturbed by twice weekly therapy. There is the problem of over-stimulation for some clients, particularly those who have been abused as children – too much contact may make them feel very disturbed, and for such people, once a week therapy is safer. The same is true for many people who are completely new to therapy. Going straight into twice a week therapy may be very frightening to begin with, and once a week can seem more manageable.

At the same time, I encounter some clients who have so much psychological material going through them, that three times a week therapy is required simply to deal with it all. This is relatively unusual, but it may develop in long-term clients, who may start to find that their unconscious is responding to the therapy by producing a huge amount of feelings, fantasies, dreams, memories and so on, and then one simply has to find the format that contains this material.

While 'containment' is a psychoanalytic term, in that it stems from the work of Bion and others, it has become a term used outside psychoanalytic circles to denote the way in which therapy holds the client, or holds the rumbustious outpourings of the unconscious. One can argue that without containment, the unconscious is anarchic and chaotic, and this feels very threatening to most people, who will therefore tend to cut off from it as a means of control. But given the right degree of containment, some kind of surrender to the unconscious can proceed.

Endings

The ending of therapy is very important, and great care should be given to it, yet one hears of quite perfunctory endings to long therapies, which suggests that both therapist and client were colluding in covering up painful and difficult feelings. For the ending of a long therapy can bring up very dark and obscure feelings about death, separation, saying good-bye, and so on. In fact, one can trigger off a new set of regressive feelings, since an ending such as this can recapitulate all separations in life, including birth, weaning, adolescence, middle age, as well as death itself.

One can argue that a fully worked through ending in therapy is a preparation for death. This sounds dramatic, but I am sure it is true. This is because the ending in therapy is like no other, for it is voluntary and final. Usually, when friendships and sexual relationships end, there is either a kind of petering out, so that there is no single point of separation, or there may an ambiguity about it, so that one does not really know if it is an ending or not. In other words, there is often an unconscious element to endings in relationships – we are ending this, but we prefer not to know that we are. But in therapy, we know that we are ending, and we tend not to encourage further contact.

Therapy is very odd therefore in that we are able to 'work through' the ending, and because of this, it can be very uncomfortable for many clients and some therapists. It can stir up many strange feelings, such as guilt, anger, relief, joy, and so on. I say 'strange' feelings, since many of them prove to be highly irrational. For example, it is quite common for a client who has decided to stop, to begin to feel angry with the therapist, as if the therapist had decided the issue! But such reversals are common in endings, since undoubtedly they stir up many old memories of separations that we experienced as children. Thus anyone who has experienced a mother going into hospital or going away for a lengthy period, or who was suddenly taken to places without warning, or who was sent to school in a harsh manner, or sent abroad – these and many other experiences can be resurrected in a very painful manner by the ending of therapy.

This is why often we need a long time to work through it. How long? Of course it depends on many factors, including the length of the therapy, the reasons for ending, the success or otherwise of the therapy, and so on. For example, someone who decides to stop therapy after six months, and feels that they haven't got much out of it, will not be in a mood to go through a long ending! One also comes across clients who attempt to guillotine the whole thing – I can recall a number of clients who arrived for the session and announced that this was the last one. One can imagine the stormy feelings that this arouses in the therapist, and usually it is a very angry act by the client.

My own gut feeling is that long therapy needs from 3 to 9 months to end; medium length therapies, up to 3 months. But quite often a natural seeming break suggests itself – for example, if a client is talking about leaving in winter, then Easter can seem an appropriate time to aim at. If the client is appalled at the length of time left, then one has good reason to believe that there are difficult feelings to be gone through, but it can be difficult in such cases to hold the line for a long ending.

The length of ending is required to enable the client to go through all the feelings that are involved. Most clients will go through some anger and rejection, no matter how irrational this is. Most will feel sad; and many relieved. Some clients experience a kind of liberation feeling, in the sense that they feel they have accomplished something major in their life, and the end is therefore a time of celebration. But contradictions abound here – one can expect the same client to feel joy, sadness and anger almost in the same breath.

Guilt is also prevalent, since many clients feel guilty about the act of separation. There is also the fear of not being allowed to leave – this is common in those clients who feel trapped in relationships, or who dread dependency.

Another reason for long endings is to allow for a change of mind, which is not uncommon. Certainly, it allows for the testing of the initial wish to stop, which may be genuine, but may also be a kind of cover for deeper feelings, for example, a wish not to become too dependent.

Should therapists argue against the client's decision to stop? I think sometimes it would be irresponsible not to, if the therapist really believes that the client is running away from something, but this is a very difficult area, since one must be very careful not to impugn the client's independence and autonomy. I know that sometimes I feel a client is wrong to leave, but I can also acknowledge that they probably need to make that decision for themselves, wrong or not.

There is also the phenomenon of 'rehearsal' therapies. I mean that sometimes clients do a short therapy, then have a break, then do a much longer one with a different therapist. It's as if one wants to withdraw for a while, and then consider whether one really wants to commit oneself to a major self-examination after having had a 'taster' experience. The first therapist might well feel some chagrin at this, but it is a valid approach on the part of the client.

Endings are like nothing else in bringing out the real feelings of therapist and client for each other. They may have become important to each other; love may be felt mutually; there may be grief at the separation from someone who has been central to one's life. At the same time, there may be ambivalent feelings as well, involving anger and resentment. One might also say that material which has not been dealt with may suddenly emerge in something of a rush. There is also the phenomenon of recapitulation: that is, it is quite common to go through again the phases which occurred in the therapy itself, but of course this time considerably speeded up.

Many clients are reminded of how their romantic relationships have ended, including marriages. They may find that this time they are able to go through a proper ending, whereas previously they could not, and brought down the guillotine so as to avoid many feelings. Many insights may emerge into how and why endings have occurred previously, and thus this can be a stormy and intense time.

At the same time, feelings of relief and looking forward to the end are good signs, and show that good work has been done, and both parties can value the experience. Sadness is mixed with a pleasure and a satisfaction that a real achievement has been made.

One can relate this discussion to the notion of boundaries, since the beginning and the end mark the most important boundaries which exist in therapy. Certainly an endless therapy would be frightening and disturbing for both therapist and client, and there is a sense that just as life acquires its full meaning because of its finiteness, so does therapy. It gives us a sense of urgency maybe; and a sense that we have a goal or a set of goals, even if these are rather diffuse. Of course, the sense of therapy as microcosm is reinforced by the ending, since we are being taught here, as elsewhere, that change is one of the most dominant forces in existence, and cannot be avoided. We do not dwell in an endless paradise, where all decisions can be postponed, and where the harsh exigencies of the world do not intrude. That is why therapy costs money; that is why it consists of quite short sessions; and this is why it comes to an end.

Are there clients who go on forever? I would yes, but they tend to be those who are disturbed in some way, mentally ill, or in some other way, not equipped for adult life. For example, I have seen a number of schizophrenic clients for very long periods. However, painful decisions may still have to be made one day, for most therapists eventually want to retire! What happens then? One has to go through very painful endings in this case, and hopefully transfer the client to another therapist, who can bear the brunt of recrimination and grief for a period.

One may also decide in such cases that the therapy has become pointless, for such clients often do not show signs of improvement, and may well go through cycles of hospitalization, when therapy is impossible, followed by a better period, when it is. Obviously, this is a personal decision. I have not found it a problem with certain clients, partly because I am convinced that therapy does improve the quality of their lives, and also, and importantly, I got on with them sufficiently to make it alright. In other words, I like them enough!

One of the perennial questions which comes up is about contact after the ending. Most therapists who have tried this have found that it doesn't work. The shock to both parties, if a meeting is arranged in a café or somewhere like that, can be huge, in the sense that one is meeting for the first time in a completely different milieu. However, I do recall meeting ex-clients accidentally in all sorts of strange places, and sometimes we have had a very good chat and the experience was a good one. On the other hand, for many clients it is anathema, and that is what counts.

If an ex-client makes contact, it might be better to suggest having a session in the same place as formerly. Social occasions tend to be disastrous, although bumping into an ex-client at a party or wedding or public meeting can be perfectly alright, especially if it's easy to avoid each other! But there have of course been examples of ex-therapists and clients becoming friends, and even getting married.

Space

Whether the therapist works at home or in an institutional setting or in a hired room affects considerably how the space is regulated. To take the extreme example of working at home – I say 'extreme' since here the therapist has complete control over the physical environment – the therapist has to ensure that the room is neither disturbingly individualistic nor too antiseptic. There is a kind of middle way between these two extremes. One does not want to pretend that it is not one's home, but one does not want to produce too cosy an atmosphere.

> A therapist had a guitar artistically draped across a sofa in his consulting room. Some clients commented favourably on it; others looked rather askance. The therapist began to feel uncomfortable about the guitar himself, and after discussion with supervisor and colleagues removed it from the room.

It is clear that the guitar was too intrusive a personal detail. For some therapists, it is tempting to introduce such details into their room, as if to say that 'this is my space', or some such message. But it is too personal. There are many similar examples – I know therapists who have giant crosses on the wall, or fishing rods in the corner, or who have their dog sit next to them (shades of Freud!), and so on, and there are those who have their cup of coffee and cigarette at hand in every session.

My own reaction to such arrangements is quite negative, but then I can also grant that it may well work for them. But I see the physical setting as a balance between the personal and the impersonal. We do not want a monastic cell, painted white, with no pictures on the wall; but neither do we want a screaming modernist pad with nudes on the wall. For me, the cup of coffee for the therapist begs too many questions – of course the client is going to want one as well, and then we are into all kinds of murky waters about nourishment, starvation, and so on.

The therapist working at home has many decisions to make – what kind of lighting, what kind of pictures on the wall, what kind of chairs, is there going to be a clock, and if so, where? Through all this, some kind of balance has to be struck between comfort and formality.

My own taste is perhaps rather formal – I work at home, and I have few personal items in the room, except for books. This in itself is quite contentious, since one might have quite strange tastes in reading, which may be best kept out of the consulting room. On the other hand, a formal row of psychological textbooks strikes me as rather forbidding, but this is a subjective matter.

The therapist also has to think about their own appearance, and this is again a very personal issue, and one has to balance between the formal and informal. I never wear suits or ties, but that is to do with what I feel comfortable with, and I would not lay it down in any way as a rule. I know therapists who wear jeans, which I would feel uncomfortable in, but they seem to feel perfectly alright.

I suppose 'subdued' is the word that comes to mind here – one is not trying to make a fashion statement as a therapist. But then I know that today there are therapists who dress very casually, wear earrings, have ponytails (men), and so on, so it is difficult to generalize.

The most important thing about the spatial arrangements is that both parties should feel safe. Note that I say both parties – it is common to say that the client should, but so should the therapist. Obviously, if the therapist feels ill at ease in the room, that does not augur well for the therapy.

Those who work outside home, in hired rooms, in institutional settings, such as hospitals, mental health centres, prisons, and so on, face quite different issues, for here one is much less in control of the environment. The main thing is to achieve consistency. I know that some therapists have problems with hired rooms, when the furniture keeps changing, chairs appear and disappear, and so on. Some people have to go in early to rearrange the room. These are not ideal arrangements, and one needs to come to an agreement with the hirer about the constancy of the room and its furniture. Similarly, one needs to make sure that the room is reasonably sound-proofed, and this can be a big problem in hospitals and other institutions.

Working on the couch

The couch is one of the important technical adjuncts to therapy, which can completely alter the way therapy proceeds. Again we find the familiar divide between the more and less psychoanalytic therapists, and traditionally the use of the couch amongst non-analytic therapists was minimal. This is changing as more and more therapists do analytic therapy themselves.

The couch encourages regression; it is much more private, and hence permits the release of material that might be difficult in face-to-face therapy;

one can simply be in one's own space. The therapist has to decide where to position his/her own chair in relation to the couch. Some sit at the side; probably more sit behind or at an angle – the issue here being whether there is still some element of face-to-face contact. I sit behind clients on the couch, since I find that a kind of half and half position, whereby I am half in view, feels rather peculiar, but this is a matter of personal judgement obviously.

Nonetheless, it is clear that the use of the couch marks a radical disjunction from face-to-face therapy. The client is lying down, head supported by cushions; the therapist may be out of sight or at an angle, but sitting up in a chair. The whole ethos leans towards a less adult, less cognitive type of process. One has literally lowered one's head, so that it is no longer 'top dog' as it were. One permits the rest of one's body to function in the therapy, so that one is more aware of sensations in the stomach, belly, genitals, legs and arms.

There is a much greater tendency to reverie in this position, since one is not continually monitoring the other person; in this sense, one is treating oneself less as an object for others, and more as a self for itself. The process of allowing the imagination to flow, and the unconscious to yield up its contents, is greatly facilitated.

At the same time, many clients need the contact provided by face-to-face therapy, although this may change as the therapy progresses, and the need for one's own space comes to the fore.

Your time and space

In humanistic psychology it is a time-honoured custom to say to clients that 'it's your time and space', which although sounding rather clichéd, contains some profound truths. For many clients are used to time and space not being theirs. Those who had domineering parents, who went to schools that were rather 'cramming', which seems to denote most schools today, and those whose work is something of an imposition, may find the statement odd, may not really believe it ('where's the catch'), or quite frequently, may find it totally incomprehensible.

Added to this, there is the related phenomenon of client passivity – I mean that many clients come to therapy in the expectation that they will be told what to do. Again, this seems to be the product of child-rearing and education systems that do just that, and hence this unwonted freedom is disconcerting. One can see people run out of things to say, and then begin to panic at the silence or their own emptiness or stuckness. What now?

Clearly what could happen now is that we discuss this silence or emptiness or stuckness. What does the client feel about it? Is it a common occurrence in their life? We have a golden opportunity to get beneath the normal façade of social chit-chat, but this is for many people embarrassing or frightening and these feelings have to be dealt with.

One might say properly that there is a resistance to the time and space being a creative area for one's own activity or free spontaneity. Say what you like, think what you like, do nothing if that seems right – these are strange injunctions in our culture, despite its much vaunted cults of 'pleasure' and 'freedom'. Many people feel very constrained and non-spontaneous, and therapy is able to get to the heart of these constraints in quite a simple way by positing a time and place which is for the client. Many clients simply cannot make use of this freedom, showing how much their spontaneity has been inhibited.

It takes most people an appreciable time therefore to grasp how they can use the time and space to explore those issues which are important to them, or if they so wish, explore nothing. I think one should always be alive to people who are tired of doing, and who may come to relish the time and space as a place where there is no pressure to produce anything. I have had a number of clients who fell asleep in sessions in a way that struck me not as an escape or avoidance, but as a surrender, a period of relaxation that was rare in their lives.

Therapy is therefore, in my book, client-centred. Of course this does not mean that the therapist adopts a totally passive attitude – if something strikes him or her as important then they are duty bound to bring it up. But I use the phrase 'totally passive' carefully, for I think there are occasions when it is appropriate for the therapist to be relatively passive, to allow the client their own exploration or silence, or whatever. We are trying to get away from the idea of the therapist as a stern parent, or a directive parent (or headmaster).

But of course there are gradations of directiveness in therapy, and while I am positing a fairly freewheeling and open-ended approach, some therapies are much more directive and goal-oriented. These will usually be focused on particular issues and problems, which can be looked at, explored and solutions found quite quickly. There is an obvious tie-up here with length of therapy, in that the short-term therapies have to focus quickly and directly on specific issues. They cannot meander or stop dead, or go into unknown areas.

Longer therapies can do these things, and one may have to cultivate not-knowing as a definite practice, for it is important not to rush to judgement, that is, make premature interpretations or analyses.

> Helen began to explore certain themes in her childhood, and one which came out quite strongly was the confusion which filled the air. She had been unclear what kind of work her father did; her mother's background was pretty unknown

to her; they had given her conflicting ideas about right and wrong; they'd both had affairs at various times, and had concealed these rather clumsily. She became very confused in the therapy, and at first her therapist felt obliged to correct this, but after considerable discussion in supervision, she became able to tolerate the confusion.

This example shows how too much clarity and too much consciousness can be premature and harmful. Many people have similar experiences of confusion, feeling blank or numb, and so on, and these will come up in therapy and have to be allowed some breathing space, not instantly interpreted and got out of the way.

I recall a client of mine who seemed to be surrounded by a kind of mental fog, which infected me as well as him. We talked about it a lot, but it still pervaded the room at times, and as we got used to it, we became able to tolerate it and allow it to occur. Of course, part of me felt this was wrong, and as a therapist I should be clarifying things, clearing up the murky atmosphere, and so on. But this in fact would be a disservice to the client's truth.

But not all clients find it difficult to use the time and space; there are others who can seize it gratefully and use it to explore many issues, and with such people the other problem may arise – that there is a workaholic feel to the therapy. They are unable to rest or stop; they cannot be as well as do. But this is a very subjective judgement, since there are very active clients who do not feel workaholic. I think the key here is the driven quality of the workaholic, and this is something which will be picked up by the therapist intuitively and subjectively. Sometimes one starts to feel tired and exhausted by the constant work done by the client, as if one is being driven oneself, which may well be true.

We can refer to the microcosm principle again – ideally, we might suggest that life should be full of work and rest, and that people who cannot give themselves both need some correction in their life. However, generalizations like this are usually eminently falsifiable – and one does meet both people who do little work and seem quite happy, and those who take little rest and seem to thrive.

Money

Money is probably the most contentious of the parameters dealt with in this chapter. This is because money has deep psychological meaning for most people, and the exchange of money for a service such as psychotherapy raises many issues. In fact, some clients find the whole financial side of therapy distressing; some get enraged by it; some are bewildered that it's not free; and of course we find here too a whole array of acting out behaviours – paying late, objecting to paying for cancellations, objecting to raises in fees, and so on.

The same principle can be adduced here as with the time arrangements – that money is intensely symbolic, and distress over money often represents something profound in the client's psyche. For example, some people feel so emotionally impoverished that handing over money feels very painful, and they may try to obtain a reduced fee, ostensibly because they have little money, but also because they feel they have little to give emotionally.

The issue of reduced fees is one that gets therapists arguing and steamed up like few other things, since every therapist seems to get a number of clients who make very persuasive cases for having a reduced fee. There are different policies on this – I know therapists who basically refuse to reduce their fee, and state quite legitimately that any able-bodied adult should be able to get some kind of work to pay for their sessions. However, many other therapists can be persuaded to reduce their fee in certain cases. Obvious examples are students, unemployed people, severely disturbed people who obviously cannot work. And some therapists in fact make it a principle to do some low-paid work or even free work.

Again, one has to find one's own position here, but I do think that one has to be very alive to the underlying significance of low fees. Most therapists have had the infuriating experience of their low-fee client going on holiday to Florida for three weeks! In fact, it can be quite embarrassing to bring these issues up, but certainly the therapist cannot be allowed to stew silently in resentment at the low-fee client's expensive lifestyle. A client of mine was left half a million pounds in someone's will, and when I hesitantly suggested that we could now raise her rather low fee a little, she exploded in rage, and accused me of being another gold-digger! However, this explosion proved quite useful to her, as she was able to distinguish between the actual gold-diggers in her life, and others who simply asked legitimately for payment.

In fact, it is often the most affluent people who raise objections about the fee-paying side of therapy, since the symbolic significance of money does not diminish if one has a lot – perhaps it is greater. In particular, one often meets well-off people who have received quite a lot of money from parents, and here issues of power, control, and separation can be very powerfully associated with money.

Raising fees is difficult for many therapists, who can experience some dread and guilt about asking for more. Of course these reactions vary according to the client. There is usually one or more clients who recommend that you put your fee up – I treat this very suspiciously, as it seems far too altruistic to be true! Money certainly shows up clearly the adult/child divide in people – I mean that rationally and from the adult point of view, clients can accept that the therapist has to earn a living, therefore charges for cancellations, puts up their fees, and so on. But there may be quite a different set of reactions concealed behind it, more primitive and child-like – that I should be loved for free, that I'm being exploited, I'm not getting value for money, and so on.

Fees also hinge on the self-worth of the therapist, and newly trained therapists notoriously have low fees, and gradually edge them up as they feel more confident. If this is a severe problem, then I would recommend not simply dealing with it in supervision, but in one's own therapy as well, as this can be a paralyzing issue, which can spread into other areas. Some clients are very good at picking up these feelings of insecurity, and the more sadistic client can become expert at punishing an insecure therapist.

8
Working with Clients

There is an interface between the client's evaluation of his own problems and the therapist's evaluation of them. To begin with, the client is self-referring and defines his/her own problems. He has come to therapy for certain reasons, which may be quite specific or may be quite vague. But gradually the therapist gets to know the client, looks at the way they relate to each other, the atmosphere of the sessions and so on, and forms his own opinion of the client. How do these points of view interact?

Let us say that Joe comes to therapy because he is lonely, his relationships are rather unsatisfying, his girlfriends tend to disappear after a short while. But Joe doesn't really know why all this is happening – or rather, why good things are not happening. Of course, we can't criticize Joe for this lack of self-knowledge. One of the deductions from the theory of the unconscious is that we are indeed unconscious of many aspects of our personality and how we live in the world, how we relate to others and to ourselves, and so on. Self-knowledge generally in human beings appears to be a shadowy and often fragmentary thing.

Joe's therapist sees a man who is rather distant, somewhat intellectual in his approach to life, sceptical about the benefits of therapy, rather dismissive about women, and so on. In addition, Joe, when asked, volunteers that his childhood was very good, his parents took good care of him and his siblings – in short, the normal idealized childhood!

Clearly there is a mismatch between Joe's self-evaluation and the therapist's evaluation of him. Joe can sense that there is something wrong in his life, but tends to blame others, or fate. The idea that he blocks relations with others, is afraid of intimacy, fears women intensely, in other words, is the author of his own unhappiness – such ideas would probably seem quite alien to him.

The therapist's situation is a delicate one. One cannot recommend normally that he crashes in with all this information in the early period of therapy. I say 'normally' because sometimes one has to take emergency action, if the client for example decides to stop therapy after two or three weeks, because 'it isn't going anywhere'. Then the therapist maybe has to give a short sharp shock to Joe, and tell him that there are some serious problems to do with his personality and his ability to relate to others.

But this is shock treatment, and is not normally recommended. Somehow the mismatch between the two evaluations has to be gradually overcome, so that the client comes to see his own shortcomings and takes action to rectify them. Much depends of course on the client's degree of self-awareness. Here we find a complete spectrum, from people who are very sensitive and alive to such issues, to others who blank off from it all, and turn their face to the wall, as it were.

The word 'gradually' above is a very flexible one. How long do we mean? One cannot give any definite answer to that. I find myself communicating such things with some clients very quickly – in a matter of weeks – whereas with others, it can take years, before they are ready and able to hear it and take it in.

Many clients have a vague sense that in therapy one gets angry with one's parents, and some are quite prepared to do this, but the next stage – which is to take responsibility for one's own life – is more difficult. Again, there is a balance here between the two – the past and the present, one might say. There is a strong need for many to look at childhood and try to uncover what actually went on, what wounds still survive from that period, what feelings have lain buried for decades.

This phase of 'reconstruction' can itself last for years, but a time must come when we move on from the past to present life, where one's parents cannot be accused of causing damage. Of course, some people do go on blaming their parents endlessly, and have to be weaned off that if possible towards a more self-exploratory path.

I come back to intuition. When is it right to say to someone, 'actually, I find you quite distant/angry/cut off'? One has to feel the rightness or wrongness of that, based on one's sense of the client's vulnerability – for some people simply are too fragile to hear such things – and that point in their journey when they are ready for it.

Of course it's best if it comes from the client, and it often will, but not always. We come back to ego strength. Those who are very wounded, vulnerable, and lack ego strength, cannot take too much hard talking like this. Those who have very powerful defences and show ego strength, generally can take it – but one has to beware of those who conceal a great fragility behind tough defences.

There is also the question of the alliance that has been built up between therapist and client. If this alliance has become quite strong – if there is quite a degree of trust between the two – then it is possible to say quite hard things. It is that much more difficult if the alliance has foundered for whatever reason, and distrust is the watchword.

In other words, a client is ready to hear difficult things from somebody whom they have grown to respect and trust, and this takes time. But let me also say that one reason that clients come to respect their therapist is that they have not shirked from saying the difficult and unsentimental things. We do not go to therapy in order to be flattered or cajoled.

> Jane was quite a manipulative woman, who seemed to go around life wheeling and dealing with everybody. She was involved in various 'scams' which tottered on the edge of legality, and her therapist wondered if a time would come when she would be invited to join in one of them. This made her very apprehensive, as she knew she would have to refuse, but also knew how forceful Jane could be in her persuasions. One day Jane asked her therapist if she would lie for her about her condition, so that she could get time off work. The therapist refused, and a massive row ensued, but later Jane told her that she respected her for that decision.

This is a dramatic example, but it is surprising how often some kind of crisis comes to a head with a particular client, which summates many of their neurotic tendencies. It's almost as if the client has set up the crisis to find out if the therapist can actually deal with it, and if not, the client may well be disappointed and may leave. It's as if they're saying: 'I can't deal with my own neurotic compulsions; I'm putting you to the test to see if you can'.

Such examples show also how evaluation and intervention fuse together. Often as we perceive a certain issue or problem going on with a client, a possible intervention will suggest itself at once. We may hold it in reserve for a long period; we may need to think it over, discuss it in supervision. But there are also occasions when the two really are fused, and as we perceive something going on, we instantly arrive at an intervention and put it into effect.

One can see that psychotherapy is not a mechanical set of exercises nor a recipe book of techniques which can be consulted in a detached manner. Everything depends on the personality of the client, on the relationship between therapist and client, on the processes that have gone on, the progress that has been made (or not). These are finely attuned judgements, which cannot be reduced to simple equations. At times, one may find oneself doing something which seems bizarre or even wrong, and yet there is a conviction about it which is very powerful.

> Margaret's therapist began to experience great dread before the beginning of their sessions. She felt frightened; at times, she burst into tears. Clearly, something was going wrong – massive counter-transferences were happening, but the therapist felt powerless to do anything about it. Discussion in supervision provided partial relief, but still the dread continued and even intensified. Eventually, the therapist decided that she would have to tell Margaret something of what she was feeling, even though she felt guilty about this, felt it was wrong, unprofessional, and so on. She felt even more dread before this session, and then told Margaret of her great fear of her. To her amazement, Margaret burst into tears, and said that many people had shied away from her, had obviously found her intimidating, without her really understanding why. The discussion opened up, and both Margaret and her therapist experienced great relief that something taboo had been broached.

This example should not be taken as a standard technique. It is one of those exceptional situations which demand exceptional measures, but most therapists come across such situations at some time in their practice, almost as if they serve as initiations. Generally, one finds that after such a difficult experience as this, subsequent parallel situations can be dealt with more easily, partly because one feels more confident in the use of one's own intuition and judgement.

Aims

What are the aims of therapy? One could say there are an infinite number, since clients turn up with many needs and wishes, and therapy should be able to deal with a broad spectrum. However, without doubt there is a kind of psychological checklist or set of aims that most therapists have in mind at times. Let me describe what such a checklist might contain.

First, that the client should develop sufficient ego-strength to withstand the shocks and vicissitudes of life. By 'ego-strength' I mean a solidity and a sureness about who one is, an ability to act or not act, the sense of having a centre that is secure.

Second, a healthy relationship with the unconscious. By this, I mean that one is able to receive the communications sent to us by the unconscious, in the form of dreams, images, fantasies, thoughts, feelings, and so on, without being overwhelmed by them and without having to suppress them.

Third, feeling comfortable with other people; being able to be intimate with others, including sexually.

Fourth, having work that is creative enough to be satisfying and fulfilling.

Fifth, having a relationship with the universe that is enjoyable and full of interest, whether it be through nature, spirituality, sport, music and literature, and so on.

Sixth, having a comfortable relationship with one's inner child, so that one can play easily and enjoyably; one can be frivolous, silly, and so on. One respects one's own irrational side.

Seventh, being able to distinguish between feeling and action, so that one can have feelings without acting on them, but one can also choose to act.

Everyone will want to add to this list, as I do myself, but it sets out a basic template against which one can consider the various personality disorders met with in therapy. For example, some people have plenty of ego-strength but have an impoverished relationship with the unconscious. But others are the reverse, that is, they can access the unconscious easily, but they are too vulnerable and cannot withstand the rigours of everyday life. Some people have good relationships but feel creatively frustrated, and again there are those who have the reverse problem.

Multi-functionality

By this rather ponderous word, I mean that therapy works in different ways at different times, or it has different levels, and we may move up and down these levels over time. For example, one obvious function of therapy is to solve problems, but these range from the very specific to the more diffuse. Somebody comes to therapy in order to deal with panic attacks, say. Even in this case, one can say that there is a spectrum of approaches. One could take quite a restricted behaviourial view, that is, help the client deal with their panic attacks when they occur by finding out what leads up to them, what feelings and thoughts they have been having, or what situations they are in, and then helping them to either avoid these situations or neutralize the frightening stimulus.

But it might also happen that our investigation of the panic attacks leads us into a much wider field, to do with a frightening childhood, or being left alone a lot as a child, or lack of containment, and so on. So even here, in terms of solving the 'problem' of panic attacks therapy may take a narrow or a wide view.

But problem solving in itself is clearly only one dimension of therapy. Some clients come in order to have an intimate relationship with someone, so that they can overcome certain problems they have with that. One might say that this is problem-solving again, but it is a much more diffuse problem and the 'solution' is in fact to have the relationship, and go through all the ins and outs of that, including no doubt the many difficulties which will arise.

Some people come to therapy in order to form a strong attachment to someone. That sounds rather bald, but I think it is true. I have had a number of clients who obviously wanted to do that, and did it, over long periods of time. One might make all kinds of objections to this – that they are avoiding forming an attachment outside therapy, that the therapist is colluding with their avoidance of reality, and so on. However, I find such criticisms rather peculiar and hyper-critical. Clearly, some clients have such a need, and I don't see why therapy shouldn't satisfy it.

Here we are getting close to that thorny area of satisfaction of needs in therapy, and the degree to which this is done or isn't done, or should or shouldn't be done. It seems absurd to deny that therapy does satisfy certain needs in clients – for example, to be seen and heard, to be taken care of, to be held in mind, to be loved and so on. How far this goes is problematic and does not offer an easily defined solution. I suppose one might say every therapist has to find out what they feel comfortable with and maintain their boundaries accordingly. Here we are surely dealing with the therapist's personality and their comfort zone, but we are also dealing with certain ethical areas – that in therapy we do not encourage romantic attachments, we do not get clients to take care of us, we do not exploit them, and so on. But such ethical rules do not actually clear up a very grey area.

Some clients want to be reparented, and they project onto their therapist many parental qualities. This is a very powerful projection, for good and ill, and it has a natural life cycle, in that hopefully, in the end the client is weaned off it.

The most succinct summary of the multi-level approach of therapy is to say that we are alive to issues in four main areas: the past; the present life situation; the therapy situation; and the inner world. In other words, psychotherapy may reconstruct the childhood of the client, particularly important relationships and their influence; it may look at the way the client's life works (or doesn't work) at present, in terms of relationships, work, creativity, and so on; pays attention to the relationship between therapist and client, and the way the client treats the sessions; and considers the implications of all this for the internal world of the client, and the various objects and forces contained therein.

That seems quite a task! Of course, therapists vary in the emphasis they place on different areas; and one also finds that different clients elicit differing emphases – for example, some clients are not very interested in their childhood, while others are fascinated by it. This doesn't mean that the therapist shares this lack of interest, but it can undoubtedly influence the overall direction of therapy.

Of course, it also leaves out an enormous amount – for example, there is no mention of the client's body and its revelation of emotional trauma; nor of spiritual issues; nor of symbolic expressions. Nonetheless, I believe that this scheme represents a reasonable overall picture of the repertoire available in contemporary psychotherapy.

Diagnosis

Some psychotherapists make considerable use of psychiatric diagnosis, followed by an indication as to strategies which the therapist will accordingly follow. However, I often find such an approach too defined and clear-cut, since in practice, one finds that many clients have a combination of characteristics in them, and second, one finds that one cannot follow a pre-planned strategy at all, since the client has presented one with a concrete set of issues which have to be dealt with concretely. This is particularly true of those disturbed clients, such as borderline or narcissistic people. Often with such clients, one is flying by the seat of one's pants, and the view is pretty terrifying!

The field of diagnostics is complex, but at the risk of over-simplification, one can suggest the following parameters. First, one can separate those who are neurotic from those who have a more primitive personality disorder – particularly those with borderline, narcissistic, hysterical and psychotic personalities. Secondly, one can differentiate along the gradience of severity, from mild forms of a disorder to very severe. Thirdly, one must decide as a psychotherapist which clients one feels reasonably comfortable with, which one feels decidedly uncomfortable with, and which one feels cannot be worked with at all – and obviously these decisions are very subjective and vary enormously from therapist to therapist.

The primary division between neurotic and more primitive disorders corresponds to the psychoanalytic distinction between oedipal and pre-oedipal disturbance, meaning that in the first case, the client has acquired a certain ability to relate to others, to work reasonably productively and so on. Thus most neurotic individuals can get through life adequately, although they may miss out on feelings of joy, fulfilment and profundity. They have acquired a sense of self which is reasonably solid, and one assumes their early relationships were adequate.

The more primitive conditions such as the borderline personality disorder and the narcissistic personality disorder show much more serious disturbances to the ability to relate to others, the sense of self, ego-strength, and the ability to handle boundaries.

The psychotic individual is often without boundaries, is overwhelmed by the unconscious, is often fragmented, and has little ego strength or sense of a unitary self. In such cases, early relationships are usually found to be deficient or abusive.

As with all such formulations, the above taxonomy can immediately be faulted. In particular, many people will be found to contain a mixture of several disturbances – for example, there are many neurotic people who have a borderline or narcissistic element. Second, the cut-off or schizoid individual – who is commonly found in therapy – seems to fall between two stools – they lack the quasi-psychotic features of the borderline client, but they have a more severe disturbance than the neurotic person. One should also mention here the spectrum of autism/Asperger's syndrome, which psychotherapy has become interested in, and which seems to suggest a constitutional or innate inability in some people to envisage someone else's consciousness or mind.[1] In fact, the ancient nature/nurture debate has been rekindled by such conditions, since it is likely that they are not environmentally induced.

Third, as I have indicated, an appreciation of someone's diagnostic category can often be of no help at all! I mean that one still might have to work very intuitively and subjectively with that particular individual.

One might say that all categories are ultimately false, since every individual is a unique combination of facets, and furthermore, one cannot produce book recipes. These tend to fall flat, since one has taken one's attention away from the person to an abstract categorization, and the client will often be aware of this, and will react badly. If you like, the therapist has fallen victim to a kind of schizoid reaction – moving away from the relationship to an intellectual description. This is of course very tempting in the case of someone who really gets under your skin – one tends to rush around reading lots of books about the borderline personality – but in the end one has to deal with that 'getting under the skin' experience, and somehow try to understand it, and what it means for the client's own life and inner world. I'm not saying that books and discussion don't help, but that one has to face the concrete and direct experience of the client – that is where the burning reality is found, and 'burning' can be sometimes the accurate word.

Process and return

One of the key functions of the therapist is to process or digest those parts of the client's psyche which are not processed or digested, and then return this in a comprehensible form to the client. We might say that this carries on the work of the child's mother, whose job it is in the early years to process the unprocessed, or what the analyst W. R. Bion calls the beta elements, transforming them into alpha elements.[2]

The unprocessed parts of the client are unconscious, alien, cut off. They often feel like autonomous functions of the client's personality, so much so that people talk of their own reactions as if they were a stranger's. 'I found myself being really scornful and horrible to her, and I didn't know why'. Even worse than this is to be scornful and horrible and not even know that one is.

These are profound states of unconsciousness, but of course they are fairly common in our culture, which prizes intellectual development but not emotional or relational development. The intellect in a culture like this turns into a kind of autistic prodigy, brilliant within its own narrow field, but actually clumsy and incapable of any kind of sensitive relating to others or to oneself.

In fact, it is the relationship to oneself that is lacking, in the sense that clients with a considerable amount of unprocessed material are massively out of touch with themselves. They grin without knowing it or knowing why; they are angry yet deny it; they are seductive yet are shocked if one points this out; they are compulsive liars, yet maintain a demeanour of perfect innocence; they sabotage their own development yet blame others. The list is endless, yet what these phenomena have in common is a denial of responsibility, a kind of acting as if one was a stranger to oneself, as indeed some people are. They have never been allowed to get to know their own psyche, as if somehow it were a sin or an indulgence to do that.

But to the therapist these things are clearer, not because the therapist is a brilliant therapist at all, but because he/she is the other. I mean that it is much easier to see such things in others, and all therapists have to do a considerable amount of therapy in order to find their own blind spots. Blind spots are a consequence of being human, but if they are large blind spots, and affect our relating to others, our creativity and fulfilment, then we have to seek help from others who can point out these blind spots.

The act of processing can take a long time. One may be puzzled by an aspect of a client for years, until eventually one is able to understand it and put into the context of the whole psyche. But other aspects may be digested more quickly, and can be returned to the client almost instantaneously.

Working through and letting go

One of the Freud's greatest ideas is to do with 'working through', the way in which therapy can help people explore certain issues, take them to pieces and put them back together, deconstruct them thoroughly.[3] If this is done satisfactorily, one finds that the person is able to let go of the issue. This double process can be seen clearly in mourning, where the mourner may need to spend years working over their relationship with the dead person, may be flooded with memories, images, fantasies and so on. But eventually with most people this process tapers off, although it may never end completely. One can then say that the living person has let go of the dead person, but 'let go of' here does not mean 'got rid of'. In fact, the process of mourning involves both letting go and incorporation. I mean by this that one installs inside oneself an image of the dead person which is permanent, so that they have become part of oneself.

We can relate this to the more general idea of working through, which is needed with those aspects of life which remain undigested. This can range from one's traumatic childhood to a very specific thing such as a dream. We explore that which has been unexplored; we go though it in detail; we may have to repeat ourselves again and again in order to connect things together. This can be a very painful process but also a very rewarding one, since one is making sense of what seemed senseless.

The paradox in all this is staggering – that what has not been worked through is clung to. This gives us one clue to clients' resistance to therapy – because it is hard to let go of something which we are attached to, even if it is injurious to us. Thus, we are all reluctant to let go of our childhood pain, since it connects us with our parents, and somewhere we still wish for restitution. Thus some people hold on to their depression, since it gives them an identity and a sense of belonging.

Interpretation

The use of interpretations shows as nothing else the flexibility or inflexibility of therapists, since there is a wide spectrum of clients, ranging from those who positively relish and enjoy interpretations, and are able to make good use of them, to those at the other extreme who detest them. In the middle there are a good number of clients who find some interpretations useful, but others unpleasant or unwelcome.

But what are therapists to do, confronted with a client who obviously finds interpretations irritating or painful or intrusive? Obviously one cannot simply give up on the idea of ever making an interpretation – that represents a kind of blackmail by the client. 'I agree to do therapy as long as you never do anything I don't like'. In fact, the first interpretation one might want to make would be to do with this dislike and the possible reasons for it.

In the main, I am content to go along with the client's predilections. That is, if someone obviously doesn't like too much input from me, then I become more silent and more withdrawn. I generally feel that there are good reasons for this dislike – for example, having had parents who laid the law down throughout childhood, so that the client grew up dreading and resenting any form of instruction or pedagogy. Of course, it is possible to deliver interpretations in such a way that they are not like this, but are much palatable and less intrusive, but the most sensitive clients will dislike this anyway.

I have had clients who were so opposed to interpretations that I pretty much didn't give any – in that case, one might wonder how therapy could proceed, but that is obviously fallacious, since therapy consists of a lot more besides interpretation. I personally felt OK about doing this, but some therapists may well find it intolerable not to give any interpretations at all.

I think this absolute rejection by the client is rare; more common is a kind of partial dislike, that is, a client who will accept a limited number of interpretations, but bridles at too many. Again, I find this quite acceptable. In some ways, I feel alright about the nature of the therapy being moulded by the client. I mean that they determine how the sessions should go. Of course, this is not absolute – the therapist has the right to speak!

In fact, the therapist has the right to protest at intolerable treatment – and if one is confronted with someone who is abusive, and who tries to stop any comment on this, then clearly that is not on, and the therapist must speak out.

In fact, we have come across a key criterion here – if the therapist feels content with a limited number of interpretations, then that will work for both parties; but if the therapist feels dissatisfied with it, or finds it intolerable, then some other way of working has to be negotiated, if possible. Ultimately, the two may have to part company, and the client find someone more amenable to them.

The interesting thing about this discussion is that it shows how interpretations – and therefore therapy itself – do not consist of some kind of detached cognitive truth – but are part of a subjective and personal relationship. Some clients love interpretations, and some hate them, and many clients are ambivalent about them. One has to work around that, and not force one's way of working upon the client.

Thus making an interpretation can be seen as a way of relating to someone, and one has to be careful about what that implies for one's relation to the client. If it is too cerebral or detached, then some clients will find that very painful and impossible to live with.

One of the key issues here is the manner in which interpretations are given, and the form of words used. This is a very delicate matter, and sometimes one finds oneself waiting for the right words and the right time. Sometimes I find it advisable to write down a possible interpretation, before giving it to the client, since then I am able to reflect on it and digest it.

A good illustration concerns the client's anger. Usually this begins to crop up when the therapist notices that the client seems heated about something, or alternatively begins to 'receive' the anger via projection. How should this be communicated? It is often said that questions are too abrasive, and hence 'Are you angry?' is inadvisable. I find this too restrictive, and in some situations it is perfectly appropriate, and in fact sometimes may have the right degree of directness.

Certainly, a more indirect approach is often better – a form of words such as 'you seem angry', 'I wonder if you're angry', and so on. But one may have to improvise considerably, if the client wants more information. I find myself using rather roundabout phrases such as 'there's just something angry about the way you're speaking', 'you seem rather vehement when you talk about your wife', and so on. There are also occasions when it is completely appropriate to make a direct statement: 'I think you're angry', or even 'you're definitely angry'.

A relationship

Psychotherapy works in mysterious ways, and some clients are puzzled at the effects that it is obviously having on them. The puzzlement may be due to a lack of problem-solving or a lack of obvious 'breakthrough' moments or huge insights. Nonetheless the client may find that in the holidays, they definitely notice the absence of therapy, or rather the therapist, and they find that changes are occurring in a subtle way in their own life. What is at work here?

One can speak of factors such as empathy, caring, compassion, and in more technical language, the holding and containing function of therapy. But driving through all this is the fact that the therapist is entering into relationship with the client, is offering attention, an attempt at understanding, interest. In other words, for the short space of the therapy sessions, the client finds that he/she is the centre of attention. This may be unfamiliar to many clients, whose childhoods may have been deprived of this, who were emotionally neglected, and not made to feel special. The therapist is not saying out loud, 'you are special to me' to the client, since this would be an inappropriate and rather seductive remark to make, and would probably confuse many clients. But the client is being treated as special for that period of time. In fact, as has often been said, the therapy session reproduces the intense focus which babies and infants receive from their parents. Anyone who has observed mother and baby together, even in a casual way, will have noticed how the mother focuses often on the infant's reactions and feelings, and feeds them back to the child. I recently noticed this going on while sitting on the bus. A young child kept pointing at things, and his mother would amplify this – 'yes, that's a tree, isn't it, it's blowing in the wind'; 'that's the window, isn't it'; 'you're tired, you can have a sleep when we get home'. This process is very familiar to anyone who has raised children, but we find something similar in therapy, not perhaps at the level of trees and windows, but at the level of the client's own feelings, thoughts, reactions, bodily states, and so on. The therapist gives the mirroring feedback, which the infant receives, and needs for its own development, and which, we can assume, some clients were deprived of. The client is being cared for, and this may be very unfamiliar.

We might call this a regressive aspect of the relationship between therapist and client, but it does not work in a separate way from the adult level, which goes on simultaneously. In fact, the therapist attends to the client, and deals with whatever is being presented. The agenda is set by the client – except that this smacks too much of voluntarism, as if the client decided what that agenda should be. The agenda is set by the client's psychic needs at that time, including those things which are emanating from the unconscious. The therapist in particular reflects back to the client those aspects of their own psyche which they are not in touch with.

We can conclude that this experience is unique in adult life. It has been compared to the devotion of lovers to each other, but it is quite different, since it is not a two-way relationship. It is analogical to the experience of the infant, except that the client is not an infant, even though psychologically some parts of the psyche may be infantile. Many adults are not used to receiving this kind of attention, and therefore, as I said earlier, they are puzzled at its effects on them. They find that they develop a strong need for the therapy, and for the therapist. The breaks are difficult and painful, and when the sessions start again after the break, the client may be angry and resistant, or alternatively, may arrive in a very pent-up state, since for several weeks they have had to do without this relationship.

It is often pointed out that all schools of therapy seem to have positive effects on clients, yet we can see why this could be so, since all schools have this in common – they give attention to the client, an unusual degree of attention, they offer a relationship to the client which gives maximum centrality to the client.

Hence the puzzlement of some clients is due to their resistance to the power of the relationship they have entered into. They want to deny that another person could have such an effect on them, that someone else can actually help them. I am always alive to the negativity aroused in some clients by this help – for some people find it humiliating and irksome, and it conflicts with their traditional view of who they are. They are the person who does it for themselves; who is self-sufficient; who can work it on their own. But they have been driven to seek help, and they find that they do obtain help. How annoying this can be! The most recalcitrant clients set out to sabotage this, or deny that it is happening, since it conflicts too much with their paranoid world view.

One might say that these functions of the relationship in therapy override everything else, or subsume everything else, for it is relationship that people crave and are deprived of. It is not simply a question of 'working things out', or understanding oneself, but of doing this in the company of another. Many clients are profoundly lonely, for they have never authentically experienced their own self, and they cannot do that in solitude, but must find another who will permit them to do it and will help them to do it. The deepest loneliness is for oneself, yet how do I establish contact with myself? It appears that it is best done through another. Again we can draw parallels with young children who clearly begin to establish knowledge of who they are and what they are partly from their relationships with others.

There is something remarkable about this phenomenon, and something mysterious. One finds that with some clients it works brilliantly, with others moderately, with others poorly. It is partly a question of personality and the suitability of people for each other; every therapist knows that they 'click' better with some people than with others, and it is clear that some people are better off finding a different therapist.

However, one cannot conclude from this that therapy is really 'tea and sympathy', and that one would do just as well to visit an unqualified person who dispenses these. For the way in which the therapist offers him or herself in the sessions to the client is tightly regulated and contained. It is not some breezy hail fellow well met bonhomie; nor some patronizing invitation to 'tell me all your troubles'. Many therapists in fact have a highly technical knowledge of relationships and their faultlines; they are able to use their own reactions to the relationship as a mirror in which can be read many unconscious aspects of the client; they understand the nature of negative thoughts patterns and can suggest ways of neutralizing them. At the same time, it is the client's own abilities which are being nurtured, particularly the ability to handle their own reactions to life, without being overwhelmed on the one hand and without cutting off on the other. The therapist is not here to dominate the client, but to nurture their self-development, so that then the client's own spontaneity becomes a source of their own delight and creativity.

A companion

Part of the therapist's job is to accompany the client through the vicissitudes of life, that is, to be a companion along the way. This is quite different from the more interpretive aspect of therapy, for here the therapist is less concerned with analyzing.

> Mike went through a period of several years when he expressed great rage about his parents. He accused them of emotional abuse, soul murder, and said they had almost ruined his life. It was unclear to his therapist how much of this was actually true, and how much was exaggeration on Mike's part, but he allowed Mike to vent his rage.

This example brings up some important themes, particularly that of going alongside the client, or accompanying them. We could say that Mike needs to go through a period of rage against his parents, and in this period he may be hyper-critical of them, lacking in forgiveness or gratitude. Privately the therapist may think that he is going over the top, but is it the therapist's place at this point to point this out?

I would say not. My sense is that the therapist holds back on such judgements until the time is right, and that comes when Mike himself begins to slacken off in his anger, and begins to accept that perhaps his parents also did their best, and that he is prepared to be reconciled with them.

We might say that part of growing up is a separation from one's parents, and often that separation is accompanied by anger or rage, for anger is required in order to get away from them. Whether or not the anger is valid becomes a secondary issue. This may seem unfair to Mike's parents, and if Mike confronts them with his accusations, it can be very painful and poignant for them. But our children have to separate from us, and this separation is often full of pain and anger on both sides.

What if the therapist were to say: 'I think you're being a bit hard on your parents'? I would say that this is a dangerous intervention, for it says to Mike that the course he is now on is wrong. It injects a note that may be quite inappropriate for Mike. Of course, one can argue that the therapist is obliged to be honest about their own reactions and judgements, but this can be overridden by the need to be alongside the client.

Of course, this does not mean that therapists slavishly follow the client's path. Quite often a point does come when one feels that the client has done enough rage and accusation, and is getting stuck there, is not moving on, and then it is appropriate to intervene.

Another example can be found with certain clients who have a very bitchy period in their life, when their doormat personality turns around, and they become very confrontational. This is not pleasant for their friends and family, but it may be necessary for the person concerned, and again the therapist is in rather an invidious position, for no doubt some of the bitchiness will be directed in their direction, yet at the same time, it may be clear that this process is good for the client.

The shadow emerges. That is the bald summation of these eruptions of anger and criticalness, particularly for those people who have been too passive and masochistic. Their aggression has been held in too much, has been bottled up, and often turned against their own self, producing depression, and now the worm turns. It would be quite inappropriate at this point to accuse a client of being too aggressive.

At the same time, as I have said repeatedly, therapists are not there to be abused. However, there is a difference between anger and aggression on the one hand, and abuse on the other. There is something clean about straight aggression, and something not clean about abuse.

Another good example is promiscuity – that some clients feel the need to have a promiscuous period in their life, and it is not the therapist's job to cast aspersions on this. One might again privately wonder if something is being acted out, but one has to be very careful about expressing such a view, for again the client may need to act out in the first place. The automatic interpretation about this may be insensitive and in fact wrong.

In all these cases we are dealing with the lifting of repression, or derepression. That which has been held down is released, and this is often accompanied by great energy, feelings of euphoria, even grandiosity. But it is no good bursting in with such interpretations, since they can be experienced as envious attacks, which they may well be. They may also repeat criticisms that were heard in childhood – don't show off, who do you think you are, pride comes before a fall, and so on. For some reason, the English language is full of such sniping attacks on self-aggrandizement.

In other words, we are not here to deflate those who become inflated. A period of inflation may be necessarily and indeed healthy, as it is in children, and a premature deflation of it is damaging.

Of course, eventually it may become correct to do some deflating, or help the client become more grounded, but again here we are faced with the issue of timing which is crucial, and which relies so much on the therapist's own sensitivity to people and their needs.

Being with (or reverie)

At times, therapy does not consist of problem-solving but of being with. I mean that the client needs to spend time with the other in a state of relatively silent communion. Without doubt, this is because this was lacking in childhood, and the client is now seeking some kind of restitution. The signs of it are unmistakable. The therapist will tend to lose the more logical side of the mind; intellectual solutions tend to die away; in fact, the inner noise of the mind dies away. Both parties may feel tired, and are often silent. If this state is permitted, it will often deepen, and then both may notice that they have entered into a very different kind of meeting, which is wordless yet very intimate. One might argue that it is a regressive state for the client, but I am not sure about that. It is certainly to do with intimacy, being not doing, and being with, rather than problem solving.

In fact, it does solve some problems, particularly to do with how to be with someone else, since many people in our culture find it very difficult simply to be with someone. They have to be doing something, they have to find some distraction, in order to avoid the other person. And so we go on, avoiding each other with a myriad number of activities, and we end up feeling very lonely and unmet.

Being left alone

Reverie connects with being left alone, for some clients come to therapy and find, often to their surprise, that they want to be left alone most of the time. This may be a surprise to the therapist as well, who may have conflicting feelings about whether or not it is really permissible to do this in therapy. Inexperienced therapists may feel that they should be 'doing something', and just allowing the client to be is not enough.

I had a client who for years followed the same pattern – she came to the session, talked for a bit, then fell silent, went into a reverie, and often fell asleep. I never interrupted this process, but in fact she did quite often, as she would get quite strong guilt feelings, and would argue that it wasn't 'proper therapy', she was wasting her time and mine, she wasn't making progress and so on. I would often argue the opposite – that she was learning how to let go with someone, how to be intimate without intrusion.

The obvious analogy to this state is the child and mother situation, when the child is playing with its toys, and mother is in the vicinity doing something else, and is not interfering with the child's activities. Of course, she is available if the child needs something, wants to show her something, feels upset or bored, and so on. But this is the classic state of non-intrusive intimacy, and children seem to need quite a lot of it.

One can surmise that those people who did not get enough of it as children will unconsciously seek it out in therapy, but then there are often guilt feelings about it, since there is the sense that not enough work is being done in the therapy, if the client is dozing off.

Crucial here of course are the therapist's own feelings, thoughts, and so on, and also the bodily state. If the client drifts off, and the therapist feels uncomfortable, afraid, tense, angry, and so on, then it is likely that the client is hiding something, or is 'cutting off'. But if the therapist has feelings of contentment, peace, and is able to let their own mind wander as well, then it is likely that both parties are in a state of reverie which is both intimate and separate.

This is surely one of the important aspects of the analogical child/mother situation. The mother in that scenario is not intruding on the child's play, but remains available. The child needs to feel that she is there, but not breathing down his neck. They are together, but separate.

One could say that children do much experimentation with closeness and separation, and have to find out how much of each they like. One can also say that many clients have to do the same, and therefore being left alone is a valid, indeed crucial aspect of therapy. Those therapists who insist on analyzing every silence, who have to interpret the client's falling asleep, and so on, are being very intrusive, and may well prompt the client to leave.

Silence

Silence is one of the most powerful forces at work in therapy for several reasons. In the first place, it is when we are silent that unconscious feelings, thoughts and images are allowed to rise to the surface. Secondly, silence can be a very intimate state between two people. Thirdly, for many busy people, falling silent may be something they rarely do – it can be a time of rest or reverie.

Of course, all of these factors mean that some clients dread silence, and fill it up with conversation, or are able to 'do therapy' very convincingly for the whole session and never allow a silence to develop. I usually make a point of asking clients whether they find silence disturbing, particularly those who never allow it. But most clients do find it disturbing in the early phases of therapy, and I see the ability to allow silence as one of the hallmarks of a successful therapy in its later stages.

But silence is not only valuable for the client but for the therapist as well. It is a time when their unconscious process can be allowed to flow, when the focus which is usually maintained can be relaxed, in other words, when a mutual reverie can develop. But this is a sign of intimacy of course, and is impermissible for many beginning clients. It is too frightening, and many of them will argue that silence is 'unproductive', that no work is being done, time is being lost, and so on. And of course that they are not getting value for money!

However, one cannot obviously force a silence into being, with a client who finds this difficult. But one can point out the lack of silence, and also enquire whether this pertains to the client's life outside, whether they can allow silence in their own life, whether they are ever still. It is astonishing how many people do not allow this. When asked, they may say, 'oh yes, I sometimes pick up a book and read, or I watch TV for relaxation, or I play computer games'. If one persists with the question as to whether they ever do nothing, they are genuinely puzzled as to what that means.

Doing nothing, being in silence, means above all being with oneself, and our Western culture finds that inimical. We are doers not contemplators, but a certain amount of contemplation is very beneficial in our daily lives, and also in therapy.

One of the chief enemies of silence is the workaholic tendency, which is common in therapy. Quite a number of clients see it as work, and of course, therapists speak of 'working through' and so on. But therapy should also be play, and sometimes should be nothing at all, or should be allowed to follow its own path. I am very wary of those clients who pursue agendas, or who want 'focus' and direction. Of course, we do need focus, but we also need to allow the psyche its own path, without steering it too directively. Many clients have a very top-heavy ego (and super-ego) control over their psyche, and this comes out vividly in their sessions, where we find they are unable to allow things to come up unannounced. In other words, their spontaneity is under lock and key.

Silence can therefore be seen as a very creative state to be in, since it allows the repressed to surface. Of course there are also strained and embarrassed silences, angry silences, fearful silences, and so on, and these have to tackled and explored.

Using therapy

Sometimes, when people ask the inevitable question 'does therapy work?', I make the retort that it's you who works – or not. What I'm trying to say with this rather provocative reply is that one cannot go into therapy in a passive way. One must be prepared to work on oneself, to use the insights gained in therapy, to keep in touch with oneself, to set time aside for oneself. It's amazing how many people don't even do this, but rush around being endlessly busy, so that there is no space for their being, their own feelings and thoughts and fantasies. But we can't go from this into a therapy session and demand that it put things right!

Of course, people do make that demand, and one can make all kinds of inferences from it – that their attitude to life is rather like an infant at the breast, demanding that it be fed instantly. It's rather peremptory, and also has a built-in dissatisfaction to it, as if failure is almost guaranteed.

Does therapy work? It's like asking if marriage works – well, yes and no. It works if you are compatible and you put your energy into it.

Areas of difficulty

1. Confrontation

The negative feelings which exist in clients can come up surprisingly quickly – as in the first session! One can generalize safely in saying that the therapist has to keep one eye and ear cocked early on for signs of resistance, opposition, sabotage, and so on.

There are a surprising number of clients with whom one finds oneself having a confrontation very early in the therapy – I mean in the first six weeks or so. I am now convinced that this is a testing procedure used by some clients to see if the therapist can take their intense feelings and problems. It can take the form of strong resistance to some aspect of the arrangements for therapy – for example, paying for cancellations or having a regular time each week – but it can also just flare up in relation to something being discussed about the client's life. Often the therapist can feel that this is make or break – that there is a possibility of the client leaving, and this may well be correct, in the sense that the client is subjecting the therapist to an intense scrutiny.

> Peter began a very sadistic attack on the therapist early on in the therapy. At first, the therapist felt puzzled and intimidated by this attack, but felt quite quickly that he had to respond to it or Peter would feel that he couldn't deal with it. He simply pointed out that Peter was being sadistic, although he didn't know why, but the attacks subsided, and Peter settled into a long period of much more reflective self-examination.

One can say in such a case that the client is possibly desperate to see if the therapist can deal with his aggression, because in some ways he can't. If the therapist can show that he can resist it, will not play masochist to the client's sadist, then the client can feel much safer, since he doesn't have to look after the therapist, and also knows that the therapist will not retaliate in an equally sadistic manner.

It should be said also that such confrontations can occur at any point in therapy, and can suddenly come from nowhere with no warning, and again, they often have a testing function. But they are especially significant at the beginning, when the resistance is often at its maximum, and the client is making the fateful decision as to whether he/she will stay for the duration with this therapist.

Confrontation also occurs with clients who have a lot of unexpressed anger. This will inevitably be projected into the therapist, who will find himself feeling angry. Clearly, one can channel this back to the client, but something else that can happen is that a kind of confrontation develops between the two, as if the hidden anger of the client is able to take both sides of the argument. I don't mean that the therapist becomes angry himself at the client, but he is able to use the projected anger as a kind of fuel for his own assertions. Then one can find oneself saying those really difficult things which are hard to say, since the aggressive fuel is propelling one along. For example, I recall a client who continually came late to sessions. I was convinced that he was expressing a hidden anger, and began to feel fed up myself with this lateness, so that eventually we had quite an argument about his lateness, and he was able to say he found therapy very rigid and dogmatic and the therapist bossy.

But I was able to say equally that I felt he found the commitment required in therapy difficult and frightening, that part of him wanted to sabotage it, that he was a very angry man who often hated life, and so on. It is difficult to say these things, but the friction created by the client's acting out actually facilitates it, as perhaps unconsciously it is meant to. We might say that the client brings matter to a head or to a crisis, to see what happens and how the therapist will deal with it.

2. Rubbish

There is a certain kind of client who after a good session will come back and turn the therapy and the therapist into rubbish. But this tends to happen in life generally – that there is a constant tendency to destroy what is good, and reduce it to rubble. From the rational point of view this seems extraordinary behaviour. Why would anyone do this to themselves?

It is clearly a complex act. Such clients find happiness unbearable, either because they feel great guilt over it, or fear envy, or find it uncontrollable, or perhaps fear the loss of their old personality, which was wedded to misery. It is the change that is so catastrophic for such people – better the depression that I am familiar with rather than the happiness which is new and bewildering.

There is also the factor of loyalty to one's family, who may well have inculcated this misery in the young child, so that being depressed became a kind of family ambience which it was safest to cling to. To reject it spells abandonment and loneliness.

If we approach this issue from the inner world point of view, there is usually a fierce inner critic who disapproves intensely of any fleeting happiness or enjoyment which the person obtains from life. This is condemned as decadence or indulgence, often associated with laziness, for the inner critic is usually a workaholic, and sees life very much in terms of work, effort, productivity, but not in terms of satisfaction or enjoyment or joy.

But such clients often do make progress in therapy, since they may be relatively open to the idea that their depression is often caused by their own harshness to themselves. Hence, they begin to lift this castigation, and find that life is easier and more pleasant than they imagined. But this is the point when the critic forces a backlash, returns with redoubled ferocity and hostility.

This can appear in therapy in a very graphic form, in that one session follows another as light and shade. A good session is followed by an angry self-punishing one, in which hatred of the therapist may be close to the surface also. As the client begins to thaw out, there is much backtracking, as doubts and fears and feelings of guilt strike back. Moments of intimacy between therapist and client may produce ferocious self-punishment, threats to leave the therapist, and attempts to turn the therapist into rubbish. Then nothing can be accomplished, which satisfies the envious hostile part of the client.

This part of the psyche is anti-life. It hates life, hates the therapy and the therapist. It tries to block all progress, and when progress it still made, it mocks it and rubbishes it.

It is surprising how often this force catches the therapist off-guard, because it can emerge from unconsciousness in a sudden manner, or in a veiled and camouflaged way.

> At the end of a session which the therapist had thought was quite useful, Alan suddenly announced vehemently, 'well, that was a waste of time'. The therapist ended the session, but was left with feelings of despair and uselessness and anger. The timing of the remark was very destructive, since it could not be dealt with, but was left as a kind of explosive device.

Of course, this kind of behaviour must be dealt with quickly by the therapist, who cannot afford to let it go without comment. One can also voice one's concerns about it recurring, especially when things are going well. This sounds a bit negative on the part of the therapist, but if there is a marked tendency towards sabotage by the client, then it helps to be prepared for it.

But the situation is often paradoxically optimistic. The intensity of the attacks may well stem from the forward direction made by the client, which produces these backlashes.

3. Survival

One of the key responsibilities of the psychotherapist is to survive. But 'survive' here does not simply mean to keep one's head down in the face of attacks from the client, or in fact in the face of the client's deep depression. One's task is to remain fully alive. That sounds relatively straightforward, but of course with many clients it is not, since unconsciously they seek to reduce that aliveness, to destroy it, to subvert it, and so on. In other words, some clients attempt to recruit one to their own brand of despair, rage, nihilism, and so on.

In the face of such psychic onslaughts, survival does not mean defensiveness, or simply enduring. One has to be alive, that is, to resist the death instinct of the client, or the destructive instinct.

Standing back from this, one can say that the client may try to recruit one into the same kind of psychic brew as was found in their original family. The therapist is brought into the family, and its psychological make-up and energies. Of course, there is a very delicate art here, of partly allowing oneself to be so recruited, without succumbing to the psychological poison which may lurk in that family. There is a kind of 'benign split' going on here – I notice that I am being treated as an irritating younger brother, and part of me wants to retaliate in kind, as no doubt the client's younger brother (or the client as the younger brother) did; but I am able to resist this temptation, since after all, I am not that younger brother. Of course consciousness is king here – one might also be put in the place of a younger brother, without realizing it, and then there is a battle royal between conscious and unconscious in the therapist. In fact, it is inevitable that unconscious projections of this kind will affect the therapist, but it is her job to begin to spot these projections on the radar and attempt to understand what they are.

Strategies?

Some of the therapists who I supervise have complained that their training organizations demand that they follow a strategy towards a particular client, and ask what strategy they are pursuing. In fact, some supervisors take this approach. One can see why training courses follow this course, as it makes the practice of therapy seem very hard-edged, empirical and definable. Of course, a lot of it isn't like that at all, but for trainees (and trainers), this may be comforting – there is the illusion that one can know what one is going to do. In fact, as therapy moves into a deeper phase, one may well not know at all what is going to happen. That is part of the fascination in following the profession of psychotherapist – that one is constantly improvising, as one battles with the forces of the unconscious both in oneself and the client.

So I can understand both points of view – the need to have a 'strategy' for clients; and also the need to have free-flowing attention, which is not focused at all. We need both in therapy – the skill or art, is knowing when one is appropriate, and when the other, and when in fact one might pursue both simultaneously.

Certainly, I shrink from being too defined and clear-cut about many clients, since I think this can inhibit the unknown forces which may be lurking under-neath the surface from coming out. I mean that many clients come into therapy for ostensible reasons, and at a later date, one finds deeper and less clear-cut reasons, which may be the more important.

> Cliff said he wanted therapy to help him find a new career, since he was tired of working in the City. He also talked about his divorce, and the rather difficult relationships with his children. But after several years, it began to emerge that Cliff had been very artistic as a child, but had put this away under the drive to become a successful business man. He said that he had been his parents' child in doing this, and being artistic was seen by them as not really a serious profession. Cliff began to draw and paint again, and said that he felt fulfilled for the first time in his life.

Examples such as this show that one can never be too sure what the main agenda is, and one cannot lay the law down, or predict the directions which a client may move. One might distinguish small scale 'tactics' and large scale strat-egy here – obviously, one must have certain responses in mind for certain issues, but at the same time, not be blind to other issues or the possibility that some-thing quite unexpected may surface. Hence I see it as unwise for therapists to push too hard in one direction, and not wait to see which direction the client will begin to go in, which may be quite different from what has been assumed.

> Jane began therapy by announcing that she had done quite a lot of therapy before, and her main issue was the abuse she had received from her father – both physical and sexual. For several sessions, she stated this firmly as her agenda. However, her therapist thought it best to not rush in, and to wait to see where Jane moved to next. In fact, Jane became very silent for a period of several months, and started to say that she was tired of remembering the past, and she wanted to get on with her life. Her therapist trusted this statement, and did not see it as an avoidance, as there was little emotional 'charge' when the subject of childhood came up.

This example illustrates several of the points I have made. In particular, the therapist waits to see which way Jane's energy will go, for it may go in quite a different direction from the expected. I worked with a bio-energetics therapist who used to say 'follow the energy', and I have always remembered those words, not in a bio-energetic sense, but in the sense of following the psychic energy of the client. And this energy may move off in a way that surprises both client and therapist.

The above example also shows the way in which conscious agendas seem quite clear -cut and even obvious, yet still may not be the correct way forward. On the other hand, one might meet a number of clients who do want to talk about the abuse they suffered as children, and who go ahead with that intention.

The same can be said about the modality of therapy. Does one encourage clients to bring dreams to the sessions, or to think about their childhood, or their next creative project, or the state of their marriage, and so on? My instinct is to say no. In fact, there is no need to set any goal, for at every session the client brings not only their body but also their life into the room. For that hour, we have the client's life in front of us, whatever that might consist of. I mean that if the client is silent, or bored, or confused, or doesn't know what to say – that is their life at that moment, and it is something we can work with, if the client so wishes. The therapist is never short of material, but of course must find some meeting with the client as to what that material is to be.

This is the reason that therapists do not need to seek a kind of continuity in the sessions with a client. Because Alan has talked about his childhood for the past sixty sessions does not mean that he will on the sixty-first, nor that he should, nor that the therapist should direct him to. Of course, there are themes and patterns which emerge over time, but one has to be very wary about expecting too close a continuity. In fact, the fact that somebody has talked about something often suggests that that topic will disappear for a while, as it has been dealt with.

I am not obviously advocating a chaotic jumble of sessions, with no sense at all being made, but I am advocating a laissez faire attitude by the therapist towards the agenda of each session, and the overall themes which emerge. We must expect the unexpected, and treat the expected with caution.

These ideas connect closely with one's attitude to the psychological un-conscious. If one feels sceptical about its existence, then one might expect a greater degree of continuity, and a greater thematic coherence, but if one trusts in its existence, then one is prepared to put up with non-coherence in the hope that the unconscious has its own narrative, which perhaps is being slowly prepared off-stage. Certainly I feel that the client's narrative must be allowed many non sequiturs, many gaps, many contradictions, and the therapist must not rush in as too zealous an editor.

Notes

1 See Paula Jacobsen, *Asperger Syndrome and Psychotherapy* (London: Jessica Kingsley, 2003).
2 W. R. Bion, *Learning from Experience* (London: Karnac, 1984).
3 S. Freud, 'Remembering, Repeating and Working-through' in J. Strachey (ed.) *The Standard Edition of the Complete Psychological Works of Sigmund Freud* Vol. 12 (London: Hogarth, 1986).

9 The Relationship between Therapist and Client

Whole books can be and are written about the therapeutic relationship. This is not surprising since it functions as a laboratory in which many of the client's basic problems are revealed and can be dealt with concretely. This is the great value of using the relationship in this way – whereas the client's descriptions of their problems in life have a second-hand flavour, since they are only descriptions, when these issues come up between the two people in the room, then we are thrust into the thing itself.

> Simon kept saying he couldn't get angry with people, including people at work, his wife, his children, his parents. Quite a lot of useful work was done on these areas, and Simon began to feel more assertive towards people. Eventually the therapist suggested that Simon sometimes felt angry with her, over issues such as payment for cancellations, the length of her breaks – she took six weeks' break in summer – and so on. Simon prevaricated, but eventually said that he did feel irritated sometimes, and began to express his anger directly.

This example leaves out something crucial – why Simon found anger difficult. But again, in the therapeutic relationship we are able to go through the blocks on anger, whether it be fear, shame, guilt, or whatever, before the anger itself is touched on. The example also shows the value of delay – the therapist does not immediately jump in with the interpretation that Simon is angry with her. That would be premature, and possibly too frightening for Simon to take on board to begin with, or possibly quite meaningless to him.

Of course, one of the interesting things about anger is that it is an intimate emotion, so we would not expect clients in the early phase of therapy to be prepared to risk being angry with the therapist. As so often there is a spectrum here. One also meets clients who are angry in the first session, begin to object to aspects of the therapy, tell the therapist directly that they're not very good, and so on. Such clients are probably familiar to most therapists, and can be very difficult to deal with, but again, their attitude to life is being brought into the therapy in a very concrete way.

Thus the therapeutic relationship is a mirror held up to life. Many issues to do with intimacy, trust, closeness, separation, many feelings such as anger, fear, sadness, liking, love – are brought up directly in the relationship going on. One would say that they are inevitably brought up, as soon as two people meet regularly and in such intimate surroundings. How much attention is brought to bear on these issues is up to the two people involved.

One can also say that the relationship is a real relationship. It is not just a device, or a laboratory, or a working tool, but a genuine meeting between two people. This was one of the standards hoisted by humanistic psychology when it began its onslaught on the perceived aridity of psychoanalysis – that it (humanistic psychology) dealt in a real way with a real intimacy between people. However, today it would be meaningless to make this division between schools, since many analytic therapists are also interested in the authenticity of the relationship.

How authentic does the relationship get? Here we come up against some of the extraordinary paradoxes found in therapy. Its authenticity is quite different from that found in other relationships, since it is organized in such an artificial way, with boundaries carefully set around it to encourage safety. Thus the therapist does not intrude into the client's life; the therapist is generally careful not to reveal too much biographical information, which simply gets in the way, and proves a distraction and a seduction towards clients; the session takes place in the same place, and we do not move out into the street or the park or the pub or the client's home, except in unusual conditions, such as severe illness.

However, none of these restrictions prevent intimacy and authenticity taking place. Indeed, all the arguments about boundaries and safety which we have looked at seem to show that intimacy can develop because of these restrictions. We are rationed in therapy. We meet for an hour and then stop. This gives both parties a very safe boundary, beyond which we do not stray. We do not meet at weekends normally nor in holidays. This rhythm of presence and absence can produce great feelings of deprivation in some clients, but generally it allows for concentrated periods, when we are able to focus quite intensely. Clients are able to open up within such tightly restricted limits, who might not be able to do so in a open-ended relationship.

There is no doubt that therapists become important to some clients, and some clients become important to therapists. The first issue is a familiar one, the second much more difficult and threatening to many therapists. Yet it is palpably true, and one finds that as therapists become more experienced and older, they are able to accept the importance of some clients to them.

After all, therapy at times in its openness and closeness approaches a state of love between two people. The word 'love' is itself a difficult one in the therapy context, since for many therapists the admission that they love certain clients is rarely made explicit, since it can seem very seductive. Yet again, it seems intuitively clear that if therapy is a healing practice, this is in part because feelings of love, compassion, caring, are elicited on both sides. Thus therapists have to be prepared to love and be loved; otherwise they will find that with some clients, their own blockage of these feelings prevents the client from releasing theirs.

What about the opposite – feelings of dislike and hatred? I would say that they are extremely useful! Certainly, the client's negative feelings towards the therapist are often very important, and if they can be made explicit, a leap forward often takes place in the therapy. But the therapist's own negative feelings provide vital clues about the client's emotional state, and often form a mirror of equivalent feelings.

An amalgam

The therapeutic relationship is an amalgam of many elements. The therapist gives interpretations, reassurance, advice, but also sometimes acts as a someone simply to bounce off, with no intervention. The therapist is sometimes rather detached, as when there is discussion of something going on in the client's life; but at other times, there may be an intense involvement between the two parties, for example, a fierce row or strong feelings of fondness.

The therapist permits the client to use their psyche as a sounding board or radar screen, on which the hidden aspects of the client are revealed. This is a strange kind of opening up made by the therapist, one which has to be handled very carefully so that the therapist is not harmed by it and the client not overwhelmed by it.

Sometimes there is a feeling of equality and mutuality in the room, but at other times, the client may regress to a very child-like state, and then the therapist takes on the role of adult. But there are occasions when this may reverse, and the therapist may realize that they are being punished or rewarded as if they were the child!

The degree of distance can vary astonishingly from an icy coldness to an undeniable feeling of love between the two people.

Psychotherapy is in many ways a metacommunication, that is a communication about communication. As a relationship, it is self-reflexive; it is able to look at itself, to investigate its own workings, to examine the intricacies and hidden dark corners that exist in all relationships, but which normally go unnoticed. Thus the therapist is always in two or more positions at once: both involved with the client in a relationship, and also observing this involvement, including one's own reactions, feelings, thoughts, fantasies and so on. I say two or more, since as soon as the therapist makes a comment about this self-observation, then a new role of interpreter, has emerged. Thus a kind of benign splitting is a prerequisite for the therapist's position: I notice that I like/dislike the client today, or I feel bored or angry or afraid, and then I am able to use this information in order to make some kind of intervention.

The therapist permits him or herself to be treated as an object by the client, so that the client's way of treating other people and also their own attitude to themselves, is brought into the open.

Clearly, one of the requirements for being a therapist is to be fairly quick-witted and to be able to think on one's feet, since the nature of the relationship may shift quickly in one session. With some clients, this is not so, since there may be a conservative unchanging quality to them, but one always has to be alive to more subterranean feelings and thoughts emerging, and possibly being projected into the therapist. But with other clients, things may change rapidly. One of the clearest examples of this occurs with those clients who find positive developments difficult. The therapist may be feeling rather pleased, even complacent, about the progress of a session, and then suddenly find themselves under attack from the client.

I have deliberately set out the above differing aspects of the therapeutic relationship in a rather brainstorming way, since this is how they can occur in reality. One can of course make some theoretical classification of the different kinds of relationship going on, but it is important to grasp the living variety that actually occurs. In other words, one is involved in a number of relationships at once with the same person![1]

Transference

The term 'transference' denotes the misrecognition of the therapist by the client, or the fantasy perception of the therapist. There are two theoretical ways of tackling transference – that it represents material from the past, so that I see my therapist as my father or mother or some other important person; or that it represents something in the inner world, so that I see my therapist as a critical figure (corresponding to my inner critic), or as a child to be chastised (corresponding to the inner child) and so on. The second approach is clearly a more modern or post-Freudian approach.[2]

Of course, these two theorizations of transference are intimately connected, since the inner world is populated in part by figures derived from one's child-hood. But one finds that some clients are interested more in one than another: for some, mention of their childhood seems to produce little interest, but the idea that one is projecting an inner figure can be stimulating for many people who are less interested in the past.

Transference is of course an invaluable source of information about the client's relationship to reality. So we find people who are suspicious, and doubt the therapist's intentions; those who are seductive, and want to disarm the therapist; those who are jokey (a kind of seduction); or resentful and blaming; or masochistic, and so on. Often such transference projections are stimulated by coming to therapy, since the fearfulness felt by many people produces a strong defensive reaction, and transference is in part a defence.

> John was angry in the first session. He also seemed frightened and very distant. It was difficult to find out what the basis of this was, but clearly John expected the therapist to punish him, and he was making a pre-emptive strike, by getting his aggression out first.

But such transference reactions do not end because the initial fear and suspicion is dispelled – we may then find different projections arising, so that a kind of layering may be found to exist in the client's fantasies about reality, and their customary way of dealing with it.

Transference has an intimate connection with resistance, in the sense that the client will often deny in the first instance that his or her reactions are repe-titions from the past, or projections from the inner world. Many clients to begin with cannot make that leap, and assert stoutly that they are simply the feelings and thoughts that go on in their mind. If you like, there is a kind of positivist stance being taken here – this is what is, this is who I am. Thus the process of psychotherapy makes a giant step if one can help the client to see that our reactions to others and to life are not simply 'as is', but have a history, have a hinterland, and that therapy can explore that hinterland, and can there-fore mitigate and reduce fantasies about other people and other aspects of life.

In other words we are trying to restore choice to the client, so that instead of relating to the world in an automatic blind manner – which means being in the grip of one's fantasies and beliefs – one can choose whether or not to act on them.

> Susan had a very seductive attitude to her therapist. This showed itself in the way she dressed, which was often provocative, and in her relations to the therapist,

which often consisted of lots of laughter, personal references, attempts to find out information about his private life, and so on. Susan's therapist tried to find out the background to this, but at first Susan resisted this fiercely, and told him that he was being destructive, and he was salacious in suggesting that she had a seductive attitude. However, eventually it became possible to get behind this façade and explore Susan's powerful feelings of inadequacy, and her belief that it was only through a kind of sexual stimulation that she could make an impact on others.

The transference relation here clearly conceals deeper psychological information, about Susan's own self-esteem, the way she relates to others, and hidden feelings of inferiority and shame. One can say that Susan has learned to act seductively, both as a concealment and as an inducement. The transference fantasy has this contradictory quality – on the one hand it is a means of relating to others and influencing them, but it also serves as a mask or barrier behind which more vulnerable feelings lurk. We may not be able to completely get rid of Susan's feelings of inadequacy, but it is possible to help her to stop the automatic nature of her seductiveness.

Seductiveness is a rather obvious transference relation, and there are other character traits which leap out at the therapist, for example, intellectuality, jokiness, coldness, and so on. But to get in touch with more subtle transferences, quite a passage of time may have to elapse, so that the full flavour of them can be experienced.

There is clearly a very complex relation between transference and resistance. As we have seen, many clients resist the idea of transference at first – this is a kind of resistance to the notion of unconscious, since the analysis of transference often reveals a very complex set of unconscious thoughts, fantasies, motives, and so on. Thus in the case of Susan above, her sexual approach to her therapist concealed both her own sense of inadequacy, and her deduction that the only way she could influence others was through being seductive – otherwise she didn't count. But this analysis comes later in the therapy – to begin with, Susan denies it, and in fact denies that she is being seductive. There is a kind of opacity which characterizes such early work, whereby clients refuse to accept that there are psychological processes going on beneath the surface.

But this shows us also that transference *is itself a resistance*, and in psychotherapy it can be seen that the transference relation rises up in order to prevent intimacy, to prevent the therapist acquiring a deeper knowledge of the client, indeed in order to prevent the client's deepening self-knowledge. Historically, or biographically, it has arisen as a means of facing the world and controlling the world, and without doubt all human beings have such methods

of dealing with reality. It is not that the neurotic or psychotic person is neurotic or psychotic because they exhibit transference fantasies, but that their
particular fantasies are self-harming and debilitating. One could argue in fact
that the optimistic person, who goes through life largely expecting and receiving good things, is equally in the grip of a fantasy, but in this case the fantasy
tends to promote the well-being of the individual. The paranoid person, who
sees the universe as malign, tends to ensure that it is, since their suspicion and
hostility makes others react badly, and since they often sabotage their own life.
This is a kind of closed loop, which can be difficult to break into, since the
paranoid person will deny that their suspicions are anything but well founded.
In other words – there is no transference; people just hate me; in fact, you hate
me. And of course, the therapist may hate the paranoid client at times, but that
is not the end of the story, since the paranoia denies any responsibility for cre-
ating such a universe – whether or not this can be changed depends on the rel-
ative balance within their psyche of such negative forces as against more
positive life-affirming forces, and also depends on the client's ability to look at
their own process.

Transference often seems like the thick mud of unconsciousness, for in it we
find condensed the client's beliefs and assumptions about reality – that it is
malign or benign; that other people are envious or well-intentioned; that the
therapist is cold and detached, or cares about the client. But by drawing attention to such beliefs and their transference manifestation, therapy attempts to
dispel the mud and restore some clarity and some light. It is shocking for some
clients to appreciate that their own beliefs and projections are not universal
and are not inevitable, and can be changed or let go of.

It is clear that transference, which might at first be taken as an encumbrance
or barrier to the therapeutic process, in fact becomes one of its foci, for the
transference fantasies and relations are part of the client's habitual way of relating to the world, and now they are seen in focus in the therapy sessions and
can therefore be explored and partly dispelled.

Counter-transference

I am using the term counter-transference to refer to feelings and thoughts and
other psychic material which is projected from the client into the therapist.
Thus I am distinguishing it quite sharply from the therapist's own reactions to
the client, which is also often given the term 'counter-transference'.

As with transference, from having originally been seen as problematic,
counter-transference is often seen as an invaluable tool for the therapist, but
beginning therapists find it something of a minefield, and often complain that

they are not sure which feelings are their own and which are being projected from the client.

If the therapist has a strong intuition, or 'radar-screen', so that they pick up quite quickly and sensitively what other people are feeling, then using counter-transference can become one of the most important tools in their armoury. Generally, what is picked up are the feelings and thoughts which are repressed in the client, or which have been split off. Projection of this material is then automatic, as if the unconscious is desperate to find some expression somewhere. There is also the phenomenon of 'buck-passing', whereby many people go around in life inflicting those feelings on others which they cannot handle themselves.

> Jim had had a very abusive childhood. His father had beaten him, sexually molested him, and also showed great scorn to him. As an adult, Jim was quite scornful towards other people, and his therapist felt quite afraid of him, as there was an abusive streak in him which was quite malicious.

One can say straightforwardly about this example that Jim is repeating the behaviour shown to him as a child, but part of that repetition is that Jim is passing on the hurt he experienced, and has kept locked inside himself, to others, just as presumably his father passed it on to him. It is noteworthy that the therapist feels afraid of Jim – this suggests that Jim is also afraid and again attempts to get rid of the feeling by projecting into others. Thus intimidating people are often unconsciously full of fear.

But it is not simply hurt or fear which gets passed on. Any feelings which are repressed or split-off can be projected into others. Many dysfunctional relationships are based on mutual buck-passing, whereby those feelings which have not been dealt with are projected into the partner, and can be then castigated and so on. This is an endless vicious circle, unless and until both partners begin to deal with their own feelings.

But projection is quite a normal human phenomenon; it is not simply a sign of abuse or neurosis. There is little doubt that we all project certain psychic contents; problems arise when these contents are explosive or damaging in some way to others. But one has also to be alive to positive things being projected from clients.

> Faith was a rather quiet mousy woman. But her therapist noticed that during sessions she often felt energized, aggressive and restless. She was convinced that Faith was squashing her own energy, and began to suggest this to her, with fruitful results.

This is the phenomenon of 'giving away' – some people give away their positive energy to others, out of some guilt or martyred attitude. Certainly, when one finds a quiet passive client coupled with a high energy therapist, one has to suspect this is going on, and it must be commented on. In fact, quite a number of sexual relationships are based on this dialectic, and it can prove remarkably stable, although either or both partners may well tire of the one-sided nature of it.

But this example brings up very clearly the way in which counter-transference is dealt with. One of the delicate issues here is how much one talks about one's own reactions. I think one can follow different strategies here – with some clients, it is better not to say that one is experiencing certain things which are assumed to be projected from the client. This is simply because some clients, the more fragile ones, are too disturbed by talk of the therapist's own feelings, and the projection from the client, and so on. This is pretty powerful stuff, and should not be shared with people with insufficient ego-strength.

However, I think at times it can be fruitful to make a comment such as: 'When I sit with you, I feel a lot of energy, and I wonder if it's coming from you'. With fairly robust people, this works well, and they are often interested and stimulated by the notion of projection. They are also pleased that one is sufficiently interested in them to take notice of their feelings!

Certainly with schizophrenic clients it is nearly always inadvisable to talk too much about counter-transference, since it disturbs such people too much. Some of them get overly fascinated by it and over-stimulated; others feel crushed by guilt that they have dumped something into someone else. But these reactions also occur with less disturbed clients, and often one has to dip a toe in the water, to see how the client reacts to such material. If there is a bad reaction, then clearly one must back off, or make interpretations which are much more circumscribed. However, this does not mean that one suffers the client's projections without comment – that is the sure way towards feeling dread and dislike of the client, and in fact, represents part of a sado-masochistic relationship. One simply has to find a way of commenting on the introjected feelings that does not go into detail about counter-transference. Sometimes a simple comment such as 'you seem angry' is quite adequate, rather than the more elaborate explanation, 'when I'm with you, I get feelings of anger'. But the therapist is not there to endure or suffer.

Therapists talk jokingly and mordantly about used as a toilet – the nasty stuff gets dumped into them, and this black humour shows that it's an important phenomenon, that it's unpleasant, and that therapists have to be prepared to deal with it. If they don't, they can start to feel overwhelmed by the bad things, and then resentful of the client, and then we are in big trouble.

It has to be dealt with by some kind of feedback or mirroring. For example, if the therapist starts to feel great despair in sessions with a client, it must be dealt with, or the therapist may be left with it. I say to therapists in supervision, that if they find they are having sleepless nights over a certain client, or their weekends are ruined, then it is very likely that massive projections are going on, and they must take action or the therapy will not go forward, and quite probably both parties will sabotage it.

We can argue from a more theoretical point of view that clients who project intensely have lacked precisely such a mirror in childhood. The 'mothering' function of making sense of the child's feelings, thoughts and fantasies and so on, has not been carried out, and the adult client is looking for it now. But mirroring does not mean martyrdom – sometimes I meet new therapists who feel that they are required simply to take what the client gives to them. This will rapidly lead to burnout, resentment and clients leaving.

The problem about confusion as to whose feelings are being experienced often seems to clear up with experience. But one useful tip is about the changes that one goes through as the sessions begins. In other words, if the therapist has been feeling angry all day about something, then anger in the session may well not be projection from the client. But if the therapist has not been feeling angry, and then begins to feel it as the session goes on, it is very likely to be a projection.

The other issue here is that the confusion itself is probably part of the projection. That is, if the therapist is experiencing boundary confusion – 'is this experience really mine or hers?' – then it is very likely that this also belongs to the client.

In any case, projected feelings tend to stimulate one's own. If the client is projecting guilt, the therapist will start to feel guilty, and part of this guilt may consist in wondering if one is simply confusing one's own feelings with the clients. This is very murky of course, but guilt always makes things murky. It is a very confusing feeling, and probably the most difficult to deal with in projected form. It is essential here that the therapist has worked extensively on their own guilt, first so that they can recognize what guilt is (since many people do not), and second, they do not feel paralyzed by it, and are able to send it back.

We can say then in summary that unconscious thoughts, feelings and fantasies are often projected, and can be picked up by the therapist, made sense of and communicated back to the client. The phase of 'making sense of' can last any length of time, and shows that we do not necessarily communicate projected material immediately. First, we have to try to understand it and identify it, and quite often there are projections which are mysterious and indefinable, and which may take years to understand fully.

The more disturbed a client is, the more fierce their projections may be, and then it is incumbent on the therapist to digest and return. Incidentally, one can argue that if the therapist is being used as a toilet, then it is quite likely that the client was used in similar fashion as a child. It is often the case in large families that one child is used in such a manner, and grows up carrying a huge emotional burden, and often feels very guilty if they don't continue in this way in their adult life. It is a kind of scapegoating mechanism, and then the client is likely to try to make the therapist a scapegoat.

Counter-transference is a complex and very rich phenomenon, and we can only scratch the surface of it here. For new therapists it often proves a headache, but as one grows into the profession, one realizes that it is irreplaceable as a tool, for nothing else gives one such a direct insight into the contents of the client's unconscious.

Retaliation

Whenever there are shibboleths or taboos in psychotherapy, one can infer that the taboo is holding back a powerful desire. For example, there is obviously massive anxiety amongst therapists about sexual contact with clients – one can infer that the anxiety arises out of an unconscious desire to have this. Another powerful taboo concerns retaliation, about which many therapists, and many books, state that retaliation by the therapist – to the client's anger, envy, scorn, and so on – is impermissible.[3] I have always found this puzzling and very restrictive. Does it mean that one can never have a row with a client? Does it mean that an infuriating client has to be given endless calm interpretations? How does one deal with an abusive client?

I find it suspicious that the psychotherapist's own anger is ruled out of court. Why should this be so? Obviously in the case of some clients, who are particularly fragile, the sight of an angry therapist would be disturbing, and would probably make many of them leave. But with other clients, this is not so.

> Sam had had a particularly good session early in the week, but arrived for his second session to announce that he wanted to stop in a month. He stated this in a rather breezy way, and proceeded to joke about it. Sam's therapist felt angry about this, and reasoned that probably Sam felt angry about having had the good session, but when this interpretation had little effect on Sam, the therapist allowed some of his anger to show.

Of course, it also depends on how the anger is expressed. It's not a question of coming down on a client like a ton of bricks, but of simply sounding angry sometimes. Is this really going to damage a client? In fact, one can turn this round, and argue that some clients actually need evidence that they have an effect on the therapist, that they are involved in a real human relationship, and are not simply confronted with a desiccated interpreting machine. If I am permitted to laugh at the client's joke, to feel fond of him, to feel sadness at his misfortunes, and so on, why am I not allowed to feel angry at his manipulations of me?

One can of course argue that being angry is not retaliatory, and that retaliation means something darker and more punitive or scornful. However, I think therapists are allowed, indeed they are called upon, to defend themselves against attack.

But of course anger is not the only form of retaliation. What about scorn, sarcasm, fury, hatred? Obviously we are dealing here with very powerful emotions, but I would still not rule any of them out. If one is engaged in a powerful relationship with a client – and obviously some relationships are – then such powerful feelings will come up.

One of the big problems in fact here is the therapist's guilt. It feels wrong to hate a client, or to feel scornful or sarcastic, and even more wrong to express it. However, these guilty feelings don't necessarily mean that they are wrong or inappropriate or damaging. In some cases, they are highly therapeutic, because they can bring home to the client how negative his own actions are.

But why do therapists feel guilt at their own negative feelings to clients? Partly of course this is a counter-transferential pick-up of the client's guilt, but it is also surely due to the powerful syndrome of 'empathy/compassion/caring' feelings that exist in the psychotherapy universe. We are here to help people, and to an extent to take care of them, and it therefore seems to go against the grain to get mad at them.

Yet the analogy with child-rearing helps us again. Anyone who has raised children knows that endless patience and loving kindness are not in fact helpful to children. Sometimes one feels angry or fed up with one's own child, and sometimes they need to hear it, so that they realize what the limits are. In fact, it is clear that children push against the limits to find out what they are, and if you refuse to set them, or if you endure their acting out, then they will become more and more wild, for in fact they may believe that you cannot see them at all as separate people.

The parallel with psychotherapy seems clear enough. Many clients also seek limits, want to find out what they are, push against them and beyond them. Of course, often one does not feel angry and one can point out one's boundaries in a calm manner. But then there is the client who sets out to infuriate you – are you to refuse to be infuriated? There is something inhuman about this. It strikes me in fact that some clients know that their behaviour is unacceptable or abusive, and they perpetrate it precisely to see what the therapist will do. Of course, one can make that interpretation, and a very powerful one it is too, but sometimes one is also engaged in the powerful emotions, and what is the shame in that? Some clients need to see that engagement and those emotions, otherwise they do not believe that there is engagement.

Of course, with everything that we practise, it's knowing when to allow these retaliatory feelings out and when not to. One can speak broadly of 'fragile' clients being unable to receive them, but then there are some fragile clients who are also enraged and abusive. What are we to do then? I think I have had the most furious rows in my practice with a schizophrenic client who was quite maddening, and knew that she could drive me mad, and did drive me mad. No doubt, in part she was projecting her 'madness' into me to see what I would do, but equally, I felt determined not to allow her to brow-beat me, which she attempted to do in a very imperious and even sadistic manner. Yet our furious rows always calmed her down, and then we were able to joke about it, and our habitual fondness for each other was restored. If I had made a formally 'correct' yet lifeless interpretation about her maddening behaviour, I think she would have felt I was trying to drive her mad in turn, and maybe there would be some truth in that.

There is something desperately straitjacketed about the notion of a therapist who does not allow their own anger, annoyance, irritation, sarcasm, and so on, any breathing space in the consulting room except in the form of an interpretation.

Holding

Sometimes an unusual kind of relationship develops between therapist and client, in which there is less talking and interpretation and working out of problems, and a more silent contemplative atmosphere develops. Some clients have a fierce resistance to this, feel embarrassed, scornful or disapproving of it, yet one can sense that they secretly want and need it. It's as if that aspect of mothering – just being there with one's child – was lacking for them, and now they are reclaiming it.

I said 'unusual' but one can detect it in many therapies. One of its key features can be described as not-doing. Both parties no longer have to 'work' in the session; there is less pressure to bring up new topics, examine new material, work out problems, analyze dreams, or whatever. Instead we are content to be with each other.

This is real intimacy, it seems to me, and one can see why resistance develops in many clients to this kind of intimacy. In fact, there is a kind of nakedness in it.

> Greg presented many problems to do with work, his girlfriend, and above all his obsessive workaholic attitude to life. But the therapist noticed also that silences would develop, and at first he enquired of Greg if these bothered him or made him feel uneasy. Greg said they didn't, and gradually they lengthened and deepened, until it was plain that something very healing was taking place.

The word 'healing' here is important, since this kind of atmosphere cannot be described in terms of problem-solving, interpretations, or any of the normal tools of therapy. Yet it is unmistakable when it begins to happen, since the feeling of the session is very different from busy sessions.

With some clients, such a holding or containing atmosphere becomes very important, and may dominate the therapy for a period. One might argue that it is regressive, since arguably the client has adopted the attitude of the infant, content to be with its mother, without demanding any stimulation. I think sometimes it is regressive, but I think also there is a less regressed kind of holding which is about adult intimacy.

'Not-doing' seems critical also here. So many people in Western culture are used to seeing life in terms of what they do, what goals they achieve, how much work they get done. Yet now they find themselves in a very different place and state of being. 'Being' is a crucial word, since some people may never have really experienced being with someone in this way.

Regression

Regression is often triggered off in therapy, since the client is the focus of attention, is invited to say whatever is in his head, may be lying on the couch – in other words, there is something quite different about therapy time from our normal lives. It represents a kind of suspension of normal rules of engagement – we don't engage in chit-chat, we are focused on the client's psyche, we attempt to get beneath the normal surface layer of adult rationality in people's character – one might say that we are looking for the non-rational and the non-adult aspects of the client.

But regression has many forms. I have found Searle's description of it useful, although he developed his theory mainly in relation to schizo-phrenic people.[4] He describes ambivalent and pre-ambivalent regression. Pre-ambivalent refers to state of bliss and fusion, where there is no conflict between therapist and client or within the client. This must be allowed to occur, since it may be very healing for the client, who is going back to a time when such a fusion state could have existed between self and mother, but for whatever reason did not happen. The therapist may experience strong feelings of love towards the client, may have powerful maternal feelings, impulses to hold or cuddle the client, and so on. In other words, the client is projecting a very strong need to be looked after in a quite non-adult manner, and this is entirely appropriate and healing.

However, it does not last forever, and just as children grow into stormy adolescence, when they may need to argue with their parents, feel scorn for them, want to be very different from them and so on, so clients do the same. Fusion is changing to separation, and both parties may experience this as a painful change, as it is for parents and children. Nonetheless, it is obviously a necessary one, since the client cannot stay in a pre-ambivalent state for ever.

Intimacy and lightness

Many clients have problems with intimacy in their relations with others, and therapy provides a very concrete forum where this can be looked at. The therapist is able to judge directly how intimate the client can be or not. But by intimacy in this context, I do not just mean the ability to be open emotionally, to describe what is going on with oneself, and so on. That is one kind of intimacy, which could be described as a state of psychological openness with another person. But there is another much lighter kind of intimacy. One of my therapists used to say that having a cup of tea was extremely intimate, and also that the British were experts at this kind of intimacy.

This might strike us as odd, since therapists are used to thinking of social occasions, and social 'chit-chat' as very non-intimate. Of course this is often true, but they can also be times of intimacy, in which we are able to indulge in a kind of play activity, or a lightness of touch which is not emotionally intense.

'Intimate' does not therefore denote 'intense'. In fact, some intense people use their intensity as a defence, which protects them from true intimacy – a kind of operatic melodrama which actually masks the real person. In fact, if one feels comfortable with oneself and with life, one does not need to be intense. One can touch another person lightly; one can enjoy the company of someone else without great emotional outpourings, one can allow one's conversation to be spontaneous and lively.

The interesting thing about this kind of intimacy is how frightened many clients are of it, since they believe it is too frivolous for therapy. There are also therapists who believe this! There is a kind of puritan grimness here, which determines that therapy should be hard work, should be deadly serious, should 'make progress' at all times, should shun frivolity. There is something seriously wrong here!

This is one reason why one should look for a sense of humour in clients, and if it is not there, or exists only minimally, one should try to find out why, since it denotes a severe inhibition on having fun. In fact, any client who is humourless has serious problems, and usually suggests a fierce super-ego or inner critic, which ruthlessly expunges lightness from life. One can also say this of therapists – that those who cannot use their sense of humour in the therapy sessions are actually depriving their clients of something crucial. Obviously, one does not want a wise-cracking therapist who treats everything as a big joke, but equally one does not want a grim figure who cannot laugh. In fact, as therapy progresses, one often finds that the early heavy atmosphere begins to lighten, as the emotional load is being worked through, and then lightness and humour may be absolutely crucial aspects of the therapy, since the client may be beginning to enjoy life. We may then find that we can enjoy therapy together.

This sense of lightness can be related to play, which forms a very important area of children's lives, and in fact of adults' lives. Again, there are strong injunctions at work in both therapist and client, that therapy should not be used for play, since that denotes 'not working'. In fact, we can argue the reverse: that the inability to play, that is to be frivolous, to see the absurd in life, and so on, is a severe inhibition, and will cause many problems in adult life. For one thing, sex becomes a grim activity, rather than a joyous one. Without the ability to play, life is seen too grimly and in monochrome colours.

In fact, the relation to the unconscious, which we are attempting to develop in some kinds of therapy, can become a spontaneous kind of play, whereby both participants are able to allow their 'stream of consciousness' to pour forth, bouncing off each other in a quite unpredictable way. In such play, control is given up, and one treats the unconscious as a kind of river of water which flows along, and which need not be blocked.

The absence of play and the lack of a sense of humour are therefore quite serious indicators in any client, since we can infer usually that the same inhibitions exist in other areas of life. There are however clients who do have a sense of fun in their life in general, but feel that it should be excluded from therapy. Thus one finds clients who crack a joke just as the session has ended, or who arrive in a bright and breezy mood, but then sink in a gloomy state during the session. Of course, sometimes this is because something depressing is coming up, but there is also the possibility that the fun side of the client is being repressed, under the instructions of a zealous super-ego, which is often projected onto the therapist.

Notes

1   See P. Clarkson, *The Therapeutic Relationship* (London: Whurr, 1995).
2   See A. Bateman and J. Holmes, *Introduction to Psychoanalysis* (London: Routledge, 1995), pp. 95–117.
3   See for example, K. Lambert, *Analysis, Repair and Individuation* (London: Karnac, 1984).
4   H. F. Searles, 'Phases of Patient-Therapist Interaction in the Psychotherapy of Chronic Schizophrenia' in *Collected Papers on Schizophrenia and Related Subjects* (London: Maresfield, 1986).

10

Thinking, Feeling and the Body

A lot of therapeutic work is concerned with freeing up stuck or repressed feelings, and the effect of consciousness on feelings is extraordinary. Feelings that seemed immovable become fluid and changing. Clients find that when their awareness is placed upon a particular feeling which has come up, that it tends to register and then change or disappear. One can compare this with the rigid and inflexible emotional state that many people are in when they start therapy – we say that someone is depressed, or is an angry man, or is a fearful person. Here we are saying that certain feelings have become permanent features of that person's personality. This is indeed an extraordinary state of affairs, which could be described as the domination of the ego by a feeling, or an identification by the person with that feeling.

Another way of putting this is that the feeling is unconscious or semi-conscious, so that the person concerned is unaware or half-aware of it, although other people may be able to see it quite clearly. This of course raises the interesting and indeed crucial question of the movement from un-consciousness to consciousness. Why don't repressed feelings simply stay repressed? Why does the unconscious move towards consciousness?

In fact, this is not an inevitable process. Without doubt, there are many people who harbour repressed thoughts and feelings for the whole of their life, and are therefore completely identified with them. For example, one meets old people who are embittered, or depressed, or angry, yet show little awareness of this. Thus if we argue that the unconscious has a tendency towards consciousness, or a movement towards it, it can be defeated by the power of repression.

On the other hand, we also find that these repressed feelings 'leak', and cause a lot of trouble. That is, the unconsciously angry person tends to go around having lots of rows with people, and in fact tends to make other people angry. In other words, the anger is projected into others. The same is found with other feelings – the deeply hurt but repressed person may deal with the hurt by hurting others, and so on. This seems to show that the state of repression is not a stable one at all, since the repressed contents continually strive towards some kind of expression. They do not simply disappear or go quiet.

> Jack came to therapy as his marriage had become very tense and angry. He insisted that he himself was not an angry man, but he continually found himself having rows with his wife and his children, and also at work. He also described his parents as feuding for the whole of his childhood. His therapist found him to be edgy, irritable and producing feelings of annoyance in the therapist. They nearly had a row in the first few weeks, over the issue of charging for cancellations, which Jack claimed was a fraud.

Thus there are also personal costs when feelings are repressed. I mean that we can't simply project repressed feelings onto others, and that is the end of it – we still find that the feelings make us feel moody, or depressed, or we have violent dreams, and so on. In other words, the unconscious is an unruly part of the psyche, and as it were fights back, and seems almost determined to communicate its contents. Thus there is a continual state of conflict between the repressed and the need for expression.

This can go so far as the 'nervous break-down', when the repressed feelings can no longer be held back and spill out, for example, in bouts of prolonged weeping, or sustained fury, or great fear and anxiety. Anxiety is in fact commonly a component of these states of repressed emotional agitation, since one is perpetually anxious that the covert feeling will emerge.

We can say therefore that at the beginning of therapy, most clients have had some inkling that there are emotional disturbances going on, although they are often unclear as to what they are and what their extent is and what their origin is.

But we also find that working through the feeling, which also means eventually letting go of it, will be a difficult task for such people, for the reason that part of them does not want to let go of it. It is part of their identity; they feel unrecognizable without it. In addition, there may be feelings of loyalty and guilt towards one's family, where the feeling was inculcated in the first place.

Nonetheless, they have come to therapy partly in the hope of finding some freedom from this tyrannical grip, and therefore we find an ambivalence in them about releasing the feelings, and a conflict over it. Part of them is prepared to engage in the work which will free them, but part of them determines to frustrate it. One will find these opposing currents quite clearly in many clients, but fortunately the currents themselves are amenable to the psychological work of exploration and consciousness raising. In other words, the therapist is able to point out the simultaneous presence of repression and the drive towards expression, and show that the client is simultaneously aligned with both processes, that is, wants to repress, but also wants to express the repressed.

One might say that the ideal state to be in, is that one places one's awareness on a particular feeling and it disappears. How does this happen? I am suggesting that the unconscious material yearns for consciousness; hence when we focus on something which is at yet semi-conscious, we give it release, and it is therefore prepared to free us from its grip. The unconscious is a tyrant to the extent to which we separate ourselves off from it and refuse to have a relationship with it. If we set out on the job of forming a relationship with it, then its intransigence soon begins to melt away.

This is a striking phenomenon with tenacious feelings such as guilt. If someone is prepared to explore their guilt in depth and extensively, they will find eventually that feelings of guilt will still arise but will disappear, once they are identified and named. By 'naming' I mean that we are able to say 'I feel guilty' to someone else, maybe the person we feel guilty about. Then the guilt tends to lift. Of course, in the beginning the guilt prevents us from doing that, or in addition we may have feelings of shame about feeling guilty, or about confessing it. One can see the wisdom of the Christian churches, which incorporated various rituals of confession of guilt, which would without doubt provide considerable relief to the confessor.

This example also shows the phenomenon of 'layering' of feelings – I mean that they often exist in stratified form, so that one feeling conceals another, and perhaps there are multiple layers. For example, it is common to find that when someone has expressed their anger, they then feel sadness or grief, as if the anger was hiding the sadness. However, we can also find the reverse, that is the person who hides their anger behind sadness.

We can also see how feelings often exist in contradictory formations – that is, one can feel love and hate for the same person; one can be afraid of the thing one wants; one feels shame for one's desires, and so on.

If the work goes well, rigidity is replaced by flexibility and fluidity. We are not striving to become people without feelings – that would mean becoming dead. But we are striving to become open to feelings, and therefore able to let go of them also. They pass through rapidly and without getting stuck, especially if we are able to communicate them.

But what is the role of the psychotherapist in the facilitation of emotional expression and the lifting of repression? There are complex factors at work here. First, the therapist is there to reflect back to the client those feelings which are unconscious or semi-conscious, so that the client is able to make use of this mirroring. Second, the therapist can help in the understanding of these feelings, where they come from, what their current meaning is, and so on. Third, by being there, the therapist often helps to stimulate certain feelings, such as anger, sadness, love, and so on. In other words, the therapist is a vital object towards which the client's unconscious feelings are directed. Fourth, the therapist has feelings also, and this is vital, since therapy is not a desiccated series of interpretations, but a living interaction between two emotional beings. If the client were to believe that he/she is an emotional cauldron, while the therapist is simply a detached forensic interpreter, disaster would strike, since the essential humanness of both parties would be denied. In short, intimacy would not be possible at all.

One might say that the therapist acts as a lightning rod for all the feelings of the client which exist in a covert form, but which are now ready to be expressed and come to life. One might question this: why should the client be in such a state? What if the client is in a highly rigid and deadened state, so that there is no emotional lability? One does of course meet such clients, but in the main people who come to therapy have done so because the foundations of their personality are beginning to shake somewhat. There may not have been an earthquake, but there may well have been tremors, odd moods, agitation, or perhaps more violent outbursts, which have perplexed the client. Change is happening in other words, and those people who are heavily resistant to change tend not to come to therapy. I am reminded again of that phenomenon in large families, whereby the most damaged do not do therapy, but a family member who is perhaps more sensitive than the others, does do therapy. One can argue that there is a kind of proxy effect here as well, that this sensitive person is doing therapy on behalf of the others – but this can be unearthed and investigated in therapy as well, and often causes great anger and guilt.

Compassion

There seems little doubt that compassion develops in those people who have contacted their own pain and suffering, and in that sense have developed compassion towards themselves. Instead of taking a harsh and critical stance towards their own vulnerability, instead of seeing it as 'weakness', they begin to take care of their own raw feelings, their own inner child, and thus begin to soften a previously harsh and inflexible austerity.

This leads to compassion towards others, and indeed the presence or absence of compassion can be used as a kind of indication as to how much people are in touch with themselves emotionally. Put quite simply, those people who are not in touch with their own vulnerability, will tend to blank out other people's. Or they may castigate it, feel scorn towards it, and so on. This used to go on in some marriages – that some men had such a hard armouring to their personality, and saw their female partner as weak and pathetic, thereby exhibiting their own fortress-like personality.

But perhaps that image of marriage and relationship is not as prevalent as it once was, say in the 50s. Nonetheless, one still comes across such a dynamic, and often one hears from women in therapy that they are suffering from its effects. One might say that the men have little compassion, and the women are saddled with the entirety of vulnerability and emotional responsiveness. In fact, there are relationships which reverse this pattern – where the women are harsh and defended, and the men are in a more masochistic position.

The term 'masochistic' brings us to the issue of excessive compassion, by which I mean an over-identification with others, so that one compulsively cares for them. This is common in social workers, and other 'helping' professions, who tend to project their own uncared for side onto others, thereby denying their own need for care and love.

Thinking

Humanistic psychology has tended to emphasize the importance of feelings and the body, and has seen thinking and intellectuality as barriers to these, and indeed as barriers to personal development. This is no doubt true for many individuals in the West, who may suffer from that cerebralization which characterizes our culture. But at the same time, one meets some clients who cannot think, who are swallowed up by feelings, or who cannot discriminate between different feelings, or between thinking and feeling. In this case, one may be required to help someone to begin to think, so that their chaotic feelings can be given some order, and one can become less impulsive. For the impulsive person tends not to think or reflect on their feelings, but turns feeling into action. Thus some violent men find it impossible to contain their own feelings. They are angry – so they go out and smash someone or something. Here there is no 'pause', there is no place of contemplation, where one can actually feel the feeling, without being driven into action. In fact, in working with violent men, it has struck me that the violence actually provides a means of avoiding the feeling by going into blind action. What is difficult with such men is to get them to sit down and actually consider the contents of their own psyche.

Norman had been in prison for beating someone up, but in therapy he was a nervous and rather placating man. He kept saying how pleased he was with the therapy, that he wouldn't miss it for the world, but in the next breath he would scornfully condemn some of his friends as time-wasters and parasites. Eventually very painful feelings of inferiority began to emerge, which made Norman furious. But the more that he worked through the inferiority, the less he felt like getting into fights.

But feeling the feeling is not enough either. As a fully developed human being, one is also required to think about the feeling. Why am I feeling this now? Where did it come from? How does it tie in with my own personality and my own blind spots? This is a kind of self-analysis which eventually develops within one's own therapy, and this indicates that one is able to leave therapy, for one has learned to think for oneself.

So we are not seeking a mass of undifferentiated emotions without thought; nor are we seeking a cold and rational thought process devoid of emotion. There is a question of balance here – the person who can think and feel together, can think about feeling, and can have feelings about certain thoughts. One might say that eventually thinking becomes a vital container for feeling, so that one is not swept away by powerful emotional currents, but is able to reflect on one's own state, before acting. There is a kind of holy trinity which exists between feeling, thinking and acting, so that when one has the right balance one is able to act after due consideration about one's feelings, and what one wants to do. Imbalance occurs when one or two of these three are either excessively developed or under-developed. Thus the atrophy of feeling is common in Western culture, but one also finds those who cannot think and who rush into action impulsively. There are also those people who cannot act, but are forever suspended in a state of suspended anxiety, or who cherish a kind of provisional existence, full of plans but with no fruition. In fact, the interrelations between feeling, thinking and acting are immensely rich and complex, and each client met with provides a unique mix of the three.

But why has thinking been arrested in certain people? Usually it's a question of an early environment where thinking of this kind did not occur, where parents themselves were chaotic and often had poor boundaries. For thought in fact provides us with very useful boundaries, both between us as individuals, and also inside us, boundaries between the different kinds of psychic experience. Thus I need to know that a dream is not the same as my waking reality; or that my anger is not necessarily going to destroy someone; or that I am not going to be destroyed by your anger. All of these reactions show an inability to think and reason, and a loss of ego boundaries consequent on this.

It is clear now historically that the 'New Therapies' rose up against psychoanalysis as a perceived over-intellectual discipline, and propounded instead the therapies of the body and of emotion, but also that in the end something more in the middle would begin to emerge, whereby we could seek a balancing between thought, feeling and the body, or in Jung's terms, a kind of inner marriage.

One of the problems with working with someone who cannot think is that usually one is prevented from thinking oneself. This is both disconcerting and useful. It is obviously difficult, since the therapist makes a practice of thinking about what is going on; but it is an extremely useful clue as to the client's inner state, since he/she too is prevented from thinking, or perhaps has never really begun to think. Thus the therapist has to overcome this temporary internal paralysis of the thinking process. One very powerful way of doing this is to confess that one (temporarily) has lost the ability to think, but this kind of disclosure is not suitable for more disturbed clients.

But the therapist must also struggle to think about not thinking, and also to talk about not thinking – this sounds a bit quixotic, but it is in fact a very powerful tool, and if persevered with, will loosen up the paralysis, and crucially also demonstrates to the client that these things are not set in stone, since many clients like this are unable to think or talk about their paralysis. There is therefore a kind of double paralysis or double bind – I cannot think, but I am not able to become aware of that.

I should also point out here that this state of affairs should not be confused with those times when not thinking is in fact desirable and pleasurable for both therapist and client. The difference between the two experiences is very clear, since one is felt as a paralysis and the result of an internal attack on thinking, whereas the other is the product of a kind of blissful symbiosis.

Spirituality

Some therapists would object to the listing of 'thinking, feeling and the body' as somehow definitive of therapeutic work and of human beings on the grounds that it left out the spiritual dimension. Some Jungian and humanistic therapists would claim that psychotherapy should be involved in 'soul-work', that is the spiritual aspects of human life, but of course many other therapists would shrink from this, on the grounds that it is not part of human psychology, or that it is somehow 'extra-mural'.

In fact, spiritual issues are entirely up to the client, and it is difficult to introduce them extraneously, if a client has expressed no interest, or indeed has expressed hostility to such ideas. However, I find that with religious clients, I am interested in how their religion interacts with the rest of their life, and how certain issues such as guilt and love are connected with their religious beliefs.

Thus if we are discussing self-esteem and value, I might ask the question: 'do you think God loves you?' of a religious client. However, this would be a very odd question to ask of somebody not interested in religion or spirituality.

We could say then that such matters very much devolve on the client's own interests. This is quite different from thinking, feeling and the body, since all human beings are involved in these faculties. Of course one might argue that all humans are spiritual beings, but that is much more tendentious, since many people deny this vehemently, or are simply indifferent.

Jung argued in fact that many psychological problems had spiritual solutions, in the sense that certain clients found an ultimate meaning to life in religion and spirituality. That is a contentious issue – I have certainly found that some clients began to take such a direction in their life, but many others have not.

This issue is of course affected very much by the therapist's own leanings. If a therapist is an atheist or agnostic, or is simply not interested in spirituality, then it is going to be very difficult to go into this area in any depth.

The body

The body is the most difficult and most taboo area of psychotherapy. I mean by 'taboo' that the injunction not to touch has dominated therapy since Freud, and although there are now therapies which employ touch, and indeed therapies based on the analysis of the client's body, the strictures against bodily contact remain powerful in most therapeutic schools.

There are obvious reasons why this is so. In the first place, physical touch can easily be interpreted as seductive, since it crosses boundaries and invades personal space. Second, it tends to stimulate some clients too much, especially those who have suffered some kind of abuse or seduction from a parent. Third, it can actually get in the way of the therapy, by which I mean that if the therapist is getting that close to the client, it may become impossible to discuss what is going on in the relationship.

Perhaps the simplest indication against touch in therapy is that for many clients and therapists, it doesn't feel safe. Of course, this is different in a therapy which is based on touch, or which works directly with the client's body, but then the therapist's training will have taken them through all the fears and taboos which exist in people about touch. But for those therapies which are based on the 'talking cure', physical touch tends to seem dangerous and/or exciting.

But the prohibition on touch does not mean that the body itself is out of bounds as a topic in therapy. In fact, the client's own communications via their body are often the most obvious clues as to what is going on, and without doubt the two parties are usually making all kinds of unconscious connections via their bodies.

Training courses vary enormously in their attention to body communication. Humanistic courses have tended to pay a lot of attention to this, in the form of modules on bio-energetics and so on, and in fact this has provided one of the unique characteristics of humanistic therapy – that it paid a lot of attention to the client's body. We might say that for the humanistic therapist, the mind is intrinsically an embodied mind, and that feelings and thoughts are bodily processes. This strikes me as a satisfactory solution to the ancient body-mind duality, and the puzzle as to how body and mind connect – perhaps one can say that they were never really separate, except through a kind of neurotic wrenching apart which Western culture has inculcated.

Humanistic practitioners therefore speak of 'bodymind' or some such formulation, which propounds the idea that the two human processes of thinking (in which I include feeling) and sensating are actually connected. Of course, for many clients thinking has become a way of denying the body, but one can say that this is a particular and peculiar form of disembodied thinking. Our job therefore is to return thinking and feeling to the body. It is therefore absolutely legitimate at times to focus on the client's bodily sensations and reactions, so long as that feels safe for the client. Thus the question 'how do you feel?' can be rephrased in terms of the body at times: 'where do you feel your anger?', 'what does sadness feel like physically?', and so on. Many clients are surprised to realize that feelings are themselves physical events, and not simply mental ones.

But humanistic therapy has been weak on the issue of the therapist's body, and the importance this can assume for the client, particularly if regression takes place. In this case, the client may well have many primitive fantasies and feelings about the therapist's body, may want to attack it, bury into it, find refuge in it, destroy it, take succour from it, and so on. Here the psychoanalyst has been able to explore such fantasies, while the humanistic therapist has been largely dumb. In fact, this can be a frightening area of psychotherapy for both therapist and client, and without doubt this is one area where one has to have had plenty of therapeutic input oneself in order to practise it.

Indeed, this is true of any kind of 'body therapy' – one cannot simply learn it theoretically, but one has to have undergone it. Obviously, this is true of all major therapeutic types of intervention, but particularly true of any kind of work with the client's body, since this does arouse so much fear and suspicion. The therapist therefore has to feel confident about the work, sure about their own boundaries, clear about their own motives, in touch with their own interest in seduction and so on, and then the client can also feel safe about the work.

> Joanne had spoken with relish about castrating men, so her (male) therapist asked her if she imagined castrating him. She proceeded to describe fantasies of cutting his genitals off, taking them home and putting them on the wall as a trophy. However, later she went through considerable sadness and guilt that she had had such destructive fantasies. The therapist reassured her that they were fantasies, and she had not actually carried out the deed.

This example also shows the power of magical thinking, that is, the primitive belief that the dream-like act has been carried out in reality. One of the very useful consequences of this kind of work, that is, working with primitive fantasies, is the separation between fantasy and reality, and the reduction in magical thinking.

The role of the body in psychotherapy has always been controversial, and one solution to this traditionally has been to ignore it, so that the 'talking cure' could seem rather disembodied. However, it is bodies which talk as well as think, and this disembodiment without doubt reflects the split in Western culture between mind and body, or psyche and soma. This is in part an issue to do with social class – working class people have worked with their bodies, middle class people with their minds, and since psychotherapy has largely been a middle class phenomenon, it has been a mental and verbal discipline. Humanistic psychology, and particularly the discipline of bio-energetics has therefore been of great importance in rectifying this imbalance or split, which hopefully can be healed in the 'integrative' therapies.

11 Negativity

The client's negativity is one of the most complex and difficult aspects of psychotherapy, yet at the same time it forms one of the most rewarding areas of work, since here one often finds concentrated the root of the client's problems in life, in the sense that we find the destructive and self-destructive tendencies which blight so many people's lives. In fact, I have deliberately used the imprecise term 'negativity' so that I can subsume a number of issues – the client's negative reaction to the therapy, to the therapist, and to their own life. But one must also include under this heading guilt and shame, self-hatred, and other feelings and attitudes directed towards the self which are injurious.

This is a massive area, and can prove pretty daunting for the beginning therapist, especially in the case of those clients whose negativity is quite ferocious. Yet oddly enough, as I have pointed out before, one often comes across such clients in the early years of work. Nothing one has discussed on a training course can prepare one for this – someone who scoffs at the therapy, denies that any progress has been made, wonders if the therapist is at all competent, expresses scepticism about therapy in general, or professes an intense pessimism about life and the universe. Yet whether one is dealing with such intense negativity or a milder version, the task for the therapist is the same – to bring it out, to reflect it back to the client, so that eventually they are able to accept that the source of this attack on life lies within themselves, and not in a hostile universe. To attempt to neutralize such thinking with some kind of 'positive thinking' invites disaster, since it can stir up even more negative attacks.

But it is a shocking thing to grasp that one is the author of negative views and attitudes, and one cannot lay such things bare in the early period of therapy, at least not with many clients. In fact, one does meet some who are able to grasp very quickly and intuitively that we make our own universe, and that pessimism and paranoia are self-fulfilling, but the majority of clients must discover these terrible truths quite gradually.

Negativity is so pervasive in therapy that one can almost suggest that if you cannot see it in a particular client, then that means it is particularly well concealed. In fact, I am relieved when clients express scepticism or doubt about therapy, or feel angry towards the therapist, or exhibit some such reaction, since this shows that the client is not too ashamed about their own negativity, and it is not too well hidden. One has more problems with the overly good person, who has been forbidden expressions of anger, irritation, and so on, and who may strenuously deny ever harbouring such feelings.

Sabotage

The following is a common enough scenario. The session has gone well, or so the therapist believes. Insights have flowed, there has been a good rapport between the two people. But towards the end of the session, the client frowns: 'We haven't got very far, have we?'

Such remarks can be devastating for new therapists, who may be just about to congratulate themselves on a good piece of work, but such acts of sabotage become familiar, as quite a number of clients find positive progress irksome and unpleasant, and attempt to deny it and sabotage it. I have noticed that it is often when I am pleased with the session, that the client delivers such remarks. This is not surprising, since an enormous amount of unconscious communication goes on, and the client is probably quite aware of my complacency, and probably quite determined to prick it.

But sabotage is a complex psychological act. In part, it stems from the client's decision not to have a good life, not to be happy, and not to have a good therapy. This is partly to do with guilt, the need to suffer and be punished. One often finds with such people that they have sabotaged relationships, and pushed people away because they needed them or loved them or felt loved by them.

But there is also the factor of envy. First, the client envies the therapist's ability to help him, to give him good things, to bring about a good session. He may envy him also for keeping some of this goodness for himself, for perhaps having a better life than the client. Second, the client envies himself for having a good session, and determines to destroy it. We should say more accurately that one part of the client envies him, while another part enjoys the session and sees it as the harbinger of a good life.

But guilt and envy in such situations are like terrible twins. Guilt makes the client deprive himself of the good things of life which leads to envy that someone else (the therapist, apparently) does not deprive himself, and in fact, is able to give to others. There is also the resentment at being helped, the mortification that one is not self-reliant, in fact, for some, the humiliation of therapy. Sometimes there is a revenge motive here: I will not give you or my parents the satisfaction of having a happy life.

Some saboteurs are more subtle than others. One may realize during a session that a very gentle undermining process is going on, so gentle that one has not noticed it, and one is succumbing to it. Therapy can only do so much; our destiny is pretty fixed, isn't it? We can ameliorate life a bit, but let's not aim too high. Such phrases conceal a determination not to succeed, not to be happy.

The sting in the tail

I recall when I was quite inexperienced having one or two clients who came in and announced that they were stopping immediately, that session. Obviously I felt shocked, angry, and helpless, since there was little I could do about it. But that kind of situation doesn't happen to me now, since I have become more familiar with the 'sting in the tail', that is, the hidden negative transference in clients. The extreme version of this is the client with whom things seem to be going swimmingly, who suddenly announce their departure, or suddenly express dissatisfaction with everything.

But there are an infinite variety of negative transferences of this kind. In some ways, the openly hostile client is easier to deal with, since the negativity is out there in the open, and one has to find a way of dealing with it. But the hidden negativity poses great problems, since often the therapist may even doubt that it is there, since the client seems so agreeable, compliant, seems in fact to be enjoying the therapy so much.

One might publish a therapist's maxim: the negative transference is always present, even if it is not visible, if one gets no counter-transference indications (such as feeling bored or angry oneself), if the client denies it strenuously. Perhaps there is a second maxim as well: there are always clues to its presence, no matter how well hidden it is. One gets used to certain clues – for example, those clients who develop a keen interest in acupuncture or past lives therapy or some other solution to their life's problems. One can see hidden here – but perhaps not that well hidden – a reproach to the therapist – see how you make me seek other solutions, since what you offer is not enough or not good enough.

Another clue is the client who rails about other people, such as the boss at work, their best friend, their spouse, and so on. No doubt some of this is genuine, but one should pose the question, first to oneself, and then to the client – is some of this intended for me? Am I being covertly criticized?

Freud argued that some kinds of hypochondria expressed anger towards the carer of the sick person, that is, that the actual suffering was an indirect and covert form of punishment towards the other. This kind of masochistic punishment is also found in therapy – the client whose life gets worse; who staggers from crisis to crisis; whose good moments are always followed by disaster. One has to wonder here if some of this is a form of punishment addressed to the therapist, but addressed of course in the most indirect and deniable of forms. The deniability is crucial, since the client can argue that the therapist is seeing things, is being paranoid, and then often the therapist may begin to wonder if this is true.

One could in fact take a very hard line – that all criticism about anything is actually meant for the therapist, but this strikes me as rather narcissistic on the part of the therapist. Nonetheless, one has to bear it in mind sometimes with certain clients. For one thing, it gives their negativity some kind of edge and point: their hatred of the therapist is something we can work with and explore, whereas their hatred of their boss or husband is more diffuse.

There are of course all the different ways of acting out negative attitudes to the therapy and the therapist – being late, not paying, not turning up. Obviously one cannot adopt an automatic kind of attitude here – that one simply gives an interpretation about the negative transference, since one's position here is rather lifeless and robotic. Again, the therapist has to be particularly attentive to their own feelings, since here one often finds the most delicate clues as to the client's attitudes. Any feelings of anger, annoyance, boredom, switching off, and so on, are vital indications as to the client's own feelings.

Resistance

One of the Freud's great insights was that if the therapist could analyze the resistance, the client would be able to do most of the work himself.[1] This was a far cry from his earlier more interventionist ideas, when the analyst tried to do everything, but it shows also the importance of resistance. We might say that with some clients this comes on top – it is the first barrier, and the first impediment to the psychic processes in the client unfolding. Resistance means that the client is setting his will against that, and if it is not analyzed, then the therapy cannot proceed.

> Neil was rather sceptical and scornful about therapy. He said that he got as much benefit from going to the pub with his friends, and that after six sessions he had

obtained very little benefit. He said grudgingly that he had 'sorted out a few thoughts', but no more. The therapist pointed out that these remarks showed quite a powerful negativity to the process, and that this seemed to indicate that Neil partly didn't want the process to take off. There was a double bind at work – Neil was complaining that it wasn't working, but he had set himself against this possibility. He was ensuring it didn't work.

However, there is more to this example than this, for it is likely that Neil's defiance and sabotage are characteristic stances of his towards life. It probably conceals a lot of fear and threat about opening up to life, since what might come up might not be to his liking. He has a 'tough' attitude to life – you just get on with it and suffering is for wimps. But therapy threatens this toughness, and promises that Neil might get behind it and find pain and other unpleasant feelings. One might also guess that Neil hasn't been that happy in his life, and is determined not to be. He also probably feels humiliated by being helped.

So resistance to therapy indicates a wider and deeper resistance to life itself. Here one might speak of a resistance to the unconscious process, as part of the way in which life lives us, carries us along, if we surrender to it. People like Neil are quite averse to any notion of 'surrender', for they tend to see life in terms of cognitive control and will-power. This has no doubt worked for Neil, so that he has had a successful career, has been married with children, and so on. But there is something missing. After all, why has Neil come to therapy?

We can see clearly that one part of the client may want the therapy to go forward, while another part is set against it. When the latter aspect of the personality is dominating the therapy, it must be tackled. In fact, one meets new clients who threaten to leave almost immediately, and they will leave unless one begins to analyze this resistance straight away and possibly at length. By 'at length' I mean that the opening phase of the therapy may have to concern itself to a large extent with the resistance.

But this is quite a blatant example of resistance. There are more subtle versions, and it is not always clear when and whether they should be tackled explicitly by the therapist. So we get people who are rather jokey, or intellectual, or who analyze themselves quite well, while suggesting that the therapist is redundant. There are those infuriating people who mainly ignore the therapist and make him feel non-existent.

It is not always clear what to do about such resistances. Sometimes one can let them go for a period, since they don't threaten the process of therapy, but perhaps the biggest clue for the therapist here is how much they come into his consciousness. If one finds oneself thinking a lot about the client's defensive state, then it is obviously on top of the pile, and probably must be dealt with explicitly. But if it gets sidelined in the therapist's mind, then it is probably alright to let it be for a while.

But one also finds as one becomes more experienced and older, that one is prepared to tackle resistance directly and quite quickly. There is a kind of confidence factor here, built on experience. Certain types of resistance tend to repeat themselves, and so one becomes accustomed to dealing with them and one feels quite confident that therapy can deal with them.

From the outside in

These examples show the benefit of working from the outside in. Thus the barriers that people put up to intimacy and sharing and openness must be dealt with before they can do those things. This sounds obvious, but it has immense implications for therapy and goes back to Freud's statement that the therapist must attend to the resistance, and then the patient will make the connections generally for himself.

One can see the same principle in relation to those systems of feelings which are arranged in layers or concentric circles, with one feeling protecting another. For example, if someone feels embarrassed about crying, then it is useful to deal with the embarrassment before we deal with the sad or grievous things. The same is true of all the prohibitive feelings such as shame, envy, guilt. These feelings actually prevent other feelings coming to the surface to be expressed and released. Thus they are feelings which make us stuck often, since we can't get beyond them.

The image of 'outside in' is not really accurate, since it seems odd to say that my shame about another feeling is more external than the feeling. If I'm ashamed about feeling frightened, is the fear more of a core feeling than the shame? Maybe this is true, but certainly we can say that the shame puts a lock on other feelings.

And in the relation to the whole process of therapy, one has to continually monitor the prohibitive tendencies in the client. We can assume that all clients have such tendencies, but of course with some they are much better concealed than others, and with some they are very well concealed, and probably completely denied. Here we are definitely into Jung's 'shadow' territory, since the overtly good person is scandalized with the notion that maybe part of them is quite negative, sabotaging, envious, and so on. But it is hard to conceive of someone with no shadow.

One finds in fact with many clients that we have a good 'run' of sessions, and then the negative prohibition comes up again, and has to be dealt with again. It's as if the negative voices or demons in the inner world become dissatisfied and restless when things are going well. Maybe they are envious of the attention which they are not getting; they resent their power being diminished; at any rate, they rise up and determine to spoil the party.

I now anticipate trouble. I mean that when things are going well with a particular client, I make a particular point of wondering if there will be a backlash. Of course, this in itself can be neurotic, in the sense that I may be needlessly looking for trouble, but one finds that this anticipation varies according to different people. With the more negatively inclined person, one has to be alive to it in every session.

But of course, we are also feeding back to the client that this is how they approach life. Analyzing the resistance is not some technical kind of procedure – it goes to the heart of their attitude to life, their ratio of optimism and pessimism. If you deal with me like this, you probably do it with others and with yourself.

There is a kind of professional disappointment here – I mean that some people are expert in being dissatisfied, finding fault, seeing the fly in the ointment, and so on. And in fact one meets people who have been through a number of therapists in this manner, and as it were have notches on their gun. I am very wary of such people, since they are professional assassins of therapists, and it may well be impossible to work with them. Even if one points out their obvious predilection for destruction, it may not be enough to prevent it, and one may have to let them go.

Guilt

Many clients who do therapy for a long period – say, over five years – tend to discover levels of guilt, or types of guilt, inside themselves, which they never knew existed. In fact, it is unconscious guilt which wrecks people's lives, since this covert poison insists on expiation being made, or penance being exacted, and this often finds gruesome realization. Guilt and sabotage are closely connected then, since the guilt demands that the individual sabotages any good things which have happened to them.

One might say then rather simplistically that the way to tackle guilt is to drive it into the daylight, that is, make it more conscious, so that one can name it, take steps against it, and share it with others. These are all ways of bringing the guilt out from its dark source in the unconscious where it is at its most powerful.

In fact, one finds people who have done quite a lot of therapy who yet feel compelled to do more, and then find that they have not dealt with an overwhelming sense of guilt which they have always had yet have remained unaware of. This sounds bizarre and impossible, yet it happens quite commonly. One meets clients whose lives have been driven by guilt. One of the problems met with here is that as the guilt becomes more conscious, one is beginning to experience it for the first time, and it is extremely unpleasant. It is tempting then to stop the process of uncovering it and drive it back into the unconscious where it can carry on the work of destruction.

> Anthea was a very talented painter who had had several exhibitions, and was now poised to take up new opportunities in teaching and on television. But she was paralyzed by depression and fear, and it seemed to her therapist, a very powerful guilt. At first, Anthea didn't actually understand what was meant by guilt, but gradually accepted that she had always felt very depressed at every success, and had often punished herself for the good things she had accomplished. She described burning a number of paintings, which she had felt were not good enough, but in retrospect she wondered if they were too good. Gradually, as this uncovering went on, she became more able to take up her new opportunities.

This example shows how creative people can be beset by crippling guilt, and many cases of 'writer's block' and creative stalemates in other areas can be related to guilt. Nearly always, one can trace this back to family dynamics, in which envy and guilt formed a hellish partnership. Thus the creative person can be very afraid of being envied by the rest of the family, and also feels guilty at having this talent to develop.

But why is guilt so often unconscious and difficult to access? I think there are complex factors at work here – for one thing, there is often a family history of covert guilt. I mean that everyone in the family shares in the guilt, but it is never discussed or alluded to. One can speak here about shame as well, linking up with the guilt, so that it is never exposed to daylight, since shame refers to the dread of public exposure.

Guilt also relates to self-loathing, and one finds that this is a very taboo feeling. Many people will not admit to any self-hatred although it may be apparent to the therapist. Again, there is considerable shame about self-hatred. One can also argue that much guilt is 'laid down' at a very early age – I mean at a pre-verbal age – so that it is bound to be unconscious.

Guilt and meaning

Another complexity in the dynamics of guilt is that it has provided for the client a kind of world meaning, which is very difficult to give up, since then one is left with no meaning at all. By 'world meaning' I mean that when guilt developed at an early age, it provided a powerful explanation of the situation one was in. If childhood was painful or frightening or deprived, then one explanation for this is that one does not deserve anything better; that the bad things which happen are due to one's own fault. Of course, there is another explanation – that the adults are at fault, but generally children need to keep their parents as ideal figures, and therefore castigate themselves.

Guilt is therefore *a philosophical stance* as well as being a very unpleasant feeling. It provides an explanation for the way reality is – it's my fault, I'm worthless, and I have caused all this damage. More extremely, I don't even deserve to live.

Hence to begin to explore one's guilt, with the aim of reducing it or removing it, can prove very frightening, for what will one replace it with in the philosophical sense? What meaning can be given to reality without guilt?

It is not the job of the therapist to suggest life philosophies or possible meanings to life, but often clients begin to search them out, and may explore many different kinds of spiritual or New Age philosophies in their search for meaning. I see this as almost inevitable with some people. Others are more stoical, and are prepared to face a universe without much meaning in it; others suggest that love between human beings is a kind of motif which gives life some meaning.

Of course there is also the despair of finding no meaning in life, and some clients have to work through that, and their therapists with them.

But the more philosophical psychotherapies – such as the psychoanalytic ones, and the Jungian ones – contain their own kind of meaning related concepts. Thus psychoanalysis envisages a satisfactory relationship between ego and unconscious; Jungian psychology proposes the fulfilment of certain archetypal forces which are contained in the unconscious (and individuation). Certainly, such theoretical schemas provide us with a greater sense of significance than more pragmatic therapies, which may propound 'better relationships' or some such concrete aim as their raison d'etre.

No doubt this is one reason that Freud and Jung have acquired iconic status inside and outside psychotherapy. They did not simply construct certain technical procedures for conducting therapy, but also provided psychological and philosophical backgrounds against which the individual's struggle can be seen. Here of course, one comes up against that difficulty in therapy which we have discussed briefly – to what extent does therapy give philosophical as well as practical help in someone's life? In a sense, it is unavoidable that every therapist will provide a philosophical background, since the most practical suggestion always comes out of a theoretical stance which is conveyed consciously or unconsciously to the client.

Anger, guilt and revenge

We have already observed that some kinds of suffering are actually designed to punish someone else – say the hypochondriac whose illness acts as an irritant on someone else. We can see the same relationship sometimes between guilt and revenge – that I punish someone else by punishing myself. We have seen some signs of this in the discussion of sabotage, for here self-destruction can be designed to attack others. I sabotage my own life in order to declare to my parents that they were very bad parents – look how they have ruined my life.

This is clearly revenge, but revenge taking the form of self-harm. How many cases of suicide are vengeful acts, designed to plunge the survivor into despair and self-reproach?

It might seem too contradictory to yoke together guilt and revenge, but we can see that the common factor is anger. I am angry at others for perceived insults or deprivation, and one way I can express this anger is to turn my anger against myself. This is particularly powerful in revenge attacks on parents, since many parents have high hopes for their offspring, and quite a number already feel guilty about their own shortcomings as parents – thus a particularly angry grown-up offspring can play on parental guilt by frustrating their ambitions. I make my life a mess in order to prove to you how bad you were/are as a parent.

I have met people whose lives to me seemed like very long drawn out acts of revenge, in the sense that acts of self-destruction followed one another, and sabotage was a common theme. Of course, there may well be genuine guilt at work as well, so that success is unbearable, but this can fuel the vengeful feelings, since someone has to take the blame.

In fact, we are talking about a culture of blame. The guilty/vengeful person blames themselves, and others.

What is the solution for this knot of intense feelings and fantasies? It seems pretty clear that all of these dark feelings and wishes have to be dragged out of the darkness into daylight, for guilt and revenge flourish in those conditions, that is, in hiding. Much revenge is unconscious, and many acts of revenge are concealed in other guise, such as self-harm and sabotage of one's own life. But in working with such clients, there are strong clues as to the revenge motif, since very powerful feelings of anger are often detected.

> Ian came to a session saying that he felt very guilt and ashamed. He proceeded to lambast himself for all of his shortcomings, but gradually the therapist became aware also that there was a blaming quality to Ian's voice, so the therapist suggested that in part Ian was accusing the therapist of not having looked after him, not having 'made him better'.

This example shows how guilt, anger and revenge find their place in therapy itself, and some clients frequently turn on the therapist and demonstrate how hopeless he/she is, and how much worse they are since starting therapy. There is a kind of masochistic sadism at work – my life is hopeless and it's your fault. The quality to a session such as this is quite different from one where the client does feel guilty and ashamed, without the anger and revenge.

One of the problems with revenge is that it is very addictive. People become glued to it, and find it fascinating. This can be seen in theatre and film and novels where stories of revenge are common. But this is a far cry from ruining one's own life in order to take revenge on others.

In fact, when this involves revenge on one's parents, one can say that the person concerned has not yet separated from their parents. Their revenge acts as a bond. They are still involved in an intense drama in their original family, and cannot as yet leave it. So therapy itself is turned into a small effigy of that drama.

I think the shock of realizing that one is so vengeful can be considerable for some people. For some it is salutary. They can take stock, and begin to see all the ways in their life has been devoted to self-harm and revenge. But others cannot tolerate the idea of leaving their parents, and remain bonded to them in a desperate hateful glue.

Something should be said about the experience of working with vengeful people – it can be very wearing and upsetting, if the client turns the revenge on the therapist. Here the therapist has to make sure they look after themselves; they must not be abused; the sadism implicit in the revenge must be pointed out, and not allowed to hide in the darkness (unconsciousness).

This is definitely a case where the therapist must call a spade a spade, and must not shrink from referring to the client's sadism, unpleasant as this can be. I mean that normally one does not like to describe clients in these terms, no more than one likes to describe someone as 'seductive', but there are occasions when it must be done, if the anger is severe, and the self-harm is severe, and the abuse to the therapist likewise.

Therapist negativity

What about those times when the therapist has negative feelings about the client? They are obviously very useful, indicating in part what the client is feeling, and also some of the internal dynamics of the client's psyche. It might also indicate that the therapist simply dislikes the client, and if that is really the case, then it would seem that the two are not really a match, and the therapy will not work.

But I think this is quite unusual. It is more common to find oneself disliking (or hating) a client from time to time, so that it is a significant occurrence, rather than a generalized dislike. The sporadic feelings of negativity tell us that something important is going on – we have to find out what it is. Generally, one's first assumption can be that this is counter-transference, and that the client is disliking the therapist, and this can be suggested.

If this is not the case, then it is possible that the client is angry at someone else and is projecting this into the therapist. It is also possible that the client is exhibiting some character trait which is pretty dislikeable.

> James had a bullying streak in him which occasionally came out. He told his ther- apist a story about hectoring a guard on a train, because the train was late, and the therapist felt an acute dislike of James at that point. The therapist had several ideas in his head at once: that James was quite objectionable when he was like this; that sometimes James really disliked people; that James was in a state of hating him (the therapist).

What is the therapist to do with all this information, and these possible openings? It's impossible for an outsider to say or to choose. What do you feel like saying? What is your spontaneous reaction? It might be to say to James that he's a bully, but of course that's a very powerful thing for a therapist to say, so one has to consider within oneself the pros and cons of that statement. It is quite an abrasive thing to say to a client, but then some clients do need a shock like this to become more aware of how they are treating others, and their attitude to life, which they can be quite cut off from.

It can be seen that therapists have to spend a lot of time going over things in their own mind, that is, containing feelings and thoughts and fantasies, and not blurting them out. This in itself is a valuable training for the client, who may have difficulty containing feelings, and also reflecting on them. So the therapist is able to reflect on his dislike of James, and eventually may be able to say something about this. But this can take a long time – one might feel such a dislike for months or years, and still not understand it, nor know what to do about it.

One of the key issues to come out of this discussion is that the therapist has to develop the inner freedom to be able to dislike clients. That sounds too bald perhaps, but there is often a resistance in therapists to having such feel- ings, especially in beginning therapists, some of whom tend to be convinced that empathy will carry all before it, or who understandably feel guilty about feeling angry or negative. However, one's sensitivity to the negative feelings going on in the relationship becomes vital in the deeper levels of therapy, and this includes the therapist's dislike or hatred as much as the client's, for indeed the one is often a clue to the other.

One must also mention under the heading of the therapist's negativity those usually unconscious desires on the part of the therapist to sabotage the therapy. This may sound bizarre and unlikely, but it can crop up, especially in the more intense relationships between therapist and client. There are different reasons for this destructive attitude: the most obvious being a feeling of envy towards the client, perhaps because their life seems better than one's own, because they have made more of therapy than one did oneself, or because one envies them for receiving so much from oneself. But one must also be on the look-out for the client's envy being projected into the therapist.

There are other destructive feelings which can affect therapists. For example, competitive feelings can arise between therapist and client, and these can become quite aggressive. If this happens, it must be talked about extensively, and obviously dealt with in supervision. One may also be the recipient of a kind of projected envious parent figure (or other family member), who wishes that the client was not making progress, but again this can be worked through in supervision and in discussion with the client.

Civil war in the inner world

I have referred briefly in a previous chapter (Chapter Two) to the revolutionary analysis provided by the notion of internal objects, or the inner world. In relation to negative processes such as sabotage and guilt, this approach is very fruitful, since we are often able to suggest that the client's psyche contains a destructive force, which may seem quite demonic, which envies the client, wants to destroy his/her happiness and success, and may pour out a constant stream of pessimistic warnings. Many clients who suffer from depression and bouts of pessimism are eventually able to locate such a figure, who seems to form a kind of internal enemy or saboteur.

Two issues arise in relation to this inner enemy: how did it arise, and how can it be neutralized? The first more theoretical question has a very complex set of answers to it, since it is partly a resume of the negative experiences of childhood – so it is a kind of negative internal parent – but also represents an attempt to defuse my own anger – I will hate myself, and then my parents and others in my family are exonerated and in fact protected from my anger which I have taken on myself. In other words, the inner demonic figure arises partly as a distillation of all the anger and hatred which the child feels towards those who have neglected it or abused it, but this is then directed, not towards those adult figures, but towards the child itself. There is a strange kind of sacrifice made, whereby the child takes upon itself the negative feelings and forces, and thereby hopes to save others. Unfortunately this 'solution' is then perpetuated into adulthood with the resulting depression, lethargy and self-sabotage.

One of the interesting aspects of this analysis is that internal objects are not simply reflections of external ones. Thus the fact that someone possesses a fierce internal critic does not simply mean that one or both parents were similarly critical. This may be the case, but the psyche is able to construct its own figures and complexes, and is not a passive mirror. It is well known that children's sense of guilt can seem much fiercer than the parents' criticisms have been – but this can be partly explained as above by the child's own intense anger, which seeming unacceptable, is converted into this self-blaming figure. Clearly the psyche is dynamic, fluid and creative, and the inner world is its own universe which in many ways is self-creating.

One immediate solution to the negative internal critic therefore suggests itself in therapy – that the hidden anger of the client towards others is reawakened and mobilized, thus siphoning off some of the negative emotion contained in the inner critic. For the client's attitude towards this figure has often been a masochistic one – one can only endure, suffer and wait. Psychotherapy can take a more proactive approach however – one can suggest to such clients that their task is now to resist the inner enemy, fight back against it, tell it to shut up, and in general not put up with its criticisms and pessimism. This may well also apply to the client's external life – that they have to begin to resist those kicks and slights which they are used to accepting, and which has made them a depressed victim.

This is often very difficult to carry out in practice, partly because to begin with many clients have no sense that there is such an inner figure, and also because most people are very attached to it. I sometimes call it the 'demon lover', for it is both enemy and lover. By 'lover' I mean that it is something or someone who has been very close to the individual concerned, who knows him/her better than anyone else. If you like, the inner enemy is that figure with whom one has been most intimate, and therefore we are all very reluctant to give it up or tell it to get lost.

Often then in therapy there is an ongoing struggle – the client gets fed up with the attacks of the inner critic, resolves to fight back and does so. But then there is a relapse, as the client feels afraid to go on without that familiar figure, or feels guilty at having shouted at it. One can see the resemblance to a parental figure, whom one feels angry at, but then one relents as after all, my father is my father, to whom I owe filial obedience. There is also the question of abandonment, for to give up the ties to the inner critic can feel very lonely: better to stay with a bad parent than live alone.

This is the struggle between masochism – whereby the client submits to a bullying inner figure – and aggression – when the client fights back, resolves not to be bullied, and so on. However, if such a struggle has once begun, I would tend to say that the therapy is going well, since it means that the client has recognized the dangers present in this inner critic and has take steps to counteract it. One cannot expect overnight victory against such an old antagonist, but the fact that the client is able to take up arms from time to time, even if there is also at times a sliding back into the old masochism, is a positive step.

It marks the shift from being done to, to doing. I mean that the masochistic attitude to the inner critic is essentially passive, and probably reproduces the child's helplessness in the face of the adult world. The critic tells me that I am useless, that life is pointless, that even when I accomplish something it will go wrong in the end – and all I can do is listen and silently agree (while of course nursing a considerable hidden resentment). But if one can turn this around to a more aggressive and combative attitude, then the client is taking charge of life, is claiming some authorship over their own story. It could be said that the disengagement from the inner negative figure is a step towards maturity and self-realization.

This is clearly a critical point of change, and some clients cannot or will not go through with it. They are unwilling to be separated from the demon lover, even if the price paid is a terrible one – the continual sabotage and wrecking of one's life. It is like some awful marriage, which makes both parties miserable, but which they both cling to out of fear that the alternative is even more frightening. But many clients do recognize the state of internal civil war which I have described, and they do decide to fight against the internal enemy, as they are fed up with being criticized and sabotaged and undermined.

This scenario sounds like a science fiction film script to those who are not familiar with the workings of the inner world. It seems lurid, melodramatic, containing monstrous figures who loom larger than life. It can be argued in fact that such figures form the basis for the demonic mythological figures which exist in all cultures (for example, in horror films) – human beings have had to project them outwards, so that they can be described and partially neutralized. But it is a fact that in the quiet consulting room, such mighty battles are fought between the armies of darkness and those of daylight within the psyche of the client. I hesitate to use the terms 'good' and 'evil', but perhaps we can use the terms 'life-affirming' and 'life-denying'. It strikes me that here we have one of the central struggles in psychotherapy, which takes us to the heart of the psyche, and the ambivalence which without doubt exists in all of us – whether to live or to die, whether to take a positive attitude to life or a pessimistic one, whether to say yes or no to the universe and our own existence.

Note

1 S. Freud, 'Remembering, Repeating and Working-through' in *The Standard Edition* Vol. 12, p. 147.

12

Symbolism:
The Dynamics of
the Inner World

Working with symbolism is often associated with Jungian psychology, yet there can be few psychotherapists who do not encounter some kind of symbolic expression in their clients' lives. Of course, in short term therapy, there is not enough time to go into great depth about the client's dreams and other symbolic expressions, but in therapy of any length, it will probably be a factor.

Dreams are the most obvious example of symbolism in our lives, but we can argue that the unconscious expresses itself in many forms – including fantasy, the kinds of literature or music that the client enjoys, and in fact in relation to actual events in life.

> Dora was very struck on her way to therapy by a funeral going down the road. She stopped on the pavement and watched it go past, and felt very moved by it. Then she came into her session and immediately began to talk about this, and wondered what the significance of it was. She didn't think it was so much about death as about great change or transformation.

This is an example 'from life', where the symbol is not created internally, but is something presented to the person and perceived in a symbolic way. One can also adduce larger events in life, such as major relationships, work, hobbies, holidays, and so on, as possible symbolic expressions.

> Marjorie had worked in a primary school for twenty years, but had become fatigued with the work, and no longer felt as enthusiastic about children as formerly. She and her therapist talked at length about the relationship of this work to her not having her own children, and also its relationship to her own childhood, which had produced many unresolved issues for her, and the present status of her 'inner child'.

Examples such as this are fairly common, because people are drawn to occupations and other activities which have meaning for them, and the meaning may often be partly obscured. It may seem quite transparent that someone looking after children is vicariously dealing with their own childhood, or that part of them that is still like a child, but usually we are all quite unconscious of such connections. In other words, it is quite sophisticated psychologically to be able to make such a connection, and therapy aims in part to give us that ability.

Of course the interpretation given to various symbolic expressions is a very delicate issue, since the client must be the chief interpreter. Nonetheless, the therapist cannot help bringing in their own ideas about symbols, and here one's own predilections will be revealed – for example, whether your view of symbols is Freudian, Jungian, eclectic, and so on. But the therapist has to be careful not to be too domineering in this area.

> Fred dreamt about going to Mecca and walking round the black stone. His therapist gave a quasi-Freudian interpretation that the black stone represented his mother, or even her breast, but Fred felt unhappy with this, and suggested that the dream had a spiritual dimension, and represented his own search for some kind of spiritual home.

But this example shows a client who is fairly sophisticated and able to challenge the therapist's own interpretations – other clients will not be able to do this, and one has to be careful about a kind of indoctrination, particularly with clients who are rather passive, and who receive such interpretations all too readily. In that case, it might be as well to not make any interpretations of this kind, since one must first deal with the client's inability to interpret their own dreams and other symbols.

One finds of course that some clients, particularly very intellectual or rational people, are quite resistant to the whole idea of symbolic meanings being found in their lives, and will be averse to dream interpretation in particular. One cannot be too heavy-handed with such people, since their rationality has probably served them well during their life. However, the therapist has one advantage here – that it is quite likely that some non-rational feelings or thoughts have been disrupting this rational approach to life, hence their entry into therapy. If you like, the symbol has made its entrance, and cannot be shoved back into the dark recesses of the psyche.

But such people may well not bring dreams to therapy, and I do not recommend pushing them to do so. One has to work with what is, and if a particular person is very intellectual in their approach to life, and dismissive of symbolism, then that is what we are working with. In other words, one has to work with the scepticism before one can begin to approach symbolic expressions or the idea of the unconscious, which in fact frightens many people, since it seems so uncontrollable.

There is an opposite danger, particularly with disturbed people, that too much symbolic interpretation can actually make them feel upset, confused or even mad.

> Sam took to dream interpretation enthusiastically, and began to comb the Bible for other possible symbolic meanings about his own life. The therapist began to realize quickly that the sessions had a very unstable 'giddy' atmosphere when symbols were discussed, and therefore decided to keep the sessions very practical.

This is a good example of 'non-democratic' therapy, where the therapist has to make a professional decision, that a certain course of therapy is proving to be bad for the client, and decides to shift away from it. This attitude to symbolism is found with many schizophrenic people, many of whom are fascinated and also disturbed by such issues. One could argue that they are already too flooded with material from the unconscious, and that their therapy should present them with something more grounded and down to earth.

These examples show us clearly that psychotherapy often attempts to find a rebalancing in the client's psyche, so that those who are already infatuated with symbolism probably need a dose of ordinary life, and those who are over-intellectual may usefully look at their dreams. In other words, there is a kind of balance between the rational and the non-rational, and between the pragmatic ordinary aspects of life as against the symbolic and dream-like aspects. One can have too much of each polarity, and one can have an insufficiency as well – and in relation to many Western cultures, the balance seems to have tipped towards the rational and the pragmatic, so that dreams, fantasies, myths, fairy-stories and so on, strike many people as bizarre or childish, and not likely to be sources of wisdom. Yet in fact it may well be from these sources that new wisdom emerges, particularly if our rational or intellectual side has been 'burned out'.

Free association

The power and validity of the concept of free association is seen most clearly in relation to dream interpretation, and other symbolic expressions such as fantasies. For it means that we ask the client to associate to the dream, and we do not issue interpretations ex cathedra. There is a fundamental principle here –

that the dream emanates from the client's unconscious. It is 'their' dream, and there is the assumption that its significance is concealed in the client's psyche too. For the therapist to throw in premature interpretations is quite harmful, since it interrupts the client's own creative process, or their relationship with their own unconscious.

However, this does not mean that the therapist is completely disbarred from contributing to the interpretation of a dream or other symbol. The key word here is 'contribution' rather than 'domination'. But free association goes on for both parties in therapy, and in some mysterious way, the associations of the therapist may link up with those of the client, and may function as an invaluable aid. One might suggest that the therapist *loans* his unconscious to the client for the extent of the session.

> John kept dreaming of wild animals such as tigers, and related this to going to the zoo when he was a child, holding his father's hand while he explained where the animals came from. His therapist also had the association of primitive energy, and shared this with John, who found this a puzzling connection, partly since he had held his own energy tightly repressed. But the therapist suggested that the dreams indicated that something was on the move in John's psyche.

One can also suggest here that both sets of association are valuable and offer insights into the dreams about wild animals. Thus it is not an either/or situation, and symbols in general admit of many interpretations, some of which may be contradictory.

The idea of free association is of great interest in the general theory of the psyche, since it assumes that the dream or the symbol is not a random or casual production of the unconscious, but emerges from an organized structure of symbols which are interconnecting. Thus in the example above, the symbol of the tiger has links in the client's mind with his father, going to the zoo and so on; but it may also be part of other structures, which are more unconscious, indicated by the therapist's interpretation – wild animals suggest primitive energy, sexuality, and so on. But the image of a tiger could suggest a beneficial energy as well as a destructive energy – our associations are fluid and cannot be captured in dictionaries or lists of dream-images.

Inner world structures

The ramifications of the theory of the inner world are enormous. Put simply, the less conscious we are of the structures and processes going on in it, the more we are identified with them, and the more they are projected onto the outer world, sometimes with disastrous consequences. Let me give an example from the fairly common phenomenon of bullying.

Bullying is common in schools, workplaces, relationships, in fact, anywhere where human beings have contact with each other. Of course, when a client is being bullied, one has to deal with all kinds of practical issues, to do with assertiveness, standing up to bullies, and so on. One will probably also need to go back in time, to investigate any possible history of being bullied in the home or at school.

There are also those clients who are bullies, and this often becomes apparent as they bully, or attempt to bully, the therapist! This is in fact quite common behaviour, and therapists have to be able to resist such pressures, and point out what is happening.

But it is essential to spend some time pondering and hopefully discussing the inner world structures that are concealed behind the manifest bullying. One can suggest that there is a sado-masochistic structure in the psyche, which is then enacted in the outer world. In other words, the bullied client is also being harassed by an internal persecutor. But one can also suggest that the client who is a bully is also being bullied internally, and deals with this by bullying someone else externally. But this is a very unconscious process of reversal and identification – I mean that the ego takes the part of the internal bully and vents it on other people. The internal bullying is dramatized (acted out) and reversed, so that the victim of bullying may represent for the bully that part of himself which feels victimized. But the acting out has the function of keeping all of this in a state of repression – the bully must deny that he is afraid, feels inadequate, and so on. Is the victim of bullying also denying something – his/her own anger for example? Certainly the victim often wants to be punished, and bullies are usually good at picking this guilt up in others and acting on it.

Thus bullying is often associated with fear and guilt. Someone who is intensely guilty may well attract bullies, who see a chance to vent their sadism. But bullies themselves are quite likely to be afraid and guilty, and are tormented themselves by an internal bully, and therefore reverse the relationship in order to deal with it. To put it rather simplistically, the bully externalizes the victim; the victim externalizes the bully. Both of them act out the inner world in order to avoid it.

To put it simply, if I feel hurt, one of the ways I can deal with this, is to hurt someone else, and then it appears as if I have transferred the hurt to them. In fact, it's a kind of bogus solution, since the inner hurt cannot really be transferred; furthermore, the process is addictive – one has to keep doing it to keep getting relief. In fact, many of these projective solutions are addictive, since one is only finding a kind of pseudo-solution. One is not tackling the hidden trauma, but merely acting it out. One can argue that many sexual perversions have this addictive quality, and conceal a traumatic history.

One might argue that the investigation of the inner world is more important than the past, since the past cannot be changed, whereas one can make changes to the inner dynamics of the psyche. The inner critic can be neutralized in various ways; the hurt child can be cared for; the enraged child can be listened to, and so on. Just to realize that one has these objects and structures and process inside one's psyche is itself a great relief and lessens the nightmarish sense that one is out of control.

The 'reverse logic' of projection is quite clear: 'I am being bullied, therefore I will bully you'. It gives us a clue to many kinds of perversion which enact various hurtful situations in order to lessen the hurt for the victim by perpetrating them on someone else. If I tie you up and hurt your body, I appear to be lessening the hurt to my own body. I say 'appear' because this solution is temporary and illusory.

But there are many such reversals of emotional logic. Someone who has a dread of being rejected may well go through life rejecting others; someone who is very guilty may be very critical of others; someone who feels uncared for may work in the caring professions. Some of these observations seem rather trite and obvious, but the basic principles behind them are of immense value in the psychological understanding of neurotic behaviour. We might say that the basic logic is that *the victim seeks out other victims, either to punish or comfort*. This principle can also be seen at work in the larger world, for example, in the political arena. How many countries which were formerly colonized or tyrannized by another country celebrate their new-found freedom by tyrannizing another people?

One learns to dread the intensely guilty client, since their unconscious guilt and anger drives them to seek others to persecute. The key word here is unconscious, for if the guilt is brought into the daylight – a very painful process – then the drive to punish others and oneself is lessened considerably. One often meets couples who are engaged in a mutually destructive cycle of punishment and guilt; each feels great guilt, finds this unbearable, and therefore punishes their partner. But in addition, those who feel this degree of guilt positively welcome punishment, since they believe that they deserve to die, or at least to live in great discomfort.

The origin of symbolism

It is clear from the discussion so far that the human capacity for symbolism is far ranging and complex. One cannot hope to give a comprehensive view of it in such a short space, but let me run through some of the more obvious kinds of symbols, and those which particularly interest the psychotherapist.

In the first place, it is clear that human beings must have an innate symbolic ability, since human language is replete with it. For example, English is full of dead or dying symbols, whose symbolic quality we are no longer aware of. If we talk about the 'root' of a problem, or the 'bottom line', we are hardly aware that we are using metaphors and similes. Poets and other artists show an ability to produce original symbols, which present us with a challenging interpretive problem. Thus when Shakespeare speaks of pity 'like a new born babe striding the blast', we are thrown into some confusion maybe, but it is hopefully a creative and stimulating confusion.

We are not far away from dream symbolism now, and here we enter into a much more mysterious realm, for where the poet is consciously producing images, the dreamer is producing streams of images in a completely unconscious manner, and the opacity of dream symbolism is well known.

But we can suggest an even more far-ranging symbolic ability in humans – that certain events and situations have a metaphoric quality, even though they are not 'images' in the sense in which a poetic image or a dream image is. For example, the man who has a fascination for prostitutes could be said to be exhibiting a symbolic attachment to the feminine, and for him the prostitute is a symbol of femininity, although why he chooses the prostitute, which might be seen as a degraded substitute, and doesn't choose a partner, requires further examination. One might also such cite such trite but prevalent examples as smoking cigarettes as candidates for symbolic behaviour – the cigarette seeming to represent a kind of oral dummy or other symbolic nipple.

We arrive at the rather stunning idea that our lives themselves could be construed as symbolic narratives whose meaning we are relatively unaware of. This might strike some as taking the idea of symbolic too far, but I believe it represents a very powerful tool in our struggle to understand people's lives.

> Anne-Marie had a reasonably happy marriage, although she had not been able to have children. But she had fostered children, and was very good at it, but had arrived at a point in her life where she felt dissatisfied with this, and yearned for something else that would express her creative side. But to begin with, we kept coming up against the meaning of her fostered children. Obviously they made up for the children she couldn't have, but we also began to stumble against the idea that they represented creative 'children' who had not yet been born. Eventually, Anne-Marie took up painting, something which she had abandoned at the age of 18, and she began to see her paintings as a new type of 'child'.

Examples such as this begin to emerge in people's lives, or in their consciousness, at certain critical turning points in life, often when an old way of life is coming to an end, and the person is searching for something new. Then it is often imperative to grasp the meaning of the old life pattern, before one can go on. Even marriages, jobs, leisure pursuits, and so on, can be investigated in this way.

One might exclaim that this kind of analysis goes too far, and that one could become overwhelmed by a surfeit of 'symbolic' interpretations. However, as so often, we are reined in by the exigencies of the therapeutic situation. One goes in for extensive symbolic work only when it is required. It is not incumbent on the therapist to introduce it willy nilly. Hence I do not even like to suggest to clients that they bring dreams to sessions. For some people have no interest in dreams, and one can make them feel uneasy or guilty that they are not meeting the therapist's requirements. But how counter-therapeutic that is, to speak of the therapist's requirements in the first place!

Hence one deals with symbolism as and when it arises, and particularly when it is pressing, as with some clients it undoubtedly is. Of course, this does not prevent the therapist from pointing out symbolic qualities to certain events and situations as they come up in therapy. But if some clients seem uninterested in this, then generally it is best to leave it alone.

Undoubtedly, the degree to which therapy is conducted along these lines is a personal issue for the therapist, as with so much else. Those who gravitate to the Jungian point in the psychological spectrum may have a particular interest in symbolism; whereas say a bodywork therapist may have less. There is a kind of poetic or 'mythological' element in Jung which attracts some and repels others, but certainly it is difficult to conceive of a lengthy psychotherapy which ignored symbolism completely. In this sense, I am happy to accept that human beings are intrinsically myth-making animals.

However, the range of symbols is clearly quite enormous, and we are presented with the interesting question as to what mental organ or faculty produces them. Does the same mental organ produce dreams and jokes and poetic metaphors? Freud himself was concerned with these issues, and inferred that the unconscious was the womb of such images, although that still leaves us rather mystified as to which part of the unconscious is able to do this.

But Freud also saw dream images as products of distortion, since the emissions of the unconscious are censored by the repressing mechanism in the psyche, which cannot permit their too free and open expression. This is a theory of symbols as concealed signals.

One might even say that some symbols represent compensatory phenomena, whereby human beings, unable to gratify certain basic desires and needs, produce substitutions for them. Thus the cigarette seems to fit here. One might also cite the person, who instead of getting involved in life, spends their time day-dreaming. One meets quite a number of 'provisional' clients, who are full of good ideas, but never actually put any of them into execution. The 'Peter Pan' scenario is closely related to this – people who tend to float above the ground, again full of ideas and fantasies, but unable to come down to ground.

Clearly, symbols and metaphors and images can represent a kind of escapism for some people, and even creativity itself can sometimes be seen as such an escape. I have had very creative clients who seemed to shun human contact in favour of the contact with their own image-making process. This is all very well, but it can reach a position that is quasi-autistic.

However, the idea that symbolism can be used as an escape from life is a quite different notion from saying that symbols are inevitably compensatory and escapist. I find this too negative a theory for the fundamental production of symbols.

Jung accepted that human beings were innately and instinctively producers of symbols and myths, and in particular, that the unconscious was a kind of crucible in which such images are produced. One might say that the Jungian unconscious produces symbols as the lungs breathe air: it is part and parcel of its nature. With the notion of the archetype, which Jung sees as a kind of universal or collective organizer of experience, the symbol reaches its fullest flowering in psychological theory.

In fact, one need not accept one theory and reject all others. It is perfectly possible, and indeed seems advisable, to adopt a kind of pluralistic view of symbol formation. I mean that symbols are produced in the Jungian sense, by the very nature of the psyche; but also that they can be manipulated and used by human beings in all kinds of ways, including the avoidance of life itself.

I have already mentioned those schizophrenics who have an unhealthy interest in symbolism. I recall the feeling of disappointment I would have when one of my clients would produce his Bible for the nth time, and proceed to prove to me that the contemporary Israeli Palestinian conflict was prefigured in the Bible, and would lead to world war and the apocalypse. With this client, any discussion of dreams or fantasies was highly fraught, since he would go away and brood on this, and would develop our discussion into an ornate and incomprehensible farrago of private symbols. Here the unconscious seems to have triumphed over the ego and over ego values, and it is quite chilling to see this happening to someone. This client could quote great chunks of Revelation; but he found it impossible to pay his bills or hold down a job. In the end, with him and with others like him, I would recommend that they get a job, preferably of a mundane nature, that they cook, do some gardening, play pop music – in short get immersed in a very material world.

Clearly there is a wide spectrum in people's relationship to symbolism. No doubt many people have an inadequate relationship with their own unconscious; we could say they steer clear of symbolism. Maybe they are afraid of it, they are in denial of it, in effect they are tormented by it and hence block it out. At the other end of the spectrum, there are those unhappy people who are persecuted by symbols and cannot escape their tyrannical grip. I suppose most of us find an uneasy place in the middle, where we are half-conscious that certain images and symbols seem to recur in our lives, but are perhaps reluctant to grasp their full significance.

But it is clear that human culture is saturated with symbolism. We only have to look at contemporary cinema, television, the visual arts, the modern novel, the pop video, design, and so on, to see a plethora of images, metaphors, similes, many of which seem quite mysterious, yet which without doubt touch some part of our psyche.

We might say there is a hunger for symbolism in human beings. It seems quintessentially human to make paintings on the wall of a cave, to decorate rocks, to wear animal skins and bird feathers, to construct myths of creation and destruction, to describe our own history. In psychotherapy, this hunger should not be underestimated. Many people feel starved of the symbols of their own life. Somehow they have been denied them. They have lost the ability to tell stories, and particularly their own story. They are lived by symbols, but they are unable to separate from them and hence have a relationship with them. They have lost any sense of being the author of their own story, yet psychotherapy – which consists in part of the telling of many stories, and in fact the continual retelling of them – can restore the sense of authorship, so that the client can feel their life is indeed their life, and not the alienated or meaningless tale of a stranger.

It is this need to have a relationship with symbols which seems crucial in human beings, and often seems to need healing and rebalancing. It is not that symbols are absent, but that they are not seen, not heard, not attended to. The dreamer must look at his own dream and interrogate it, and not simply be dreamed by it. We are neither the master nor the victim of our own symbols, but hopefully a kind of partner.

This discussion shows how widely and how deeply we can take the notion of symbolism, ranging from a fragment of a dream, or a fantasy, to the telling and retelling of one's own life as a coherent narrative, with its own interconnections, its own key images and metaphors. Without doubt the latter view of symbolism is quite 'full on', and it does not suit some clients, but it can provide that sense of meaning which is so often lacking in our culture.

13 Difficult Clients

It might seem redundant to have a separate chapter on problems in therapy, since every client brings their own problems, and presents special problems for the therapist. But clearly there are problems and problems. Some kinds of clients pose unusual difficulties for their therapists, either because of the tenacity of their deep-rooted problems, because of an unusually negative attitude to the therapy itself, or because of a chaotic mental state, which can easily infect the therapist.

In fact, many serious problems for therapeutic technique stem from infection from unconscious to unconscious. That is, the therapist may feel invaded by some feeling or sensation or mode of thought possessed by the client, which is relatively unprocessed, and therefore tends to be projected into the therapist. Of course, this process happens all the time, but creates unusual difficulty when the projected material is more intense and less digestible than usual.

Fifth gear

I have what I call my fifth gear for very difficult clients – who can generally be termed borderline, or extremely ambivalent people, or those who are very chaotic. Generally this group does not include schizophrenics, most of whom come to therapy under medication, and are therefore not in massive turmoil. But the first group often are, and one key identification of them is that the therapist tends to feel tormented, crazy, very tense, and so on. Words such as 'infuriating', 'maddening', 'driving me crazy', are sure signs of very fierce projections from client to therapist, and the projections stem from intense conflicts in the client's unconscious.

The fifth gear that I refer to developed out of a realization that normal therapeutic techniques do not work with such people, or at any rate, when they are at their worst, the normal techniques do not work. Interpretations leave them cold, or are seized on with relish and demolished; any discussion of their day-to-day life is impossible, because of the welter of emotional intensity which is spilling out; chaos and confusion are palpable in the room. There is often intense anger towards the therapist, and towards life; nothing works; and anything that seems to work is overturned rapidly.

However, quite often there are more tranquil periods when normal therapy work is possible – the problem is how to get to these periods. My fifth gear technique is to be much more open about how I feel in the session. That is, if I feel crazy, tormented, explosive, very tense, and so on, I am open about this. I am emotional as well – I don't just report my feelings dispassionately. I say that I can't stand the session, that it's unbearable, and so on, and without doubt, I am reflecting how unbearable things feel for the client. But these are clients who do not respond if one makes such a comment – 'things seem to be unbearable for you'. If anything, such interpretations make things worse.

Of course, this technique is a way of returning the ferocious projections of the client, but not in a reported manner, but in an emotional way. And it works – it seems to shock many disturbed clients to find that they have such an effect on others. I conjecture that they are so caught up in their turmoil and drama that they lose sight of other people completely, and especially the effect they have on others. The therapist's self-disclosure is therefore a kind of reality check, which brings them back from the land of fantasy and melodrama to a more present world, where there are two people in the room, trying to deal with each other.

It seems odd at first that the most disturbed people are the very ones with whom one might become more emotionally open, yet these are people who cannot be contacted by normal means. They are in another place entirely, not in an adult world of reason and discussion at all. One might say they exist in a very infantile state, they are gripped by powerful unconscious feelings, they are almost paralyzed by their own psyche. The presence of the other person is discounted, but when the other one makes their presence felt powerfully, then some contact can be established.

Of course, this technique cannot be used with those people who would be overwhelmed by the therapist's self-disclosure, but generally therapists are able to make that distinction. In fact, the indications as to when such unorthodox methods might be used are usually unmistakable – in particular, that the projections from client to therapist have a very fierce, destructive quality, and tend to lodge in the therapist's mind, so that weekends are spent having internal arguments with the client, sleep may be lost at night, pages and pages of notes are written in an attempt to rid oneself of the psychic onslaught. In other words, the end of the session does not mark an end at all, but the psychological input of the client continues in an intense, not to say burning, manner. This shows us how normal boundaries are being disrupted – both the boundaries of the session and the boundaries of the individuals concerned. The very disturbed client has a remarkable ability to break these down, so that the therapist can easily feel invaded and overwhelmed.

It is clear that the client is communicating something very important about their own psychic state and their own history, but unfortunately whereas with 'normally neurotic' people one is able to refer such issues back by means of interpretations of various kinds, with disturbed clients, this does not work. This is the second criterion for the use of unorthodox methods – that orthodox ones do not work. In fact, many therapists come to use methods which are abnormal as a result of their own sense of stress, helplessness, or even despair. In extremis, one has to emerge from therapeutic anonymity, and confess that one is being tormented by the therapy, just as the client without doubt is tormented by life and their own psychic demons.

Depression

Depressed clients do not normally require such unorthodoxy, since while they may be plunged into despair or even feel suicidal, their psychological boundaries are usually fairly secure. Some clients arrive in therapy already depressed, but quite a number arrive with their defences intact. In particular, an underlying depression, which probably goes far back into childhood, has been well concealed, both from others and from the person concerned. In this case, part of the therapeutic task is to unlock this depression so that it can come to the surface, and then can be worked through. This is the sense of the term 'therapeutic depression': one might almost say that one hopes that the therapy will eventually plunge the client into depression. This is partly behind those macabre jokes which one hears that therapy made me feel much worse. To begin with, that is desirable, in the sense that we want to find out what your 'worst' is, where it stems from, and how it can be worked through.

One can make a distinction between temporary depressions, which are occasioned by the normal upsets of life, such as relationship problems, work issues, creativity blocks, and so on, and a deeper underlying depression. Normally, there is quite a different quality to the latter: one senses its greater depth; quite often it is non-verbal, and therefore, one suspects, preverbal; in other words, it is an ancient feeling which has been locked away in the recesses of the psyche for the entirety of adult life.

One might describe life as a parabola, which ascends in the first part of life, and then descends to death, but one of the paradoxes about this is that in the ascension, feelings are often ignored and repressed, and it is only in the second part of life that the really deep feelings can be tackled. It has often been said that the mid-thirties are a critical time for many people, since this marks the end of youth, and the end of irresponsibility, certainly in the psychological sense. In other words, most young people – people in their twenties – ignore depression, and find distractions from it quite successfully. But a decade later, this strategy often begins to fail, for the depression demands attention as a neglected part of the psyche.

One has to be careful with a deep ongoing depression. I mean careful not to over-interpret, but also careful not to ignore it. These are the two dangers – first, that one might be intrusive, and not actually allow the client to be depressed in one's presence. This is of great importance, since many people have had the experience in childhood and adolescence of not being allowed to be depressed, so that they learned to hide these feelings from their parents. Part of this concealment often consists of a wish to protect one's parents from feelings which might be felt as a reproach to them – 'I am depressed because you didn't love me enough'.

It is important therefore to allow someone to be depressed without too much interpretation. I mean that the depression must be allowed breathing space or room to be. If the therapist jumps in immediately with comments and interpretations, there is a sense in which the old taboo is being repeated, and the interpretation is a kind of nervous stifling of the feelings. Sometimes silence is the best response.

The other danger is that the therapist might actually neglect the client's depressed side, might not be sensitive to the client's needs in such a state. These needs often consist of wanting to be seen and heard in this depressed state, perhaps for the first time in one's life. This also involves referring the current depression to one's past, particularly childhood, finding out what went on in the family, how cared for and wanted the client felt (or not), the particular relationships with each parent and with siblings.

I sometimes call such depressions 'life depressions', in the sense that they form a nodal point or a core emotional complex in the client's personality. They have probably determined many aspects of life, certainly in an unconscious way, for example, in the choice of partners. And the need to conceal such feelings may have taken up huge amounts of energy, which can now be released hopefully into more creative enterprises.

People vary in the slowness with which they release such deep depressions. There is an old adage that it takes two years with many clients before one gets to the underlying problem, but that is not always true. There are a few people who are 'ready and ripe' for therapy, and begin to explore such uncomfortable feelings from the start, but they are a minority. For the majority, one must first deal with the defences against the depression coming out, which can obviously vary enormously.

Depression is particularly subject to 'layering', in the sense that it often conceals other feelings, such as anger, guilt and sadness. The word 'depressed' itself suggests that something has been driven down, and the therapist's own feelings are a vital clue in this respect as to what lies beneath the surface.

> Dawn poured out a terrible story about her childhood, with parents fighting each other, hitting the children, sometimes leaving them for days on end, so that Dawn had to look after the other children. However, her therapist noticed that he began to feel irritated by Dawn's litanies, and suggested to her that under her depression (the reason she had come to therapy), she was furious with her family and the responsibilities she had been prematurely given. At first, she found this confusing, since anger had been the prerogative of others in her family, but eventually she was able to articulate her own sense of indignation.

If there is any sense of martyrdom about a depressed client, this usually suggests hidden anger, as the martyr wishes to punish others with their own suffering. Depression is something of a catch-all term in this respect, in that it can be found on top of many different emotional configurations, and the 'flavour' of the sessions with a particular client is an important indication as to the feelings which have been 'depressed'.

Severe cases of depression lead us to consider those with suicidal thoughts and feelings, and the normal procedure is to ask such clients to find medical back-up, in case there is the genuine wish to commit suicide. But some clients refuse to do this, and some suicidal people refuse all suggestions from medical staff as to the taking of medication. In this case, therapists have to be fatalistic in a sense, and remind the client that suicide is their choice. At the same time, the suicidal feelings have to be explored urgently, for again, it is likely they conceal other feelings, for example, the wish for revenge on others, a sense of hopelessness and so on. If a therapist feels guilty about a client's suicidal thoughts, ('why haven't I helped him more?') then the issue of guilt must be explored, even if the client denies feeling guilty, for it is very likely that intense counter-transference is going on.

Ambivalence

All clients have some ambivalence about psychotherapy, and this is not surprising, since it is often not comfortable and can prove to be quite threatening to one's traditional ideas about oneself and about life. However, some clients have a high degree of ambivalence, and this often shows itself in small ways, such as not turning up for sessions, turning up late, making payment late, constantly changing the time of the sessions, and so on. Even more important is the quality of being with such people – one picks up their ambivalence, and one senses someone who is not really here, present in the room. There is a Peter Pan quality, an ethereal quality, compared to someone else who is more grounded and rooted. The therapist's fantasies are often important here – one often has fantasies of the person not turning up, or stopping quite soon, and so on. Such fantasies are reliable indicators of the client's wish to leave.

After some years of experience one becomes quite attuned to ambivalence of this kind, for such people usually carry this attitude into all areas of their life. So in their relationships, their work, their friendships, the same half-out, half-in attitude can be found, as if they have not quite made up their mind to be committed to life.

But what do we do about ambivalence? Clearly, it must be discussed, and discussed at length and frequently, otherwise the client will begin to act it out without realizing it. One can safely say that if one does not begin to explore the ambivalence in this way, there is a high likelihood of them leaving.

I find that my own fantasies are extremely useful in this respect. I say to people: 'I keep imagining that you're going to stop'; 'I thought maybe you couldn't come this week'; 'you feel as if you're not really here'. It can come as quite a shock to hear such feedback, for the person concerned is so used to their own ambivalence, they often don't realize how debilitating it is, and how much impact it has on others. In fact, someone who is markedly ambivalent in relationship makes the other person withdraw in turn, for it is unsafe to trust oneself to them. Of course, some people chose ambivalent partners and lovers, for then their own ambivalence is catered for.

It can be pretty exasperating working with such people, for their energy turns on and off, they blow hot and cold. They turn up for a period and then miss a few sessions. They go missing and then return full of apologies. Fortunately the therapist has certain things on their side, particularly the fact that quite often the person's ambivalence has spoiled their life, or has left it unfulfilled. They can look back on a series of unfulfilled opportunities in work and relationships. They may be full of regret for those things that didn't work out – although the regrets themselves can be highly addictive, and become a means of avoiding life in the present.

One has to plug away, pointing out the underlying fear of commitment, or being pinned down, or rooted to the spot. In addition, one must explore the background to these feelings, for one usually finds that the person's childhood was full of disconnections, either parents who weren't really present, or being sent away, or other kinds of insecurity. The client's ambivalence is a defence against committing oneself to somebody or something which may let one down. Ambivalence is therefore a kind of pre-emptive strike – if I'm not totally committed, I can't be let down.

Borderline clients

Borderline clients have the reputation of being the most difficult to work with, since their projections are often fierce and unpredictable. The word 'infuriating' is often used, since such clients are often full of fury, which is projected into the therapist, who is often left holding it rather helplessly. There can be a paralyzing quality also about such people, which is particularly distressing for therapists, who can feel that their own value and ability is under attack. This is because in part one's normal armoury of therapeutic techniques is refuted by the borderline client, who is often a very clever person, adept at spotting what one is trying to do, and adept at ruining it.

The term 'borderline' suggests an instability, since such clients tend to veer between what can be called 'normal neurosis' and a more psychotic sense of chaos, rage and despair. The term 'borderline' is also useful in suggesting the great problems with boundaries which often occur with such people, since they may have an uncanny ability to dissolve the normal interpersonal boundary, so that one feels conflated with them, or fused with them, or somehow tangled up in their unconscious. The phrase 'under the skin' seems appropriate, since such clients do get under your skin, and are able to produce confusion, anger and excitement in the therapist, and it can be quite difficult to know what to do with these projected feelings.

Clearly such personalities are the product of very disturbed childhoods, and one often finds evidence of parents who are themselves unstable, with poor boundaries and poor contact with their children. However, attempts to historicize the client's issues in this way may often be met with either scorn – which is one of the great weapons of the borderline client – or a kind of chaotic confusion.

The shift from the neurotic to the psychotic can happen very quickly in such people, and can be very disturbing for the therapist. If it proves too disturbing, then one can suggest that the therapist does not work with such people for a period. Of course, there is the problem of spotting the borderline client at the beginning, for sometimes it is not immediately apparent. However, there is no shame in realizing that one has bitten off too much – and if the therapist does feel ashamed of this, then it can be worked through in supervision and one's own therapy.

Certainly, I find that my 'fifth gear' is very important with such people, since frequently normal therapy does not work. It is a kind of emergency measure, and if again the individual therapist feels that they cannot cope with such extreme therapeutic methods, then it is appropriate to send the client on to someone else.

The emergency here is that the therapist, confronted with the borderline client, can begin to experience intense feelings – of panic, rage, grief, guilt, and so on. These are being projected from the client, but with such ferocity, and such apparent lack of boundaries, that the normal reflective treatment of projections is very difficult. If one attempts to 'return' the projected material in the form of an interpretations, it may provoke further fury, scorn or despair. One can end up feeling that one is in the grip of an endless cycle of madness and rage. No doubt that is what the client is trying to convey – that that is their own experience.

So with some clients I confess my own sense of despair, fear, rage, or whatever feelings are besetting me. It has usually worked well, partly because the client is stunned to realize that they have such effects on others. They are often so caught up in their own world, that such effects are ignored or not even considered. If you like, the shock treatment is designed to stop the client in their tracks, and get them off their own cycle of craziness, which is very addictive to them. One gets the feeling that no-one has ever actually tried to engage honestly with such people, and honesty and authenticity may be vital tools.

> Margaret was telling her therapist for the umpteenth time what a failure he was, and how she had thought of reporting him to his professional association, and suggested that they tape a session to demonstrate how inadequate he was. Her therapist was used to this treatment, but on this occasion felt it was unbearable, and exclaimed out loud that this was so. Margaret was shocked, and her tirades abated after this session. She said she had never thought he could be affected by her in this way, as he was a 'professional'.

It is also clear that many therapists have used such 'extreme' techniques, often in a state of despair, and feeling at their wit's end, since normal psychotherapy does not work, or is met with derision and destructiveness. One can mention the amazing work done by H. F. Searles with very seriously ill patients in hospital, in which he found that his own authentic personality was absolutely crucial in the work.[1] The cool neutral therapist, with a certain amount of empathy, will simply get demolished by such people, as in fact will the warm sympathetic one.

In a sense, the borderline client is making a serious demand – stop using your intellectual therapeutic techniques with me, and get real. Show me your real self; show me what you feel, before you start telling me how to get in touch with my feelings. This can be exciting work, but also frightening, intensely challenging, and often full of despair, since often just as one thinks one has made progress, the infuriating client wrecks it all again, pours scorn all over it, goes off into another crazy relationship, as if to say to the therapist – I defy you to help me, since I am infinitely cleverer than you, and I am a brilliant saboteur.

Some clients undoubtedly want to drive the therapist mad, probably to demonstrate how they were driven mad, and the therapist has to respond to this with appropriate feelings. One cannot simply report dispassionately, 'I think you are trying to drive me mad', for that will in turn drive the client crazy, since with such an interpretation one has refused to be engaged personally. The terrible quality of their experience has to be met with by the therapist in authentic terms, and cannot be explained away or interpreted dispassionately.

At the same time, those clients with a severe borderline disorder may have to be dealt with in an institutional setting, thus providing a degree of safety and containment, which cannot be found in a private practice. Furthermore, serious cases may require periodic hospitalization, and such cases have to treated by very experienced psychotherapists.[2]

Narcissistic clients

Many clients have a narcissistic element to their character, but the fully fledged narcissistic personality has a peculiarly self-contained existence, which often seems impervious to other people, or to life itself.

> Nigel spent a number of years in therapy, and never made any comments about the therapist, the room they were in, the weather, the trees outside, and so on. At first, the therapist was not aware of this, but gradually realized how Nigel's reality seemed filled only with his own thoughts and feelings. At the same time, Nigel projected an air of extreme vulnerability, so that the therapist hesitated to bring these observations to his attention.

Here is that strange mixture of self-containment and fragility that one often finds in the narcissistic person – they often seem to erect 'keep off' signs all around, so that one hesitates to make comments which with other, more robust characters, would be said quite casually and as a matter of fact.

A key concept here is the 'narcissistic wound', which phrase conveys eloquently that mixture of fragility, and even rawness, with an imperviousness which can be infuriating. Indeed, one can detect behind this defence many intense feelings such as anger, envy, and often a very powerful sense of despair. But the narcissistic person shrinks from sharing such feelings with others, and tends to revolve them endlessly round in their own head.

Doing therapy with such people is a strange affair, since one often feels left quite alone. I have had a number of clients who carried out a kind of self-analysis, while I sat there as a kind of witness. I felt relaxed enough about doing this, but of course every now and then, one's own vanity and self-esteem rears up and demands some attention back. The narcissistic client is always startled by this, as if the infant on the breast were to suddenly realize that the breast itself has its own rights and needs and communications.

The image is interesting, suggesting the primitive nature of many narcissistic people, who seem to see other people not so much as living subjects in their own right, but as convenient adjuncts to themselves. The disregard and indeed coldness of such attitudes can come as a shock, and seems at times almost inhuman.

We can see how the therapist's own feelings, and general state of mind in the therapy is very important in the course of the work. One may well be prepared to go along with the client's self-analysis for a period, but one must be on the look-out for feelings of discomfort, anger, loneliness, and so on. These are in part projected from the client, but undoubtedly they also reflect the feelings which the client arouses in others. Being married to someone like this must be very challenging indeed, since one is like the moon circling the earth.

Progress with narcissistic clients is usually slow, since the defensive system is set like concrete, and is not going to be given up lightly, if at all. My sense is that such people do not make dramatic changes, but tend to become a bit less narcissistic over time, and a bit more aware that someone else is in the room. Yet there is always the curious feeling that in fact they would be swamped by the full presence of someone else.

It is clear that the narcissistic personality disorder is a severe one, which often does not lead to full psychological health, but can be ameliorated to a degree. That may sound pessimistic or overly cautious, but one can also see it positively, for such people have lived grey half-lives, and if one has helped to bring back a bit of colour to them, that is good news.

There are clients who show both borderline and narcissistic traits, and one may well feel puzzled by them, or in fact deranged by them, but one has to work very pragmatically with such clients, that is, working with the material that they bring, paying attention to one's own feelings and thoughts and fantasies, taking care of oneself, if there is a psychic onslaught, and so on. Each session may present a different challenge, and there may be little sense of continuity.

The phrase 'taking care of oneself' has an important theoretical aspect, since one is saying that one's inner child must be looked after, suggesting that the client's own inner child is in torment, and therefore shuts everyone out, reacts with coldness to them, cuts off, and so on. The client has not learned how take care of this part of themselves, and therefore the therapist must take care of their own child, and that will gradually help the client do the same. Here projection and repetition come together: the despairing child (still present from the client's own history) is projected into the therapist, who must show how it can be looked after and refuse to let it be abused.

There is always an element of despair in this work. I mean that from time to time the therapist will feel a despair that nothing has changed much, we are not going anywhere, the client remains locked in a closed world. The despair is in part projected from the client, and can often be usefully fed back, but it also belongs to the therapist, since one is involved in a very difficult relationship, which often seems to bear little fruit, and in which one seems to receive little recognition. At the same time, such people can elicit great compassion, since their world seems so constricted and in fact at times so bizarre. If in fact one feels indifferent to such people, then it is best not to work with them, since progress is slow and the therapist may have to endure considerable isolation.

Introversion

Introverted clients become difficult to work with if one pathologizes their introversion. This can happen with some object relations therapists, who are convinced that the ability to relate to others is the be-all and end-all of personal growth, and therefore fail to see that for some people, relating to themselves is a top priority. This need to be with oneself increases for many people as they get older, and they may find that they are labelled anti-social and so on, as they enjoy being alone more, avoid parties and groups of people, and see their friends less.

Alan gave up his job and rented a house in the country, where he saw few people. Friends and family expressed their concern that he was cutting himself off, and his therapist was worried by Alan's solitariness. But Alan said that he had been with people for the whole of his life, and he now wanted to find something in the silence that existed when he was alone. In his therapy also, while he would talk animatedly at times, at other times he would become silent, would drift off and so on, and his therapist learned to leave him to it.

One of the problems with this kind of client is that their withdrawal can closely resemble someone who is cut off from human contact, shuns people, withdraws into a kind of protective solitude, and so on. But I am convinced that for some people, introversion is not pathological, and not simply a kind of optional life-style, but becomes absolutely necessary. We can refer back to the ideas about individuation discussed in Chapter Two, for the person who is beginning to find out more about themselves will often move away from group activities, may spend less time with their family and friends, may simply disappear into their own space.

And it starts to show up in the therapy sessions. Such clients do not remain engaged for the whole of the session. They may become silent or fall asleep. They may begin to go into silent reverie, and not communicate what is going on. Therapists who are too possessive or demanding can begin to crowd such clients, with disastrous results, for one must be able to leave them alone when they need it. Of course, this doesn't mean one is prohibited from speaking, but one can usually tell when such clients have had enough contact, and want their own space.

One might say that introverted people are a problem for our culture at large, for they don't fit in, they tend to give up the normal goals, which we are meant to pursue, they tend to become more contemplative than workaholic. We can refer again to 'being not doing', for the introvert is moving into a period of being, and this can be disconcerting for others.

This process is particularly difficult for those people who have lived a fairly extrovert life, and then discover a kind of hidden introversion inside, and begin to express it in their life. Other people may object to this, may say that they are mentally ill, or may advise a dose of anti-depressants, and so on. There can be a degree of intolerance shown to introversion, and it is therefore important that psychotherapists are sensitive to it, and are able to give it breathing room.

Notes

1 H. F. Searles, *Collected Papers on Schizophrenia and Related Subjects.*
2 See Bateman and Holmes, *Introduction to Psychoanalysis*, pp. 222–34.

14 Conclusions

This book is highly selective and has to be. I mean that psychotherapy is such a rich and in some ways bewildering field of knowledge and practice that one cannot encompass the whole of it. As a practitioner, one gravitates towards those areas which suit one's own personality; and the potential client does likewise.

However, we can point to certain unifying factors in all the different schools of psychotherapy, and the word 'foundation' in the title suggests that certain things operate universally. What are they?

I have explored a number of foundational themes, which I can summarize here.

1. First, in psychotherapy there is an enquiry into intimacy and the resistance to intimacy. I mean that every human being has the need for human intimacy, but also probably has some resistances to it, and clients who come to psychotherapy probably have such resistances in abundance. One might say that many human problems are concerned with our neurotic self-harming barriers to others, or the ways in which we push others away, cut off from them, scapegoat them, and so on. In other words, we partly refuse to be intimate, and turn others into villains or victims or even things.

The psychotherapeutic space is an astonishing invention, since it sets up from the beginning a kind of intimate environment. That is, two people are ensconced in a private room, hopefully in an atmosphere that is quiet and non-intrusive. In the beginning, the client may be called upon to suggest why he/she has come to therapy. In other words, all the conditions exist for an intimate conversation to take place, which can be the beginning of an intimate relationship, of course a very special kind of relationship, which does not find sexual expression, which is not romantic, but which nonetheless may attain a considerable openness.

For many clients this is both desirable and frightening, and naturally most clients react initially by pulling away, or by bringing into play their habitual defences against intimacy. Thus, in the first session (or after the first phone call) we can argue that the therapy has already begun to elicit the client's neurotic (or psychotic) resistance to others, and indeed to life. We can begin immediately to study these defences, and to consider whether they should be dismantled, and how. I say 'whether' since it is obviously true that some people's defences should be left intact, since behind them exists a chaotic or raw person, who cannot as yet face others, or indeed cannot face too much reality. In other words, some clients need considerable ego-strengthening before we can consider any question of the lowering of defences.

Nearly all psychotherapeutic schools use the therapeutic space, which can be defined as a private intimate dyad. Of course, the actual techniques used by the therapist vary enormously, but one can argue again that many of them are concerned with indicating to the client the barriers which they have erected against others, and against life, and ways in which these can be taken down or modified. For example, it may be an issue of choice – instead of one's defences being automatic, so that one is controlled by them, one can learn to acquire some choice over them.

2. Second, most therapies use some kind of reflecting back or mirroring. One can call it simply feedback, but it goes further than that, since it often attempts to help the client digest and assimilate that which remains undigested. In the extreme case, we are speaking of aspects of the personality which have been split off and disowned, but in less extreme cases, we are referring to elements of the personality which are covert, and which the client is not in touch with.

One of the most powerful means of doing this is the interpretation, which originated in psychoanalysis, but which has spread to many other schools. We have seen that this is a most delicate instrument, which must not be used too intrusively, but which can be very powerful in effecting the shift from lack of awareness to awareness. But clearly, interpretations do not work unless the client is ready for them. Hence the danger of the premature interpretation, for which the client is not ready, and which may produce strong reactions and even the threat to leave therapy.

3. Third, many therapies use interventions which are more directive than interpretations. These vary from the mild to the brutal. Sometimes one might suggest an alternative way of dealing with someone or with a certain situation;

but equally, in extremis, one might insist that the client stop treating the therapist in a certain abusive manner. I had a client who used to go to the toilet and leave the door open, and when I objected, he insisted that he had the right to do this. I demurred vehemently, and I was prepared to stop the therapy if he continued to do this.

How insistent one's interventions are depends on many factors, including the behaviour in question, the length of time it has been considered, the desperateness of the client (or the therapist), and so on. But the point here is that therapists are not simply passive observers and interpreters. At times, they need to intervene more forcefully. There is a kind of parental role here which is important.

4. Fourth, therapies rely on some kind of alliance between therapist and client. There is an ethos of cooperation, without which it is difficult to see how psychotherapy can work. Hence therapy is not like some medical procedure, which involve an expert 'doing something' to the patient's body, which is fairly passive.

5. Fifth, the alliance has a shadow side, in that all clients resist therapy, resist the therapist, and covertly set out to wreck things. One might object to my use of the word 'all' – since surely some clients are not destructive? This takes us back to the maxim of the negative transference – that we should assume it is always present.

This is a wise assumption, since I am saying really that it is human to be destructive, just as much as it is human to love. In fact, this means that we also have to consider the therapist's own resistance to the therapy being successful. This is obviously a very shadowy and unconscious area, but one has to attempt to penetrate into it, since factors such as envy and seductiveness in the therapist can derail therapy.

6. Sixth, there is a relationship going on between two people, and the authenticity of this will have a greater or lesser importance in different styles of therapy. We can certainly argue that some clients are looking for a sense of realness from their therapist, and will find too much detachment and coolness to be a barrier to their own opening up.

7. Seventh, and this is the most mysterious, covert and least discussed foundation of psychotherapy, one can say that it is based on the view that the individual has absolute value. This sounds strange, and perhaps sounds too abstract or too idealized, but I believe that as a principle it has pervaded psychotherapy from the beginning.

One has to ask – why do we practise psychotherapy? No doubt there are many personal reasons, both conscious and unconscious. There certainly are unconscious mechanisms at work – for example, the projection onto the client of the therapist's own wounds, which are then vicariously healed. There is also the need to make a living, which should not be underestimated or denigrated.

But surely the simple act of sitting down in a session with a client says something about one's views of human value. Is it not saying that you have value as you are? Not because as a client you are productive, work hard, or you are attractive, or poignant, or whatever, but simply for being what you are.

Of course, for many clients (and therapists) this is a terrifying and even repellent notion, for many people believe that value is earned through hard work, through being attractive, or through some other means. The notion of absolute value seems alien in our culture. It also seems to suggest that there is no need to change or to be 'cured', since things are all right as they are. I don't think it suggests that at all, since the urge to change and become healed is surely a basic human drive, but part of that healing is self-acceptance, and this means accepting that one has value.

Again, it strikes me that the invention of the therapeutic space embodied this notion of value, since by sitting down together we have already paid each other considerable respect; we have acknowledged each other; in the end, we have set out on the long road towards the acknowledgement of love.

I/Thou

In general it is true that clients look for a human being in their therapist, not a desiccated interpreter or solver of problems. Many clients are themselves suffering from a kind of atrophy of human contact and relatedness, and are therefore seeking real contact with someone else, and yet a contact which gives them space and time, and does not intrude. Many clients need to go at their own pace, which may be quite a slow one, if they are particularly fragile or confused.

I also think that as therapists become more experienced, they become more authentic. Whereas in one's immaturity, one might have sheltered behind book knowledge, clever interpretations, and so on, one finds with experience that this is not necessary, in fact that it is counter-productive, since the client does not respond to it.

Somehow, our civilization has produced vast amounts of inauthenticity and alienation. That is, people are alienated from their own bodies, feelings, needs and desires. Psychotherapy has arisen as one way of restoring these things to people, and the practitioners of that discipline have no doubt struggled to overcome their own alienation. It is like the Olympic flame – it is handed on from one generation to the next.

Psychotherapy is an empirical, pragmatic discipline. It is concerned with the subjective experience of the client, and as a therapist one is also concerned with one's own subjective experience, as a way of opening doors and windows into the client's. After all, one is faced with the enigma of another person. What is it like being them? What is it that they want? What is it that stops them finding that? To travel this road is a mysterious process, since often one does not know the way, but then again perhaps something present in both the client and the therapist does know the way, for often one finds that a door is opening that one never knew existed.

I see the pragmatic nature of psychotherapy as meaning that one hopes to get closer to the client's experience, their subjectivity. If you like, one becomes immersed in it, one takes it into oneself temporarily. This may seem dangerous at times, or boring, or exciting, or pointless, but in the end it is also a privilege. But even more importantly, that process of getting to know someone seems to help them know their own self a bit better.

Something from Martin Buber's I/Thou relationship comes to mind here, for without a Thou I cannot truly be an I, and if that consummation went badly when I was a child, then in therapy I can find another Thou who may help me to find myself.

Index

accreditation 48
acting out 15, 89
agency 157–8, 171
alliance, therapeutic 106, 196
aloneness in therapy 120–1
ambivalence 143–4, 171, 182, 187–8
anger 114–5, 118, 124, 140–1
  and guilt 166–7
aphasia 68
archetype 26
association of ideas 12
authenticity 34, 45, 81–2, 131, 197
autism 111
automatic thoughts 52–3

beliefs, irrational 54–5
bio-energetics 41–2
bodywork 41–2, 154–6
borderline disorder 110, 182, 188–90
boundaries 96, 131, 152, 184, 188
brain damage
  and personality 67–8
brain of infant 62–4
brain/mind interaction 61–2, 69
breaks 90–1
bullying 176–7

catharsis 39–40
censorship, by ego 15, 179
centrifugal forces 72–3
centripetal forces 72–4
childhood
  feelings from 20, 169
  reconstruction of 105
  trauma of 61
child-rearing 65–6, 141
civil war, in psyche 169–71
client-centred therapy 100
clients
  abusive 167
  difficult Chap. 13
  passive 99

cognition and emotion 65–6
cognitive analytic therapy 52
cognitive faults 50–4
cognitive therapy Chap. 4
  techniques in 58–9
commitment 89–92
compassion 150–1
complaints procedures 79–80
confidentiality 76–8
confrontation 123–4
confusion 139
containment 76, 87, 90, 93, 152
couch, working on 98–9
counter-transference 12–14, 78, 136–40, 159
covert/overt distinction 15, 52
crop circles 42–3

death of God 2
defences 20–2
deficits in childhood 64–5
depression 52, 184–6
derepression 119
despair 165
destructiveness 34, 157, 169
diagnosis 110–1
difficult clients 123–6, Chap. 13
diversity 80
dreams 128, 172–4, 178, 179
drives 13, 41, 61
drugs 68

ego-strength 107
emergency action 78, 105, 107, 182–4,
  189–90
empathy 34, 46, 81
endings 93–7
enriched environments 68–9
envy 158–9, 164
European Commission 74
existential philosophy 44
existential therapy 44–5
exploitation of clients 78–9

fantasies 78–9
feelings 147–50
  layered 149, 162–3, 186
  release of 147–50
  of therapist 121, 150, 191
fees 102–3
Ferenczi, S. 25, 34
flexibility 83, 113–4, 149
free association 174–5
frequency of therapy 92–3
Freud, S. Chap. 2, 41, 73, 112, 160, 165, 179
  and Jung 31
  and neurology 61, 67
  paradox in 24
  see also psychoanalysis

Gestalt therapy 35, 41
guilt 83, 149, 163–7, 177
  and envy 158–9
  and revenge 166–7

Hamlet 25
hatred by therapist 167–8
healing 143
here and now 35–6
holding 87, 142–3
homework 58–9
hospital 76
humanistic psychology 3, Chap. 3, 77, 99, 155
  anti-intellectual 46
  criticisms of 45–7
  critique of psychoanalysis 34–5
  eclecticism of 48
  focus on experience 37–8
  optimistic 34
humour 145

incoherence of psyche 11
individuation 29–30, 73
inner child 13, 108
  of therapist 192
inner critic 13, 124–5, 170–1
inner world 13, 22–3, 47, 133–4, 169–71, 175–7
internal objects 13, 22–3, 170
interpretation 113–4, 173–4, 183–4, 195

intervention by therapist 36–7, Chap. 8, 195–6
intimacy 12, 61–4, 66, 108–9, 131, 144–5, 194–5
introversion 192–3
intuition, use of 105, 137
irrational beliefs 54–5

Jung, C. G. Chap. 2, 42, 154, 162, 165, 180
Jungian analysis Chap. 2, 72, 172
  and psychoanalysis 3, 30
  and transcendence 26

Klein, Melanie 13, 23–4
Kohut, H. 24

Lacan, J. 73
Laing, R. D. 45
language learning 62
length of therapy 91–2
letting go 112–3
lightness 144–5
long-term therapy 91–2
love 95, 132

magical thinking 156
management of therapy 87–8
masochism 151, 170–1
Masson, J. 40
mavericks 73
metacommunication 132–3
microcosm in therapy 19, 101
mirroring 139, 195
money, symbolism of 101–3
mother/child interaction 62–6, 120
mourning 112–3
multi-functionality 108–9

narrative 178–9, 181
narcissism 110, 190–2
narcissistic wound 191
needs in therapy 109
negativity 34, 45, 52–4, Chap. 11
  in client 124–5, 157–8
  in therapist 140–2, 167–8
neurology 61
neuro-psychoanalysis 67–9
neuroscience Chap. 5

neurosis
  sexual aetiology 13
  as self-damage 40, 194
  trauma theory 40
NHS 75, 91
not doing 143

object relations 13, 22–3, 192
organizations 72–4
over-generalization 55–6
over-stimulation 93

panic attacks 108
parent/child relation 63–4
persona 21
personal qualities 81–2
pessimism 56–7
phenomenology 44
plasticity in children 62–4
play 66, 83, 144–5
power trips 88
pre-ambivalence 143–4
prejudice 80
pre-oedipal disturbances 64
problem-solving 35, 108–9
process and return 111–2
professionalization 48, Chap. 6
projection 137, 174–7, 176–7, 183–4, 189
psyche, creative 170
psychoanalysis Chap. 2, 52, 65, 75, 80
  causative 11
  criticisms of 25–6, 34–5, 152
  fantasies about 43
  and Jung 3, 30
  rebellions against 33–4
  reductive 25
  relational 24
  schools of 23–4
psychoanalytic space 24, 63–4
psychology, behaviourist 61, 69
psychosis 110–11
psychotherapist
  as companion 117–9
  life crises 82
  as other 2, 112
  person of 5–6
  therapy for 82
  as toilet 138
  qualities 81–2

psychotherapy
  aims 107–8
  as being with 119–20
  class system in 43–4
  as confession 2
  and creativity 92
  and death of God 2
  and diversity 72
  historical view 1
  and intimacy 63–6, 108–9
  and neuroscience Chap. 5
  as profession Chap. 6
  as relationship 115–7, Chap. 9
  splits in 72–3
  and the state 74–5
  not unified 1, 2, 72
  and Romanticism 2
  unity of 2
  using 122–3
Puritanism 28–9

reconciliation procedure 80
reconstruction 105
regression 90, 98, 143–4
regression therapies 40
regulation 74–5
Reich, Wilhelm 41–2
relationship in therapy 115–7, Chap. 9
relearning 66
repetition compulsion 13–14
  in therapy 19, 88
repression 17–20, 147–8
  lifting of 119
  and repetition 17–20
resistance 12, 100, 113, 116, 134–5, 160–2,
    195
retaliation 140–2
return of repressed 14
revenge 159, 166–7
reverie 99, 119–20
'reverse logic' 177
role play 58

sabotage 124–5, 158–60
saboteur, inner 23, 169–71
scepticism 157–8
schizoid character 62, 110–11
schizophrenia 138, 174, 180
Schore, A. 66–7

Searles, H. F.   64, 143, 190
seductiveness   135
self, sense of   63, 67
Self   26–7
self-cure   22
self-destruction   157
self-disclosure   45, 182–4
self-knowledge   5, 105
setting   Chap. 7
sexuality   41
   and aetiology   13
   exploitation   79
shadow   30–1, 80, 119, 162, 196
short-term therapy   91–2
silence   121–2
sociopathy   68
space   97–8
spirituality   38, 153–4
splitting   20, 65, 73
strategies   126–7
subjectivity   3, 5, 198
suicide   186
supervision   76
survival   126
symbolism   Chap. 12

technique
   unorthodox   107, 182–4
thinking   151–3
   faulty   50–1
   and feeling   47, 65–6, 152
   paralysis of   151–3

time   88–90
   disruption of   89
touch in therapy   154–6
training   4, 38, 71, 155
transcendence   26–7, 38
transference   12–14, 46, 52, 80, 133–6
   negative   159–60
transpersonal psychology   38–9

UKCP   71
unconscious, the   4–5, 11–12, 14–17, 90,
      93, 104, 128, 179
   collective   28–9
   communication from   14–15
   drive of   18–19
   infection by   182
   leakage   15, 147
   and neurology   66–7
   and repression   15, 17–20
   relationship with   107
   therapist's   16–17
unprocessed elements   112
using therapy   14, 122–3

value   196–7
victim   176–7
visualization   58

wild fringe   42–3
work contexts   75–6, 97–8
working through   112–3
writer's block   164